IN THE SHADOW OF EMPIRE

ARCHAEOLOGY AND BIBLICAL STUDIES

Brian B. Schmidt, General Editor

Editorial Board:
Andrea Berlin
Aaron Brody
Annie Caubet
Billie Jean Collins
Yuval Gadot
André Lemaire
Herbert Niehr
Christoph Uehlinger

Number 30

IN THE SHADOW OF EMPIRE

Israel and Judah in the Long Sixth Century BCE

Edited by
Pamela Barmash and Mark W. Hamilton

SBL PRESS

Atlanta

Copyright © 2021 by SBL Press

All rights reserved. No part of this work may be reproduced or transmitted in any form or by any means, electronic or mechanical, including photocopying and recording, or by means of any information storage or retrieval system, except as may be expressly permitted by the 1976 Copyright Act or in writing from the publisher. Requests for permission should be addressed in writing to the Rights and Permissions Office, SBL Press, 825 Houston Mill Road, Atlanta, GA 30329 USA.

Library of Congress Control Number: 2021948715

Cover photograph courtesy of Mohammad Reza Domiri Ganji. See https://commons.m.wikimedia.org/wiki/File:Tomb_of_Cyrus_the_Great.jpg.

Contents

Acknowledgments vii
Abbreviations ix
Figure Credits xv

Introduction: The Long Sixth Century
    Mark W. Hamilton and Pamela Barmash 1

Success and Failure, Resistance and Submission: Nuanced Identities and Relationships during the Return and Early Persian Period
    Pamela Barmash 11

The Art of Control: Iconography of the Early Achaemenid Empire
    Ryan P. Bonfiglio 35

Controlling the Narrative: The Babylonian Exile as Chosen Trauma
    Caralie Cooke 61

Bury Me with My Fathers: A Voluntary or a Forced Return Migration?
    Lisbeth S. Fried 77

The Exiles of Empires in Prophetic Images of Restoration (and Micah 4:8–5:1 [ET 5:2])
    Martien A. Halvorson-Taylor 97

"Empire" as a Political Category and Reflections on It in Centers and Peripheries
    Mark W. Hamilton 115

The Far Side of the Long Sixth Century: Mesopotamian Political Influences on Early Achaemenid Persia
    Matt Waters 139

Remembering the Future: Prophetic Literature's Archives of Exile and Judah's Social Memory in the Persian Era
    Ian D. Wilson 161

Bibliography 181

Contributors 211
Ancient Sources Index 213
Modern Authors Index 218
Subject Index 223

Acknowledgments

A book of this sort depends on the work of several people, in addition to those whose names grace the cover and table of contents. We thank our fellow contributors as well as others who discussed the historical, literary, and theological issues surrounding the events of the long sixth century BCE and its aftermath. The organizers of the Society of Biblical Literature section Exile and Forced Migration, Martien Halvorson-Taylor and Katherine Southwood, deserve our special thanks for allowing us to present earlier versions of these chapters at the Annual Meeting. Pamela Barmash thanks Mark Hamilton. Mark Hamilton thanks Pamela Barmash; the family of Robert and Kay Onstead, who endowed the chair in biblical studies that he holds; and his assistants, Troy LaRue and before him Josiah Peeler.

Most significantly, we dedicate this book to our teacher Peter Machinist, teacher and scholar par excellence. Everyone who knows Peter knows that his extraordinary capacity to situate texts in their historical settings and find previously unexplored depths of meaning and significance is matched only by his capacity to inspire all of us not only to learn and come to know, but to understand our knowledge as something deeply human. As Hillel is supposed to have said, "in the place lacking human beings, strive to be a human being" (במקום שאין אנשים השתדל להיות איש, m. Avot 2.6). Peter reminds us that a great scholar can be a great human being as well.

Abbreviations

4Q55	4QIsaiah[a]
4Q372	4QApocryphon of Joseph[b]
AB	Anchor Bible
ABD	Freedman, David Noel, ed. *Anchor Bible Dictionary*. 6 vols. New York: Doubleday, 1992.
ABL	Harper, R. F., ed. *Assyrian and Babylonian Letters belonging to the Kouyunjik Collections of the British Museum.* 14 vols. Chicago: University of Chicago Press, 1892–1914.
ABRL	Anchor Bible Reference Library
ABS	Archaeology and Biblical Studies
AER	*American Economic Review*
AfO	*Archiv für Orientforschung*
AfOB	*Archiv für Orientforschung: Beiheft*
Ages.	Plutarch, *Agesilaus*
AH	Achaemenid History
AHB	*Ancient History Bulletin*
AHR	*American Historical Review*
AIL	Ancient Israel and Its Literature
AJSR	*Association for Jewish Studies Review*
AMIT	*Archäologische Mitteilungen aus Iran und Turan*
ANEM	Ancient Near East Monographs
AOAT	Alter Orient und Altes Testament
AoF	*Altorientalische Forschungen*
ArchS	*Archival Science*
Art.	Plutarch, *Artaxerxes*
AS	*Aramaic Studies*
b.	Babylonian Talmud
BabAr	Babylonische Archive
BAI	*Bulletin of the Asia Institute*
BARIS	British Archaeological Reports International Series

BASOR	*Bulletin of the American School of Oriental Research*
BDB	Brown, Francis, S. R. Driver, Charles A. Briggs, *A Hebrew and English Lexicon of the Old Testament*. Oxford: Clarendon, 1907.
BETL	Bibliotheca Ephemeridum Theologicarum Lovaniensium
BibInt	Biblical Interpretation Series
BICS	*Bulletin of the Institute of Classical Studies*
BIFAO	*Bulletin de l'Institut Francais d'Archéologie Orientale au Caire*
BO	*Bibliotheca Orientalis*
BRPBI	*Brill Research Perspectives in Biblical Interpretation*
BZABR	Beihefte zur Zeitschrift für altorientalische und biblische Rechtsgeschichte
BZAW	Beihefte zur Zeitschrift für die alttestamentliche Wissenschaft
CAD	Gelb, Ignace J., et al. 1956–2010. *The Assyrian Dictionary of the Oriental Institute of the University of Chicago*. 21 vols. Chicago: The Oriental Institute of the University of Chicago.
CBQ	*Catholic Biblical Quarterly*
CHANE	Culture and History of the Ancient Near East
ClQ	*Classical Quarterly*
COS	Hallo, William W., and K. Lawson Younger Jr., eds. *The Context of Scripture*. 4 vols. Leiden: Brill, 1997–2016.
CUSAS	Cornell University Studies in Assyriology and Sumerology
DB	Darius I, Bisitun inscription
DJD	Discoveries in the Judaean Desert
DNb	Darius I, Naqš-e Rustam, inscription b
DPd	Darius 1, Persepolis, inscription d
DSf	Darius I, Susa, inscription f
ErIsr	*Eretz-Israel*
ESHM	European Seminar in Historical Methodology
FAT	Forschungen zum Alten Testament
fem.	feminine
FOTL	Forms of the Old Testament Literature
GI	Great Ideas
Hau	*Hau: Journal of Ethnographic Theory*
HB	Hebrew Bible

HBAI	*Hebrew Bible and Ancient Israel*
HCOT	Historical Commentary on the Old Testament
Heb.	Hebrew
Hist.	Herodotus, *Histories*
HSM	Harvard Semitic Monographs
ICC	International Critical Commentary
IEJ	*Israel Exploration Journal*
IM	*International Migration*
Iran	*Iran: Journal of the British Institute of Persian Studies*
IrAnt	*Iranica Antiqua*
IrSt	*Iranian Studies*
JANEBL	*Journal for Ancient Near Eastern and Biblical Law*
JAOS	*Journal of the American Oriental Society*
JASR	*Journal of Achaemenid Studies and Researches*
JBL	*Journal of Biblical Literature*
JBQ	*Jewish Bible Quarterly*
JESHO	*Journal of the Economic and Social History of the Orient*
JHebS	*Journal of Hebrew Scriptures*
JNES	*Journal of Near Eastern Studies*
JNSL	*Journal of Northwest Semitic Languages*
JSA	*Journal of Social Archaeology*
JSJSup	Supplements to the Journal for the Study of Judaism
JSOT	*Journal for the Study of the Old Testament*
JSOTSup	Journal for the Study of the Old Testament Supplement Series
JTS	*Journal of Theological Studies*
KAT	Kommentar zum Alten Testament
LCL	Loeb Classical Library
l(l).	line(s)
LHBOTS	Library of Hebrew Bible/Old Testament Studies
LXX	Septuagint
m.	Mishnah
masc.	masculine
MC	Mesopotamian Civilizations
Meg.	Megillah
MUS	Münchener Universitätsschriften – Juristische Fakultät Abhandlungen zur Rechtswissenschaftlichen Grundlagenforschung
NEA	*Near Eastern Archaeology*

NEAEHL	Stern, Ephraim, ed. *The New Encyclopedia of Archaeological Excavations in the Holy Land*. 4 vols. Jerusalem: Israel Exploration Society and Carta; New York: Simon & Schuster, 1993.
NRSV	New Revised Standard Version
OBO	Orbis Biblicus et Orientalis
OBO.SA	Orbis Biblicus et Orientalis, Series Archaeologica
OBT	Overtures to Biblical Theology
Oec.	Xenophon, *Oeconomicus*
OG	Old Greek
OIP	Oriental Institute Publications
OLA	Orientalia Lovaniensia Analecta
Op.	Hesiod, *Opera et dies*
Or	*Orientalia*
ORA	Orientalische Religionen in der Antike
OrAnt	*Oriens Antiquus*
OTL	Old Testament Library
OtSt	Oudtestamentische Studiën
PDRI	Publications of the Diaspora Research Institute
PEQ	*Palestine Exploration Quarterly*
Pers.	Aeschylus, *Persae*
PHSC	Perspectives on Hebrew Scriptures and Its Contexts
pl.	plural
PSPCAIH	Proceedings of the Second Payravi Conference on Ancient Iranian History
r.	reigned
R&T	*Religion and Theology*
RA	*Revue d'assyriologie et d'archéologie orientale*
RB	*Revue biblique*
RBL	*Review of Biblical Literature*
REB	Revised English Bible
RG	Reihe Geschichte
RIMA	The Royal Inscriptions of Mesopotamia, Assyrian Periods
RINAP	Royal Inscriptions of the Neo-Assyrian Period
SAA	State Archives of Assyria
SAAS	State Archives of Assyria Studies
SAN	Studia Aarhusiana Neotestamentica
SAOC	Studies in Ancient Oriental Civilization
SBLMS	Society of Biblical Literature Monograph Series

SBLStBL	Society of Biblical Literature Studies in Biblical Literature
SemeiaSt	Semeia Studies
sg.	singular
Song Rab.	Song of Songs Rabbah
SPCCS	Sheffield Phoenix: Critical Commentary Series
SPQ	*Social Psychology Quarterly*
TM	Textes et mémoires
Transeu	*Transeuphratène*
UF	*Ugarit Forschungen*
UNINO	Uitgaven van het Nederlands Instituut voor het Nabije Oosten te Leiden
VT	*Vetus Testamentum*
VTSup	Supplements to Vetus Testamentum
WAW	Writings from the Ancient World
XPh	Xerxes, Persepolis, inscription h
XPl	Xerxes, Persepolis, inscription l
ZA	*Zeitschrift für Assyriologie*
ZAW	*Zeitschrift für die alttestamentliche Wissenschaft*
ZTK	*Zeitschrift für Theologie und Kirche*

Figure Credits

1.1. Relief on the inner wall of the gateway of the Hibis temple, dedicated to the Theban triad (Amun, Mut, and Khonsu) in the Kharga oasis, depicting the gods Amun and Mut. Copyright 2004 NYU Excavations at Amheida (used with permission). Image published on the authority of Amheida project director Roger Bagnall. Published by the Institute for the Study of the Ancient World as part of the Ancient World Image Bank (AWIB). For further information, see https://tinyurl.com/SBL1735a.

3.1. Close-up of the victory stela of Naram-sin, twenty-third century BCE. Source: Ryan P. Bonfiglio, *Reading Images, Seeing Texts: Towards a Visual Hermeneutics for Biblical Studies*, OBO 280 (Fribourg: Academic Press; Göttingen: Vandenhoeck & Ruprecht, 2016), 211, fig. 5.5.

3.2. Sphinx of Thutmose III reclining on the nine bows, fifteenth century BCE. Photograph by Rama, Wikimedia Commons, Cc-by-sa-2.0-fr.

3.3. Close-up of one of nine bound captives, Ramesses II's temple at Abydos, thirteenth century BCE. Photograph by HoremWeb, Wikimedia Commons, Cc-by-sa-2.0.

3.4. Bisitun relief, near the modern-day city of Kermanshah in western Iran, late sixth century BCE. Source: Ryan P. Bonfiglio, *Reading Images, Seeing Texts: Towards a Visual Hermeneutics for Biblical Studies*, OBO 280 (Fribourg: Academic Press; Göttingen: Vandenhoeck & Ruprecht, 2016), 66, fig. 3.1; see also Brent A. Strawn, "'A World under Control': Isaiah 60 and the Apadana Reliefs from Persepolis," in *Approaching Yehud: New Approaches to the Study of the Persian Period*, ed. Jon L. Berquist, SemeiaSt 50 (Atlanta: Society of Biblical Literature, 2007), 114, fig. 15.

3.5. Bottom left: Detail of the base of the statue of Darius, Susa, late sixth century BCE. Source: Margaret Cool Root, *The King and King-*

xvi   Figure Credits

        ship in Achaemenid Art: Essays on the Creation of an Iconography of Empire, Acta Iranica 19, TM 9 (Leiden: Brill, 1979), pl. XI.
3.6. Relief of the king's throne, south door of the Hundred Column Hall at Persepolis, late sixth century BCE. Source: Bonfiglio, *Reading Images, Seeing Texts*, 72, fig. 3.3; see also Othmar Keel, *The Symbolism of the Biblical World: Ancient Near Eastern Iconography and the Book of Psalms*, repr. ed. (Winona Lake, IN: Eisenbrauns, 1997), 351, fig. 476a.
3.7. PFS 0113*, court style. Source: Mark B. Garrison, "Achaemenid Iconography as Evidenced by Glyptic Art: Subject Matter, Social Function, Audience and Diffusion," in *Images as Media: Sources for the Cultural History of the Near East and the Eastern Mediterranean (First Millennium BCE)*, ed. Christoph Uehlinger, OBO 175 (Fribourg: University Press; Göttingen: Vandenhoeck & Ruprecht, 2000), 130, fig. 3.
3.8. PFS 0007*, court style. Source: Mark B. Garrison and Margaret Cool Root, *Seals on the Persepolis Fortification Tablets, Images of Heroic Encounter*, OIP 117 (Chicago: Oriental Institute of the University of Chicago, 2001), cat. no. 4.
3.9. PFS 0034, fortification style. Source: Garrison, "Achaemenid Iconography," 131, fig. 4.
3.10. PFS 0009*, court style. Source: Garrison and Root, *Seals on the Persepolis Fortification Tablets*, cat. no. 288.
3.11. PFS 0057*, fortification style. Source: Mark B. Garrison, "Achaemenid Iconography," 133, fig. 5.
3.12. PFS 0182, court style. Source: Ryan P. Bonfiglio, "Divine Warrior or Persian King? The Archer Metaphor in Zechariah 9," in *Iconographic Exegesis of the Hebrew Bible/Old Testament*, ed. Izaak J. de Hulster, Brent A. Strawn, and Ryan P. Bonfiglio (Göttingen: Vandenhoeck & Ruprecht, 2015), 233, fig. 12.12; see also Mark B. Garrison, "Archers at Persepolis: The Emergence of Royal Ideology at the Heart of the Empire," in *The World of Achaemenid Persia: History, Art and Society in Iran and the Ancient Near East*, ed. John Curtis and St. John Simpson (New York: I. B. Tauris, 2010), 346, fig. 32.7e.
3.13. PFS 0118, fortification style. Source Bonfiglio, "Divine Warrior or Persian King?," 232, fig. 12.9; see also Garrison, "Achaemenid Iconography," 140, fig. 16.

3.14. Archer series coin, type II. Source: Bonfiglio, "Divine Warrior or Persian King?," 230, fig. 12.4; see also David Stronach, "Early Achaemenid Coinage: Perspectives from the Homeland," *IrAnt* 24 (1989): figs. 1 [2, 3, 7].
3.15. Archer series coin, type III. Source: Bonfiglio, "Divine Warrior or Persian King?," 230, fig. 12.5.
3.16. Archer series coin, type IV. Source: Bonfiglio, "Divine Warrior or Persian King?," 230, fig. 12.6.
3.17. Original central panel of the Apadana (north stairway), Persepolis. Source: Izaak J. de Hulster and Brent A. Strawn, "The Power of Images: Isaiah 60, Jerusalem, and Persian Imperial Propaganda," in de Hulster, Strawn, and Bonfiglio *Iconographic Exegesis of the Hebrew Bible/Old Testament*, 209, fig. 10.11
3.18. Detail from Wing B of the Apadana (east stairway). Source: de Hulster and Strawn, "Power of Images," 208, fig. 10.9.
3.19. Detail of hand-holding gesture from Wing B of the Apadana (east stairway). Source: de Hulster and Strawn, "Power of Images," 211 fig. 10.13.
8.1. Drawing of Bisitun Relief. Source: L. W. King and R. Campbell Thompson, *The Sculptures and Inscription of Darius the Great, on the Rock of Behistûn in Persia* (London: British Museum, 1907), pl. XIII.
8.2. 8.2. Winged guardian genius, Pasargadae. Courtesy of David Stronach.

Introduction: The Long Sixth Century

Mark W. Hamilton and Pamela Barmash

Most readers of the Bible know the basic story line: during the early sixth century BCE, as we would call it, the Babylonian ruler Nebuchadnezzar sacked Jerusalem, deported its population or at least its leaders to Mesopotamia, and triggered a crisis of faith in the minds of prophets, priests, and liturgists that still echoes through the centuries. After a generation or two, the Persian ruler Cyrus absorbed the Babylonian state into his far larger empire, and the Judahites went home from their exile, giving us texts of celebration and explanation that we still read with interest and sometimes pleasure.

This straightforward story of exile and return masks many complex issues of evidence and fact, however. Some of these issues we raise in detail, while we can only hint at others. The essays that follow raise questions and explore new directions without trying to be comprehensive, reflecting our view that a new synthesis cannot exist without a thorough reassessment of the current one.[1] For instance, the problem of scope remains unsolved, not just percentages of deportees versus remainees versus the dead, but the fact that forced migrations involved populations all over the Near East. Privileging the Israelite/Judahite experience(s) may have merit under certain circumstances, since the ancient texts now embedded in the Bible do that to some extent (though not completely), but more comprehensive historical accounts ought to involve comparisons and contrasts with the experiences of other groups, conquerors and conquered,

---

1. The essays began life in presentations in the section Exile and Forced Migrations during the Annual Meetings of the Society of Biblical Literature in 2016 and 2018. We are grateful to the organizers of the section, the presenters during it (including some whose work does not appear here), and to the many respondents whose questions and comments helped sharpen our work.

to the degree that those remain recoverable. Moreover, the deportations did not begin with Nebuchadnezzar in the sixth century but with Tiglath-pileser III in the eighth. This fact means that mere mention of deportation provides no clue to the date of a biblical text, since it is utterly implausible that theological reflections on, and cultural accommodations to, mass forced migration had to wait for the Babylonian incursions following the collapse of Neo-Assyria.

Perhaps most tellingly, the elaborate constructions of exile and return that have grown like kudzu in biblical studies need hacking away at a bit. It is important at this juncture in biblical scholarship to ask what we know and how we know it. To what extent can we extrapolate from our texts to realities on the ground? How well can we read the motivations of the people whose texts we read, given the constant intrusion of our own experiences into historical analysis? And more specifically, what evidence do we have in ancient texts and artifacts concerning the recurring movements of people during the so-called period of exile, especially the sixth century BCE? How well founded are prevailing conceptions, and when do they float on airy constructions built atop one another?

One such conception must be the periodization that we employ. All history writing demands stopping and starting points, and all such points are inevitably more or less arbitrary in that human advances always carry forward elements of the past. Moreover, as the Annales school has taught us, history moves at several speeds simultaneously, not just one, with the long, slow changes of ecology, food production, and the reproduction of life evolving much more slowly than the ephemera of politics and war.[2] Intellectual traditions may move slowly too, returning as they do to their roots and then shooting forward into the future in unpredictable ways. Ideas or practices proposed in one era may have to wait for another for their full flowering.[3]

---

2. Note most famously the discussion in (and the very structure of) Fernand Braudel, *The Mediterranean and the Mediterranean World in the Age of Philip II*, 2 vols., trans. Siân Reynolds (New York: Harper & Row, 1972). For a broader survey of the evolution of the Annales school, see Peter Burke, *The French Historical Revolution: The Annales School, 1929–2014* (Palo Alto, CA: Stanford University Press, 2015).

3. For example, on the twentieth-century retrieval of Thoreau's work on civil disobedience, see Benjamin Sommer, "The Limits of Interpretation," in *The Pentateuch: International Perspectives on Current Research*, ed. Thomas B. Dozeman, Konrad Schmid, and Baruch J. Schwartz, FAT 78 (Tübingen: Mohr Siebeck, 2011), 85–86. Or

At the same time, however, tears in the fabric of history are discernable, at least in retrospect. One such occurred throughout the Near East beginning with the fracturing and then disintegration of the Assyrian Empire in the late seventh century BCE and continuing through to the consolidation of the Persian Empire under Darius I or even Xerxes. The Babylonian state, however imposing it seemed to Judahites and other subject peoples, and however fully the Bible's historiography still colors perception of that era, barely survived its founding generation. Its mark on the Bible, enormous as it was, did not match the reality on the ground. An event that affected part of a community directly and the rest indirectly became a central narrative touchstone for a whole community over centuries. The political changes and failures to change had implications for other sorts of developments as well, as patterns of urbanization, agricultural production, trade, language boundaries, and other characteristics of the human experience adjusted to new realities at the top of the successive states dominating the Near East as well as created them. Periodization matters because frameworks for understanding data matter.

The Shape of the Discussion

Contemporary scholarship on this period begins with Peter Ackroyd's Hulsean Lectures, published in his slender volume *Exile and Restoration*.[4] As the subtitle, *A Study of Hebrew Thought of the Sixth Century B.C.E.*, indicates, his is an intellectual history, or really a history of literature. He demonstrates both the dependence of Second Isaiah, Jeremiah, and their contemporaries on the older prophetic traditions, and their subsequent influence on the evolving traditions of Second Temple Judaism. Commendably, Ackroyd rescued these exilic and postexilic texts from the second-class status in which they had languished since the age of Julius Wellhausen (or arguably, earlier). For him, the retrieval meant emphasizing both their value as contributions to Christian theology in a Christian Bible and their legitimacy as Jewish texts. The commendable effort at reclaiming these texts' theological insights as intellectually respectable, and indeed stimulating,

---

consider the retrieval of Søren Kierkegaard among the theologians of crisis following the publication of Karl Barth's *Römerbrief*.

4. Peter R. Ackroyd, *Exile and Restoration: A Study of Hebrew Thought of the Sixth Century B.C.E.* (Philadelphia: Westminster, 1968).

blazed research trails still being explored.[5] The periodization he adopted continues to shape the field, despite its inherent overvaluing of the Judahite (Deuteronomistic and Isaianic, really) construction of that era.[6]

In the decades since Ackroyd's writing, the ground has shifted more than once with respect to both the evidence available for study and the methods for doing so. For example, the Assyrian, Babylonian, and Persian texts, iconography, and material culture are far better understood today than in Ackroyd's time, with new editions of primary material and critical studies of it appearing constantly. Important synthetic histories of the successive regional empires have appeared,[7] and previously unobtainable but appropriate cross-cultural comparisons can now be made.

An interesting example of the latter occurs in the Achaemenids' deliberate use of merged local traditions to portray imperial rule. So, a monumental sculpture of a guardian genius at a gatehouse in Pasargadae can portray the wings and stance of an Assyrian jinn, while wearing a Persian beard, an Elamite robe, and an Egyptianizing crown, all with a highly pleasing aesthetic effect that gives not the appearance of bricolage but of careful integration of elements.[8] Similarly, Darius the Great could sponsor a temple in Hibis, near the Kharga oasis in the Western Desert of Egypt, in which he portrays himself as a pharaoh while also highlighting the role of Seth, a deeply problematic, fratricidal god in the Egyptian pantheon, in his capacity as slayer of the monster Apep (thus foregrounding a wider

---

5. See already in Ackroyd's Festschrift the remarks of Rex Mason, "The Prophets of the Restoration," in *Israel's Prophetic Tradition: Essays in Honour of Peter R. Ackroyd*, ed. Richard Coggins, Anthony Phillips, and Michael Knibb (Cambridge: Cambridge University Press, 1992), 137–54.

6. Note, for example, the remarks of Rainer Albertz, *Israel in Exile: The History and Literature of the Sixth Century B.C.E.*, trans. David Green, SBLStBL 3 (Atlanta: Society of Biblical Literature, 2003), xi, 1–3. He points out, rightly, that "the Bible does not contain a continuous account of the exilic period." This analysis holds almost as fully for seventh century BCE as for the sixth.

7. Notably, Mario Liverani, *Assyria: The Imperial Mission* (Winona Lake, IN: Eisenbrauns, 2017); Giovanni Battista, Raija Mattila, and Robert Rollinger, eds., *Writing Neo-Assyrian History: Sources, Problems, and Approaches*, SAA 29 (Helsinki: Neo-Assyrian Text Corpus Project, 2019); Pierre Briant, *From Cyrus to Alexander: A History of the Persian Empire*, trans. Peter T. Daniels (Winona Lake, IN: Eisenbrauns, 2002).

8. See the discussion in David Stronach, "Cyrus, Anshan, and Assyria," in *Cyrus the Great: Life and Lore*, ed. M. Rahim Shayegan (Boston: Ilex/Center for Hellenic Studies, 2018), 55–58.

Near Eastern theme of the monarch as viceroy of the chaos-ending deity).⁹ And he can have erected in Susa a statue carved in Egypt with the characteristically Egyptian dorsal back and standing on a base of hieroglyphic cartouches bearing ethnonyms of his subject peoples. Their anthropoid figures stand with arms outstretched in the poses characteristic of the Bisitun and Naqsh-i Rustam reliefs, not traditional Egyptian ones.¹⁰ Again, artistic hybridity mirrors an imperial need to place Persian rule in a long tradition, downplaying its foreignness and, conversely, the non-Persianness of the various subject peoples. Local traditions survive to serve the populations whose ancestors created them, and they also migrate to serve new ends for new users (especially of high status). The local and the imperial mutually enrich each other, even while preserving the seeds of their own dissolution.

For biblical scholars, this hybridity puts texts such as Isa 44–45 and Haggai in a different light. We have known for some time, from the Cyrus Cylinder and related texts,¹¹ that the imperial chanceries sought to appropriate local traditions when possible, not perhaps on merely pragmatic grounds but for more profound ideational or theological reasons. The existence of the Israelite texts shows, however, that the subaltern peoples (surely not just in Yehud or Samaria) could employ sometimes parallel, sometimes contrasting, or even subversive strategies of hybridity for their own purposes. The merger of old and new and thereby the transformation of both characterized the climate of the long sixth century. We are just beginning to discover the forms such transformations could take or how they interrelated.

---

9. Henry P. Colburn, *Archaeology of Empire in Achaemenid Egypt* (Edinburgh: Edinburgh University Press, 2020), 114–23; and more widely, Melanie Wasmuth, *Ägypto-persische Herrscher- und Herrschaftspräsentation in der Achämeniden Zeit* (Stuttgart: Steiner, 2017).

10. Colburn, *Archaeology of Empire*, 153–62.

11. Note the fine survey of that text in Hanspeter Schaudig, "The Magnanimous Heart of Cyrus: The Cyrus Cylinder and Its Literary Models," in Shayegan, *Cyrus the Great*, 67–91; Beate Pongratz-Leisten, "'Ich bin ein Babylonier': The Political-Religious Message of the Cyrus Cylinder," in Shayegan, *Cyrus the Great*, 92–105. For a cautionary note on the relevance of this and similar Achaemenid decrees to the biblical allusions to such texts, see Lester L. Grabbe, "The 'Persian Documents' in the Book of Ezra: Are They Authentic?," in *Judah and the Judeans in the Persian Period*, ed. Oded Lipschits and Manfred Oeming (Winona Lake, IN: Eisenbrauns, 2006), 531–70.

Fig. 1.1. Relief on the inner wall of the gateway of the Hibis temple, dedicated to the Theban triad (Amun, Mut, and Khonsu) in the Kharga oasis, depicting the gods Amun and Mut. Copyright 2004 NYU Excavations at Amheida (used with permission). Image published on the authority of Amheida project director Roger Bagnall. Published by the Institute for the Study of the Ancient World as part of the Ancient World Image Bank (AWIB). For further information, see https://tinyurl.com/SBL1735a.

It has become increasingly clear, then, that scholarship needs both to follow Ackroyd and his many worthy successors in closely reading literature relevant to the sixth century BCE and to consider other kinds of evidence (art and architecture among others). A rethinking of historical periodization is also in order, since processes that came to the fore during the so-called Babylonian exile began earlier and continued later as part of a process of empire formation that radically altered intercultural relationships and intracultural practices. In the exegesis of given texts, the tendency toward later dating of all mentions of deportations (or exile) and return creates blind spots. So, much rethinking needs to occur.

The Work at Hand

The contributors to the present volume have sought to join in that rethinking by widening the focus of study both temporally and, more still, geographically. It is hard to repeat the lucid, elegant treatment of the subject seen in Ackroyd (and perhaps others). So we have not tried.

We do not offer a comprehensive treatment of the historical issues surrounding the long sixth century, as we prefer to call it. This period stretched from the collapse of Neo-Assyria in the 620s and 610s to the consolidation of Persian rule under Darius (or even his successor, Xerxes), with the Babylonian Empire being a makeshift transitional period. These include deportations and return migrations, but also the problems of imperial legitimation and consolidation, changing patterns of production and consumption, urbanization and deurbanization and reurbanization, and so on. All of these issues intermingle, not just in modern scholarly reconstructions but in the ancient texts and artifacts we study.

Instead of seeking comprehensiveness, the essays here address selected relevant issues, acknowledging the incomplete but, we hope, suggestive nature of the discussion: the nuances of group relationships to one another and to their own pasts (Barmash), the persistence and alteration of iconography across the change of imperial centers (Bonfiglio), the processes of literary creation in response to major external factors (Cooke), the possible social or political motivations for return migrations (Fried), the structures of empires and reflections on them (Hamilton), the reuse of images and ideas in prophetic texts in response to successive imperial actions (Halvorson-Taylor), the cultural appropriation at the top of society for the sake of imperial power (Waters), and the nature of social memory during this period (Wilson).

A number of important conclusions emerge from this research into the multiple media of communication employed by both elite and subject groups during this period. To summarize them in the order in which they appear in this volume, these include:

- the importance of iconography as a complement of texts in communicating the ideas, values, and aesthetic sensibilities of the imperial center to the general population;
- the complex and shifting interrelationships of centers and peripheries of successive empires;
- the inadequacy of the dichotomy collaboration/resistance to describe the many ways in which subject peoples interacted with the power structures facing them;
- the nature of culture as a commodity whose artifacts and practices could be manipulated for multiple purposes;
- the presence of ancient versions of orientalism in which the exotic served the imperial center's claims to legitimate universal rule;

- the variability of views of forced migration, not only in contrasts related to the social strata of those reflecting on that experience, but even within groups who shared aspects of it;
- the centrality of mental geography or conceptions of space, especially home space, for subaltern groups;
- the crucial need of survivors of the long sixth century to reclaim a usable past that could explain or at least make intelligible their experiences;
- the concomitant need of the imperial centers to promote their own view of the past;
- the environmental impact of population shifts and changes in agricultural practices or even plants under cultivation as populations moved about (a topic that deserves more than passing study);[12]
- the nature of ancient literary works, especially complex works such as the biblical prophetic texts, as collections of multiple voices and multiple ideas from the same author; and
- perhaps most significantly, the ways in which our modern interests in the period affect both the historical conclusions we draw and the moral implications we may derive from our studies.

Such a long list, which could be extended further, sketches lines of research that we can work on painting in for a long time as a fuller picture emerges. Some of the elements, if not all of them, deserve far deeper study than we can give them here.

Conclusions

Fuller historical pictures do not, of course, emerge simply from piling up more data points. We need not be as cavalier as Paul Veyne when he says,

---

12. Note, for example, Melissa S. Rosenzweig, "Assessing the Politics of Neo-Assyrian Agriculture," *Uneven Terrain: Archaeologies of Political Ecology: Special Issue Archeological Papers of the American Anthropological Association* 29 (2017): 30–50; Rosenzweig, "Cultivating Subjects in the Neo-Assyrian Empire," *JSA* 16 (2016): 307–34; Rosenzweig, "'Ordering the Chaotic Periphery': The Environmental Impact of the Neo-Assyrian Empire on Its Provinces," in *The Provincial Archaeology of the Assyrian Empire*, ed. John MacGinnis, Dick Wicke, and Tina Greenfield (Oxford: Oxbow, 2016), 49–58.

"Truth is the name we give to the choices to which we cling," to recognize that no historical reconstruction can ever be permanent.[13] Yet repositioning scholarship on the long sixth century from a text-centered to a multimedia discourse (including texts) should allow deeper understanding of the oft-studied (and deservedly so) biblical texts, helping us understand their theological and aesthetic programs within a larger framework. Such a repositioning does not force us to take sides on historical causality, as if factors such as class or means of production or ideology were fixed data rather than relationships among large sets of behaviors, ideas, feelings, and even accidents of life. Causality lies beyond our reach in any case.

Still, we trust that this collection of essays will provoke reappraisal of the relevant texts from Israel and beyond, of the art and architecture of empire, of the restructuring of societies following disaster, and perhaps even the present implications of all this for our own world. We seek (1) to broaden the discussion of texts to a study of the multiple media in which ancient societies communicated during the long sixth century, (2) to widen the historical time frame in which forced migrations and returns can be considered as they impinge on the biblical record, and (3) to identify the wider scope of historical phenomena considered relevant to the discussion of this period and its aftermath. Such a reframing may get us out of the cul-de-sac of research in which we find ourselves. And it may present more even richer implications for life today. For the problems of a Second Isaiah have their cognates today, as do the problems of Darius the Great. Top and bottom of society find themselves locked together now as then. Centers and peripheries find themselves closely intertwined. If we may learn something from the long sixth century, perhaps it is that.

---

13. Paul Veyne, *Did the Greeks Believe in Their Myths? An Essay on the Constitutive Imagination*, trans. Paula Wissing (Chicago: University of Chicago Press, 1988), 127.

Success and Failure, Resistance and Submission: Nuanced Identities and Relationships during the Return and Early Persian Period

Pamela Barmash

Among the most striking features of the biblical book of Ezra is its narrative shape: the chronological gap of a half century or more between the initial group of returnees and the arrival of Ezra is passed over in silence (Ezra 6–7).[1] Both b. Meg. 16b and Song Rab. 5:5 miss the extent of the chronological discrepancy and question why Ezra did not join with those returning at the behest of Cyrus. The omission highlights the tension between the success and failure of the returnees—did they succeed in their efforts at rebuilding, or did Ezra, a generation later, need to do what they could not accomplish? The text's multivocality is amplified in other dimensions. The Judahites are portrayed as both submitting and resisting imperial rule: they retained Hebrew amid an ocean of Aramaic, and they conceptualized imperial actions through their own theological lens. The cultural dynamics in play during the community's transition from the Neo-Assyrian and Neo-Babylonian empires to Achaemenid Persian imperial rule shape the biblical texts that recount and present the return from exile. The Judahites had to negotiate a complex and nuanced path between the political and economic reality in which they lived and their aspirations. They sought to uphold their cultural and religious identity despite, and perhaps because of, imperial overlordship.

---

1. Scholars have debated when the temple was rebuilt and when Ezra was active, whether slightly before Nehemiah or after, whether in the fifth century or the fourth century. See, for example, Diana Edelman, *The Origins of the "Second" Temple: Persian Imperial Policy and the Rebuilding of Jerusalem* (London: Equinox, 2005), 151–208; Lisbeth S. Fried, *Ezra, a Commentary*, SPCCS (Sheffield: Sheffield Phoenix, 2015), 289–90, 293–97.

The Nature of Historical Narrative

A crucial recognition must be kept in mind: the authors and editors of the historical texts in the Bible shaped the contours of the historical narrative they recount. This is so both for the author of the original form of a text and for any and all later editors. They organized the chronology and set its beginning and end. They selected events and people to highlight or obscure and singled out specific details. They provided explanations for the occurrences in the plot, whether through explicit articulation or by placing events next to one another, implying causation, and they integrated a variety of social, political, and religious ideas into the narrative, whether they articulated them expressly or presumed them implicitly.[2] The authors and editors constructed their (hi)story out of the historical data they knew prompted by their different motivations.

In light of how the authors and editors shaped the historical narrative, we must take into account the narrative strategies they employed to remember the past.[3] Whatever the historical reality of the community of returnees and the early Second Temple period, the historical narratives about the return reveal much about the concerns and worldview of the authors and editors. How did they perceive past individuals and events as having an impact on their circumstances? Which religious, social, and political ideas informed their view of the past, and how did they resolve conflicting influences?

For the Judahite exiles, returning to their homeland entailed conceptual complexity: they abandoned a life in which they and an earlier generation adjusted to exile, whether well or poorly, and they launched on a new life in a land that was supposed to be their homeland. But the reality of the homeland they entered was neither that of the homeland that was left behind nor the one they may have imagined.[4] They had to adjust to a new

---

2. In contrast to Greek and Latin authors, biblical historians do not disclose their theoretical reasoning about constructing their historical accounts, but it must be noted that explicit reasoning articulated by Greek and Latin authors sheds light on only part of their motivation.

3. Ian D. Wilson, *History and the Hebrew Bible: Culture, Narrative, and Memory*, BRPBI 3.2 (Leiden: Brill, 2018), 1–69.

4. Adele Berlin, "The Exile: Biblical Ideology and Its Postmodern Ideological Interpretation," in *Literary Constructions of Identity in the Ancient World*, ed. Hanna Liss and Manfred Oeming (Winona Lake, IN: Eisenbrauns, 2010), 349–50.

reality at the same time as they reshaped reality to fit their expectations. They employed the return in nuanced ways in their self-understanding, and in turn, how it was presented had a profound impact on how they constructed their social memories.

In the misprision between the anticipated and the actual, the accomplishments of the Judahite protagonists are presented as equivocal. The returnees are viewed as the main exemplar of the Israelites after the exile. The historical spotlight is focused on them, not on those whose ancestors were not exiled and remained living in their native country.[5] A set of accomplishments is credited to them. The returnees in Ezra 1 are portrayed as eagerly obeying the command of Cyrus, who himself recognizes and obeys God. They are depicted as receiving the full support of Cyrus's administration and of their community, and their transporting back to Jerusalem the vessels and implements of the destroyed temple serves to undo its loss. The returnees are portrayed as those who successfully built and maintained a permanent settlement despite the machinations of adversaries. They are celebrated as rebuilding the Jerusalem temple, but their inability to build more is obscured, partially by the omission of the temporal gap between them and Ezra.

Failures and near misses mar their accomplishments. Rebuilding the temple was delayed, not due to their laziness or disobedience but to the malfeasance and opposition of other imperial subjects. Even when they reached the high point of the raising of the temple, tears were shed, but whether these were tears of joy or tears of sadness is left ambivalent. Their incapacity to rebuild Jerusalem beyond the temple, whether due to political and/or economic circumstances, is elided; by contrast, their transgressions are highlighted. The community's failures in observance are placed front and center in the later chapters of the book. The narratives about the returnees and their descendants are placed next to one another, and this contour amplifies both their successes and their failures. Differing images of the community are woven together. The characterizations interact,

---

5. As I will address later in this essay, the identity of the exiles as Judahites/southerners and/or Israelites/northerners is a complex matter, especially in the memory of exile and return. For an analogous reshaping of history in the contrast posited between the northerners becoming the exiles never to return, while the southerners became the exiles who did return, even though many northerners fled south and the two populations mixed in exile, see Pamela Barmash, "At the Nexus of History and Memory: The Ten Lost Tribes," *AJSR* 29 (2005): 207–36.

complementing and contradicting one another. The returnees and their descendants are portrayed as multivocal and polyvalent figures.

The nuanced characterization shapes how the historical narrative in Ezra 1–6 amplifies the importance of the Jerusalem temple. The narrative could have placed the emphasis solely on the returnees and their resettlement in Judah. The restoration of Israelite rule over the entire province and the identity of specific individuals with authority in the Judahite community could have received the greatest stress in the early chapters of Ezra. But the narrative is structured so that the rebuilding of the temple is the center of attention. The major triumph of the sixth-century returnees is depicted as the rebuilding of the temple despite all odds.

Yet there is a wrinkle. Ezra 3:1–7 depicts the returnees as setting up an altar and offering sacrifices day and night, even though the rebuilding of the temple's foundations had not yet started. The eagerness of the people is highlighted as they gather spontaneously as one when the seventh month approaches in Ezra 3:1.[6] Articulating that the sacrifices were resumed before the renovations began accents the alacrity and enthusiasm of the returnees.[7] At the same time, an altar without a surrounding temple highlights their difficulties. Its solitude manifests what is missing: the building of which the altar should be a part. The altar is arguably the major feature of consequence in the temple, and its happenstances manifest the success and failure of the returnees. The narrative about the resumption of sacrifice with the altar by Zerubbabel and Joshua in Ezra 3:1–7 may have been moved from its original place at the culmination of rebuilding as narrated in Ezra 6, and in so doing, the delays and impediments in building the temple are accentuated.[8]

---

6. Antonius H. J. Gunneweg, *Ezra*, KAT (Gütersloh: Gütersloher Verlag Mohn, 1985), 10. The verse echoes Neh 7:73 and 8:1, but whether the Ezra text is borrowed from Nehemiah or vice versa is debatable.

7. The rearrangement of events in a historical narrative in the Hebrew Bible is not unprecedented. For example, 1 Kgs 11:23–25 is placed near the end of the account of Solomon's reign, yet it concerns hostilities that started at the start of his reign.

8. It is doubtful that the altar was commissioned before the temple was rebuilt. Zerubbabel, the one who set up the altar along with Joshua the high priest, is portrayed as participating in the laying of the temple's foundation in the first year of the return (Ezra 3:8–13). However, Tattenai's letter reveals that it was Sheshbazzar who was the governor who oversaw the rebuilding of the foundation in the reign of Cyrus, not Zerubbabel, who arrived only as governor in the second year of Darius (Ezra 5:14–16). Darius's order to Tattenai indicates that Darius's support of an unnamed governor

The corresponding action to the setting up of the lone altar, namely, the building of the temple, manifests the polyvalence of the success and failure of the returnees. Commissioning the altar and starting the rebuilding of the temple mark the success of the returnees. The accumulation of obstacles and interruptions signal their failings, even though the historical narrative is arranged to demonstrate that the delays are not of their own doing. Ezra 4 interrupts the successes of Ezra 1–3 and 5–6 with accounts of how adversaries suspended the rebuilding. But Tattenai's letter (Ezra 5:8–17) and Haggai and Zechariah do not mention the work stoppage during the reigns of Cyrus and Darius (presumably Darius I) narrated in Ezra 4:1–5, and Lisbeth Fried argues that this incident was fabricated in order to create a reversal of fortune of the protagonists.[9] Unnamed adversaries are deemed those responsible for suspending the work, not the returnees. The returnees have laid the foundations of the temple at the conclusion of Ezra 3, and other local worshipers of YHWH ask to participate in its rebuilding and are rebuffed in Ezra 4:1–3. The rejection provokes antagonism, and according to Ezra 4:4–5, the rebuilding of the temple is halted due to fear on part of the returnees and the interference of royal ministers.

The narrative of Ezra 4:6–24, the letter of complaint by the Judahites' adversaries, is shifted out of chronological order of Ezra 1–3 and 5–6, again to accentuate the failures and successes of the returnees. The correspondence deals with the rebuilding of the city's walls, not the temple.

---

of Judah may be an indication that Zerubbabel was active in his reign, not Cyrus's. Furthermore, oblique evidence may also shed light on when the altar was dedicated: Haggai, a prophet active in the reign of Darius according to the incipit of the book bearing his name, declares that from a certain time forward, the people will be blessed and no longer be defiled from what they touch, implying that corpse contamination was no longer an issue because the altar was rededicated as part of the rebuilding of the temple (Hag 2:18–19). Until that point in time, the people were in a state of defilement (Hag 2:14). Corpse contamination, a type of ritual impurity incurred by touching, is overcome by the ritual of the ashes of the red heifer, a ritual that requires the use of an altar (Num 19). This may signal that the altar was set up during the reign of Darius, not during the reign of Cyrus. One may also wonder whether the start of the rebuilding occurred during the reign of Cyrus, since the ceremony in Ezra 3:10–13 lacks the mention of a prophet. It stands to reason that Haggai and Zechariah (or another prophet) would have taken part. These pieces of evidence signal that the installation of the altar should be chronologically integrated in the close of the account of the rebuilding of the temple rather than precede it (see Fried, *Ezra, a Commentary*, 22–23, 154–57, 162, 238–40).

9. Fried, *Ezra, a Commentary*, 194.

It is included as proof, and it is most likely authentic because if the biblical author had forged it, the author would have written a letter dealing with the building of the temple, not the city walls. Ezra 4:1–5 address the cessation of temple building during the reigns of Cyrus and Darius, and the narrative about the temple is taken up again in Ezra 5–6, an account portraying Haggai, Zechariah, Zerubbabel, and Joshua in the time of Darius I. In between is placed an account (Ezra 4:6–24) relating how work on rebuilding the city and its walls was stopped in the reigns of Ahasuerus (presumably Xerxes I, r. 486–465 BCE) and Artaxerxes I (r. 464–425 BCE).[10] The insertion further deepens the tension as to whether the Judahite community can succeed in building the temple.

Polyvalence shapes the figure of Ezra as well: he was not alive at the time of the rebuilding of the Jerusalem temple, so that achievement cannot be ascribed to him. The narrative, however, constructs the portrayal of his administration so that he emerges as the triumphant leader and rebuilder. His authority is generated by his personal character and is emphasized in a way that the status of previous leaders (Sheshbazzar, Zerubbabel, and Joshua) is not (Ezra 7:1–6). His relationship to God is specifically articulated (7:6), and the direct authorization for his leadership from the Persian king is given ample space (7:11–26). His journey to Judah is portrayed as a second exodus.[11] The travelers depart in Nisan, the month linked to the exodus and the preparations for leaving Egypt (7:8), embodying the old exodus in their journey. Ezra's confrontation with the community about their transgressions both enhances his status as an expert in Torah and highlights the failings of the community and his effectiveness as leader. Yet his depiction as a subordinate to Nehemiah in interactions with imperial hierarchy further serves to lessen Ezra's status and emphasize his failures.

---

10. The letter and the response ordering a work stoppage are assigned in Ezra 4:23–24 explicitly to Artaxerxes I (r. 464–425 BCE) and Darius II (r. 423–404 BCE). An editor presumably tried to tie the overall narrative together by assigning the end of the work stoppage in Ezra 4:24 to Darius I: this ruler cannot be Darius II because Ezra 5 is tied to Zerubbabel and Joshua, who are named in Ezra 2 as part of the initial return. Ezra 6:14 is presumably another editorial addition, with the naming of Artaxerxes as an attempt to create an uninterrupted chronology.

11. See Pamela Barmash, "Out of the Mists of History: The Exaltation of the Exodus in the Bible," in *Exodus in the Jewish Experience: Echoes and Reverberations*, ed. Pamela Barmash and W. David Nelson (Lanham, MD: Lexington Books, 2015), 2.

Ezra and Nehemiah are presented as heroes in their time and models for the future, both secure and insecure in their authority. Ezra's authority derives from his expertise in Torah, a criterion internal to the Jewish community, as well as imperial authorization based on his expertise, while Nehemiah's authority derives from his status in the imperial hierarchy as well as his demonstrated accomplishments in the community. Yet they lack the jurisdiction that a Davidide monarch could claim. They are nondynastic heroes for a political situation in which independence under a native monarchy is impossible. The reestablishment of the Davidic dynasty was a forlorn hope. And despite their leadership, the community remained errant.

The polyvalence in the portrayals of the returnees and Ezra and Nehemiah is mirrored in the weaving together of the distinct images: Should the city and territory be seen as ruined, or as the temple rebuilt and the city and territory repopulated, or a combination thereof? Is the community supported by the imperial administration, or is the community imperiled by local and regional adversaries, or both at the same time? Is the community successful, or is the community endangered, or both one and the other? Is Ezra and/or Nehemiah a success or failure as a leader? The congeries of images was undoubtedly shaped by the reality and perception of the community as to its successes and failures.

There are two ways to approach the multivocality of the texts under discussion. We can adopt a diachronic approach, and from the twists and disjunctures that they manifest, we could infer compositional history: differing views developed due to political, socioeconomic, and cultural transformations over time. In contrast, we can adopt a synchronic approach that situates a text in a single historical context, one of multiple, even contradictory, viewpoints. The diachronic approach posits that the multivocality developed over time and that a single slant dominated at a time, while the synchronic approach holds that Israelite and Judahite readers maintained diverse and at times contradictory viewpoints at the same time. The validity of the diachronic approach is based on the premise that a single point of view prevailed at a time, an assumption that can be questioned and requires proof, while the synchronic approach is inherent in the final form of a biblical book and in its presence in the biblical canon, one of multiplicity in a single era. Even if the texts are diachronic in their composition and redaction, their preservation in holistic form means that their composite texture affected the individuals and communities that read them.

Polyvalence creates dynamic potentials for generating meaning.[12] Judahites of the Persian period would see themselves in the multivocality of the returnees and the rebuilding of the temple and the city; the hesitant success and failure of the community and its leaders, Ezra and Nehemiah; and the need to accommodate empire. The texts' multivocality may mean that readers were comfortable with and may have even needed the multiplicity of viewpoints. Perhaps they saw their identity as twofold, part Judahite, part imperial subject. They were used to ambiguity, and perhaps they needed the multiple dimensionality of their texts because they, too, were both successful in a number of areas and wanting in others. The multivocality of their texts affirmed their own complexity. They were both secure and insecure, safe and compromised, at ease and ill at ease as imperial subjects, protected and disquieted in subjugation. The multivocality fitted the reality of their lives in the Persian period, and helped them negotiate the dissonance of their identity.

Multivocality in texts recounting history worked because the Judahites' connection to the past was deep: the past offered possibilities for the future. Historical accounts were intended as a way of reaching into the past to lay claim to the future.[13] The memory of the past was intended as a blueprint for the future, not an antiquarian reminiscence. The figures of the returnees and of Ezra serve as inspiration for the future, as models of conduct and behavior. Recollections of what they did were to be consulted again and again for guidance. The past was to serve as explanation for contemporary situations and as guidance for future conduct.

The multivocality of the historical accounts meant that it was nuanced and flexible to meet a greater variety of contexts and quandaries. The nuances opened up more possibilities. It maximized options, rather than minimized them. Historiographic writing is rooted in the past, yet is intended to offer guidance for the present and future. It uses the past as a means of proposing alternate futures. Ian Wilson argues persuasively that "the multivocal narratives ... can be subjects of historical inquiry and can provide valuable historical information about Israelite/Judean culture and its concerns, regardless of the historicity of the persons and events described therein."[14]

---

12. Wilson, "History and the Hebrew Bible," 56.

13. Pamela Barmash, "The Exodus—Central, Enduring, and Generative," in Barmash and Nelson, *Exodus in the Jewish Experience*, ix.

14. Wilson, "History and the Hebrew Bible," 34.

Multivocality may have been intended because no one knew whether and how return would work out. No one knew what Persian dominance would signify in the long term. Multivocality allowed for multiple possibilities. Multivocality expressed what the returnees and their descendants were experiencing.

What is not multivocal is the sharp focus on the returnees, and it is a telling aspect of these historical accounts. Only a segment of the Judahite deportees and descendants took part in the return. A significant number remained in their native land and never went into exile.[15] Many of the descendants of the deportees remained in exile as well. Yet the story of the returnees has become the story of the whole Judahite society.[16] Two factors precipitated this shaping of memory. First, the trauma of exile and the sense of dislocation were so profound that they shaped the self-perception of all. People who have not experienced trauma but are members of a group, part of which has experienced shock, find that that shock has become part of their story as well. Second, the trauma of exile was resolved by return, and the focus of the shared cultural narrative is on the returnees. Even those who remained in the land or in exile saw themselves through the lens of the returnees.

The exclusive focus on the returnees constructs and shapes social memory. Nonreturnees adopt the story of the returnees because exile and return is the most significant event that has happened to the group.[17] It

---

15. A fierce debate has broken out over whether Israelite territory was empty during the exilic period. See Hans M. Barstad, *The Myth of the Empty Land: A Study in the History and Archaeology of Judah during the "Exilic" Period* (Oslo: Scandinavian University Press, 1996), as well as the essay by Lisbeth S. Fried in this volume. Whatever the historical reality was, 2 Kgs 24:14–16 and 25:11–12 depict the land as still inhabited, although by the poor, who eventually grew into tens of thousands. Second Kings 25:29 recounts that the remaining people fled to Egypt because of fear of the Babylonians but leaves unclear whether that flight was temporary or permanent. Jeremiah 44:1–2 depicts a land devoid of inhabitants. However, 2 Chr 36:10 minimizes the deportation, limiting it to Jehoaichin the king, and 2 Chr 36:17–19 confines the destruction to Jerusalem and does not extend it to other cities in Judah. See Berlin, "Exile," 349.

16. The books of Esther and Daniel do provide a window onto the life of the exilic community that remained behind and did not participate in the return, but their dates of composition may have been well into the Persian period, and perhaps even later.

17. Even those who did not experience it were affected by it. Furthermore, it may be that the returnees created the narrative because they were among those who were

does raise the question, of course, about the later generation, that of Ezra and that of Nehemiah, whatever the chronological relationship between them, who clearly were members of a Judahite social group who remained in exile until it was their turn to return. The story of their group remaining in exile did not become the main story, even though they were the literate cultural producers. Only when they joined the earlier returnees did they become part of the story. Their status, as authorized by the overlord, enhanced the standing of the returnees. That the overlord lent them authority and resources to rebuild prestigious sites associated with Jerusalem reinforced their status.

Accommodation to Empire

The imperial paradigm shifted during the sixth century BCE: the Achaemenid Persian Empire pursued a policy of granting local autonomy rather than aggressively incorporating independent territories under imperial rule. This seemingly more tolerant policy was ironically enabled by the belligerent program of previous empires. The aggression of Neo-Assyria and Neo-Babylonia secured the assumption and acceptance of foreign rule by formerly autonomous countries. Local populations were intimidated into submission, and the exercise of authority by an overlord became part of the ethos. Resistance, however, could assume another form besides military opposition: the ruled need not submit and defer completely but could find other ways to assert their identity. Imperial power could be subverted and forestalled in cultural life because empires in general have to tolerate enough polyculturalism to forestall rebellion while exercising sufficient force to prevent and subdue it.[18]

The Neo-Assyrian political and military administration forged an empire in the ancient Near East where there had not been one before. When the Neo-Assyrian Empire was overthrown, Egypt and Babylonia vied for hegemony, with Babylonia succeeding in seizing power. Then the Achaemenid Persian Empire supplanted Neo-Babylonian rule and expanded what had been created earlier. In so doing, the Persians were able to benefit from the imperial program of the Neo-Assyrian Empire and

---

the literate cultural producers. See Caralie Cooke's essay in this volume and her argument that the returnees were the literate cultural producers.

18. For more on the relationship between empire and subject population, see the essay by Mark W. Hamilton in this volume.

its immediate successor, the Neo-Babylonian Empire. The harsh treatment of territorial groups by the Neo-Assyrian and Neo-Babylonian empires prompted acceptance of Persian domination.

To what extent the Persian Empire adopted a less violent and authoritarian policy overall is debatable and perhaps immaterial to the assumption of imperial hegemony the Judahites absorbed. An imperial policy of dominion and subjugation was established by the earlier empires prior to the Achaemenids, and the Cyrus Cylinder shows that Cyrus utilized a strategy of restoring select cults and giving populations modest amounts of autonomy as a means of ensuring loyalty.[19] It does not demonstrate that he extended this treatment to all peoples and cults, and it serves only as a document recounting a release analogous to that recorded in the Hebrew Bible for the Judahites.[20] Whether Cyrus and other Persian kings were

---

19. For a new edition of the Cyrus Cylinder, see Hanspeter Schaudig, "The Text of the Cyrus Cylinder," in *Cyrus the Great: Life and Lore*, ed. M. Rahim Shayegan (Boston: Ilex/Center for Hellenic Studies, 2018), 16–25. Other essays in this volume offer analyses of the rhetoric and cultural context of the Cyrus Cylinder.

20. A number of scholars have cast doubt on the historicity of the Judahite return during the reign of Cyrus as recounted in Ezra and Chronicles and argue for a later return under Darius I and/or Artaxerxes I, partially because of Aramaic documents excerpted in Ezra date from a later time period (see Edelman, *Origins of the "Second" Temple*, 151–206, esp. 164). Edelman suggests that Deutero-Isaiah knew of the language of Cyrus's proclamations, one version of which is inscribed on the Cyrus Cylinder, and employed it as a hope that Cyrus would also restore the Jerusalem temple and allow the Judahites to return home. She also doubts that the repatriation under Darius was historical. See also Robartus J. van der Spek, "Cyrus the Great, Exiles, and Foreign Gods: A Comparison of Assyrian and Persian Policies on Subject Nations," in *Extraction and Control: Studies in Honor of Matthew W. Stolper*, ed. Michael Kozuh et al., SAOC 68 (Chicago: Oriental Institute of the University of Chicago, 2014), 233–64. There is no positive evidence from the records of Judahite exiles in Babylonia since there is no clear break in the archive indicating that a return occurred in the reign of Cyrus. See Laurie E. Pearce and Cornelia Wunsch, *Documents of Judean Exiles and West Semites in Babylonia in the Collection of David Sofer*, CUSAS 28 (Bethesda, MD; CDL, 2014), 5; Rick Bonnie, *Judeans in Babylonia: A Study of Deportees in the Sixth and Fifth Centuries BCE* (Leiden: Brill, 2020); Michael Jursa and Ran Zadok, "Judeans and Other West Semites: Another View from the Babylonia Countryside," *HBAI* 9 (2020): 20–40.

The tablets of a family returning from Babylonia to Neirab in Syria have resurfaced, providing a parallel instance of repatriation to that of the Judahites. See Edouard Dhorme, "Les tablettes babyloniennes de Neirab," *RA* 25 (1928): 53–82; Israel Eph'al, "The Western Minorities in Babylonia in the Sixth and Fifth Centuries BC," *Or* 47

as humane as often claimed is debatable. Cyrus was perceived as more humane by Greek historians, such as Herodotus, *Hist.* 3.89, and Xenophon, *Cyrus the Great*.[21] Yet Cyrus and others employed brutal policies at times: the Bisitun inscription mentions the rebels Darius I defeated and executed, and the relief portrays the rebel leader under his feet and the mutinous kings in fetters before him.[22]

That imperial authority demanded absolute submission is employed as an argument against the Judahites: their opponents contend that the fact that the Judahites rebelled against a previous overlord means that they will resist the Persians. It is striking that an uprising against the empire that the Persians defeated is held against the returnees. The rebellion of Jerusalem mentioned in Ezra 4:15 must refer to the rebellion during the time of the Neo-Babylonian Empire. This testifies to the nature of imperial hegemony: a city that rebels against one empire is considered one that may rebel against another. Because imperial domination is to be unquestioned, a city that rebelled against an overlord, even one that rebelled against a prior overlord defeated by the prevailing superpower, would still be deemed rebellious. It should have remained submissive. So the prevailing view is not "the enemy of my enemy is my friend" but "the enemy of my

---

(1978): 74–90; Frederick M. Fales, "Remarks on the Neirab Texts," *OrAnt* 12 (1973): 131–42; Joachim Oelsner, "Weitere Bemerkungen zu den Neirab-Urkunder," *AoF* 16 (1989): 68–77; Gauthier Tolini, "Le rôle de la famille de Nusku-gabbê au sein d'une communauté de déportés originaires de Neirab en Babylonie au VIe siècle," in *La famille dans le Proche-Orient ancient: Réalité, symbolismes et images; Actes de la 55è RAI (Paris 2009)* (Winona Lake, IN.: Eisenbrauns, 2014), 591–98.

21. By contrast, the Neo-Assyrian Empire cultivated a violent image, even if it did not impose its religion on subjugated nations. See Morton (Mordechai) Cogan, *Imperialism and Religion: Assyrian, Judah, and Israel in the Eighth and Seventh Centuries B.C.E.*, SBLMS 19 (Missoula, MT: Scholars Press, 1974); John McKay, *Religion in Judah under the Assyrians* (London: SCM, 1973). Albert T. Olmstead originated the idea that the Assyrians imposed their religion. See Olmstead, "Oriental Imperialism," *AHR* 23 (1918): 755–62.

22. Elizabeth N. von Voigtlander, *The Bisitun Inscription of Darius the Great* (London: Lund Humphries, 1978), fig. 1. For an analysis of the violence of the revolt, see Yannick Müller, "Religion, Empire, and Mutilation: A Cross-religious Perspective on Achaemenid Mutilation Practices," in *Religion in the Achaemenid Persian Empire: Emerging Judaisms and Trends*, ed. Diana Edelman, Anne Fitzpatrick McKinley, and Philippe Guillaume, ORA 17 (Tübingen: Mohr Siebeck, 2016), 197–227; Uzume Z. Wijnsma, "The Worst Revolt of the Bisitun Crisis: A Chronological Reconstruction of the Egyptian Revolt under Petubastis IV," *JNES* 77 (2018): 157–73.

enemy is also suspected of being my enemy." The ideological assumption is that a vassal city must be submissive. There is no conceptualization that a city could rebel justifiably. A city should always demonstrate unquestioned allegiance to its overlord, no matter who.

Nevertheless, the ruled could resist in nonmartial ways, and so the Judahites reconceptualized their world. Persian imperialism is reimagined in content and terminology through Judahite eyes. Cyrus's edict is in particular reshaped in biblical memory. One way Cyrus's actions are assimilated to Israelite needs is how the Edict of Cyrus is articulated in Israelite terminology:

1. The phrase indicating direct discourse "thus says (personal name)" is a phrase occurring many times in the Hebrew Bible, both for a human speaker and a divine speaker (e.g., Gen 15:5; 32:2). It does not appear in Neo-Babylonian inscriptions, and in Achaemenid Persian only starting in the reign of Darius (r. 522–486 BCE).[23] The phrase does not appear in any Achaemenid inscriptions dating from Cyrus's own time (r. 559–530 BCE).[24]

2. The title given to Cyrus, "king of Persia," is one that would only be employed in texts written by non-Persians in the time of Cyrus.[25] It becomes common from the reign of Darius on.

3. The term "God of heaven" is found in 2 Chr 36:23 and Ezra 1:2 as well as in Neh 1:4, 5; 2:20; Jonah 1:9; Gen 24:3, 7. The Israelites did not adopt this term from the Persians since the Persian god was never called as such in a Persian inscription.[26] The phrase is employed in the Elephantine papyri, and based on its appearance there and in Jonah and Genesis, Israelites employed it in their accounts of interactions with non-Israelites.

Even more conspicuous is how Cyrus's act is refracted through Judahite concepts:

1. The Persian emperor acts at God's command, not for his own political reasons.[27] Ezra 1:1 observes that Cyrus was roused by God to fulfill

---

23. Matt Waters, "Cyrus and the Achaemenids," *Iran* 42 (2004): 73–78.
24. Fried, *Ezra, a Commentary*, 54.
25. Peter Ross Bedford, *Temple Restoration in Early Achaemenid Persia*, JSJSup (Leiden: Brill, 2001), 120–22; Fried, *Ezra, a Commentary*, 54.
26. D. K. Andrews, "Yahweh the God of the Heavens," in *The Seed of Wisdom: Essays in Honour of Th. J. Meek*, ed. William Stuart McCullough (Toronto: University of Toronto Press, 1964), 45–57. Auramazda's name means "Lord of Wisdom."
27. The statement that the Persian king was favored by a foreign god is echoed in a number of other texts commemorating the rebuilding of temples. The Cyrus Cylinder recounts Cyrus's rebuilding of the Esagila temple, which he had destroyed

a prophecy of Jeremiah: "And in the first year of Cyrus king of Persia in order to fulfill the word of YHWH spoken by Jeremiah, YHWH roused the spirit of Cyrus king of Persia to issue a proclamation orally and in writing, as follows."[28] But which oracle was meant? Ezra 1:2–3 presents Cyrus's command without identifying the specific prophecy:

> Thus says Cyrus king of Persia: YHWH God of heaven gave me all the nations of the earth, and he commanded me to build his house in Jerusalem, which is in Judah. Every one of you of his people—may his God be with him. May he go up to Jerusalem, which is in Judah, and build the house of YHWH God of Israel, the God who is in Jerusalem.

The conclusion of 2 Chronicles, which may be based on the beginning of the book of Ezra or vice versa, references a prophecy of Jeremiah, connecting it to the Edict of Cyrus:

> And he exiled those who escaped the sword to Babylonia, and they became his and his sons' servants until the reign of the Persian Empire, in fulfillment of the word of YHWH spoken by Jeremiah, until the land has paid back its Sabbaths; during the time of its desolation, the land rested until seventy years were completed. (2 Chr 36:20–21)

The reference to seventy years of exile and/or destruction may indicate that the prophecy in question is Jer 25:9–13 and/or 29:10:

> I am now summoning all the nations of the north—utterance of YHWH—and Nebuchadnezzar king of Babylon my servant, to bring them upon this land, its inhabitants, and its surrounding nations. I will annihilate them and make them a desolation and an object of hissing, ruins for all time. I shall banish from them the sound of joy and the sound of rejoicing, the sound of groom and the sound of bride, the sound of the mill and the light of the lamp. This entire land will become

---

(*COS* 2.124:314–16). It emphasizes that Marduk selected Cyrus to rebuild the city of Babylon and the Esagila temple. An inscription from the temple of Neith in Sais commemorates its rebuilding at the behest of Cambyses and Darius and notes that Neith, mother of the god Re, countenanced the Persian conquest of Egypt and that the two Persian kings venerated the goddess. See Miriam Lichtheim, *Ancient Egyptian Literature, a Book of Readings* (Berkeley: University of California Press, 1980), 3:36–41; Fried, *Ezra, a Commentary*, 55–56.

28. Unless otherwise indicated, all translations are mine.

a ruin, and these nations will serve the king of Babylon seventy years. When the seventy years are over, I will remember the king of Babylon and that nation—utterance of YHWH—for their sin, and the land of the Chaldeans, and I shall make it desolation forever. I will bring upon that land all that is written in this book which Jeremiah prophesied about all the nations. (Jer 25:9–13)

For thus says YHWH: When Babylon's seventy years are over, I will remember you, and I will fulfill my word of favor to bring you back to this place. (Jer 29:10)

The sin committed by the Judahites is to be recompensed by a seventy-year rest. The reason for the term of seventy years rather than another number is opaque. That amount of time, seven times ten, could have been prompted by the failure to observe Sabbatical Years and Jubilees (Lev 26:34–35). According to Lev 26:18, those who transgress are to be punished seven-fold, but how this adds up to seventy is not clear.[29] The number may stem from historical reality, a time period that was imposed on the Judahites by outside political actors: (1) the period between 605 and 539 BCE, when the Achaemenid Persians conquered Babylon; (2) the time between the destruction of the temple (587/6 BCE) and its rebuilding (516 BCE); or (3) between the deportation (597 BCE) and Cyrus's edict (538 BCE).[30]

Nonetheless, Cyrus's decree is understood through Judahite prophecy. That God stirred the spirit of Cyrus is a declaration based on Jer 50:9 and 51:11:

For I am now rousing and raising up an assembly of great nations. (Jer 50:9)

YHWH has roused the spirit of the kings of Media. (Jer 51:11)

Cyrus acts at the behest of God in Judahite conceptualization.

2. The text of Ezra sets the returnees in parallel to Cyrus by terming their action as "all those whom God roused the(ir) spirit to go up to

---

29. Seventy seems more about signifying a very long time, as indicated in royal inscriptions of Esarhaddon. See Rykle Borger, *Die Inschriften Asarhaddons, Königs von Assyrien*, AfOB (Osnabrück: Biblio-Verlag, 1967), 12–19.

30. That this is an iconic time period is shown in that Dan 9:2 also refers to Jeremiah's seventy-year span.

rebuild the house of YHWH" (Ezra 1:5). Both Cyrus and the returnees are recipients of divine inspiration.

3. While other Jewish communities built temples during the Persian period, such as the Elephantine community, the temple in Jerusalem was the focus of the aspirations of the Judahite returnees.

4. The building of a temple must be authorized by a god: the god makes the decision, and the king receives the commission to build. This is a common presumption in the ancient Near East, but its boldness is manifest in the naming of Cyrus, a non-Israelite, as the king commissioned by God. Cyrus is placed in the august company of David and Solomon.[31]

5. It might be expected that Cyrus (and his scribes and/or administrators) would refer to "the God of Judah" because the exiles were from Judah. A settlement of theirs in Babylon is called "the town of the Judahites."[32] But "the God of Israel" is the term used here, mirroring the political and theological presumption of the Judahites that they are the bearers of corporate ethnic identity in place of the northern kingdom. Isaiah 45:3 refers to "the God of Israel," who selects and upholds Cyrus, and Ezekiel and Deutero-Isaiah ascribe the name Israel to the Babylonian exiles.[33]

6. The rebuilding of a temple signaled the reconciliation of God with the Judahites according to Israelite theology.[34] The Persians may have supported the rebuilding of temples in marginal sites.[35] An example may be seen in the rebuilding of the temple of Osiris and Isis at the Kharga oasis during the reign of Artaxerxes I, along with an underground reservoir and water supply system. The building of a temple at an out-of-the-way place in Egypt as a way for protecting the periphery. In the same vein, the Per-

---

31. Victor (Avigdor) Hurowitz, *I Have Built You an Exalted House: Temple Building in the Bible in Light of Mesopotamian and Northwest Semitic Writings*, JSOTSup 115 (Sheffield: Sheffield Academic, 1992), 26; Arvid S. Kapelrud, "Temple Building: A Task for Gods and Kings," *Or* 32 (1963): 56–62.

32. Pearce and Wunsch, *Documents of Judean Exiles*, 312.

33. Bedford, *Temple Restoration in Early Achaemenid Persia*, 113.

34. It is to be noted that major temples were not always rebuilt. The temple at Hamath as well as much of the city was destroyed, and the temple was not rebuilt even when the city was rebuilt in the Hellenistic period. The ʿAin Daraʿ temple was also destroyed by the Assyrians and never restored. That the Jerusalem temple would be rebuilt was not a foregone conclusion. It may be a striking exception (see Fried, *Ezra, a Commentary*, 27, 31).

35. Xenophon observes that the Persian monarch set a premium on the cultivation of land (*Oec.* 4.8).

sians may have wanted to rebuild the Jerusalem temple as a way of encouraging settlers in an out-of-the-way place. There are practical political reasons for the Persian empire to permit a return and finance the rebuilding. Nonetheless, Judahite theology understood the actions of the Persians as a manifestation of divine favor.

Cyrus's edict is remembered in distinctively Judahite tropes. It is striking, then, that Deutero-Isaiah appears to be adopting language from Cyrus's decree as evidenced in the Akkadian inscription. The Akkadian inscription asserts that Marduk called Cyrus by name and took him by his hand and that Cyrus acted as a shepherd.[36] Deutero-Isaiah avows that YHWH also called Cyrus by name and took him by his hand and terms Cyrus as a shepherd (Isa 44:28–45:1). The contrast with the version of the decree in the first chapter of Ezra is arresting.

Aramaic versions of the edict are found in Ezra 5:13–15 and 6:3–5, which basically agree with each other but not with Ezra 1:2–4.[37] They lack the prefacing text that explicitly links Cyrus's action to divine inspiration or as fulfillment of Judahite prophecy. They do not employ Israelite terminology, such as "God of heaven." The Aramaic texts are used as citations in bureaucratic texts, and only as part of the larger historical narrative do they fulfill the theological program in which the temple is rebuilt.

> In the first year of King Cyrus of Babylon, he issued an order to rebuild the house of God. Even the silver and gold vessels of the house of God that Nebuchadnezzar had taken away from the temple in Jerusalem and brought to the temple in Babylon, King Cyrus released them from the temple in Babylon to be given to Sheshbazzar, whom he named as governor. He said to him, "Take these vessels, deposit them in the temple in Jerusalem, and let the house of God be rebuilt on its site." (Ezra 5:13–15)

> In the first year of King Cyrus, he issued an order concerning the house of God in Jerusalem: "Let the house be rebuilt, a place for offering sacrifices, with its base built up high. It should sixty cubits high and sixty cubits wide, with a course of new timber for every three courses of hewn

---

36. Schaudig, "Text of the Cyrus Cylinder," 22, l. 12.

37. Ezra 6:3 includes more specific information as to the dimensions of the rebuilt temple. The fragments of another copy of the Cyrus Cylinder serve as evidence that decrees were issued in multiple copies and perhaps in multiple media and languages. See John Curtis, *The Cyrus Cylinder and Ancient Persia: A New Beginning for the Middle East* (London: British Museum Press, 2013), 45.

> stone. The costs will be paid by the palace, and the gold and silver vessels of the house of God that Nebuchadnezzar had taken away from the temple in Jerusalem and brought to Babylon shall be returned. Let each (of them) go back to the temple in Jerusalem, where it belongs. You shall deposit it in the house of God." (Ezra 6:3–5)

Neither Aramaic version seems to be the full text of the edict but appears to present only excerpts as needed for the specific reason the edict is cited. Ezra 6:3–5 includes details about the dimensions of the Jerusalem temple that would affirm the authorization of a building of that size. Other multilingual versions of Persian decrees are not identical with each other.[38] The Aramaic versions are not reshaped by Judahite terminology or theological concepts. The closest interaction they have with them is how they figure in the larger theological scheme of the historical narrative when opponents to the rebuilding of the temple are frustrated by the Persian emperor.

The return of the temple vessels is employed in biblical historiography to manifest the sincerity of Cyrus's edict and the totality of the restoration.[39] Ironically, the return of the vessels became a trope used by the prophet Jeremiah's adversary and competitor, Hananiah, to argue for resistance to empire (Jer 28:3). He highlights the return of the temple vessels as a sign of divine favor in opposing imperial rule: "In two years, I will restore to this place all the vessels of the house of YHWH which Nebuchadnezzar king of Babylon took from this place and brought to Babylon." The trope in Hananiah's utterance signals opposition to empire, but Cyrus's return of the temple vessels is viewed in Ezra as signaling the support of the imperial rule. Full restoration includes the furnishings of the temple.

The cult vessels are the singular manifestation of the Israelite god in place of the cult statue.[40] The historical narrative about the destruction

---

38. Lisbeth S. Fried, *The Priest and the Great King: Temple-Palace Relations in the Persian Empire* (Winona Lake, IN: Eisenbrauns, 2004), 140–54. One objection to the authenticity of Cyrus's edict is that it is in Hebrew, whereas the official language of the Persian Empire was Aramaic. But the Cyrus Cylinder is in Akkadian, and the inscription about the temple of Neith is in Ancient Egyptian.

39. That the temple vessels were of singular importance is manifested in the emphasis on Belshazzar's decadence in drinking from the vessels of the Jerusalem temple (Dan 5:2–3).

40. In the reliefs depicting Sennacherib's conquest of Lachish, one segment depicts soldiers removing spoils: they take away large incense burners. In the absence of a cult statue, the incense burners served as a substitute object.

recounts that Nebuchadnezzar had confiscated them as spoils of war (2 Kgs 25:14–15). These vessels, probably stored in Esagila, were then returned, as a counterpart to their being taken as spoil (Ezra 1:7): "Now, King Cyrus brought out the vessels of the house of YHWH, which Nebuchadnezzar had brought out of Jerusalem and placed in the house of his god." The vessels pass from one Persian official to another (Ezra 1:8): "Cyrus king of Persia had them brought out through the office of the treasurer Mithredath, who accounted them to Sheshbazzar the prince of Judah." In exact figures: "These are their inventory: 30 gold basins, 1,000 silver basins, 29 knives, 410 silver biform bowls, 1,000 other vessels, in sum, 5,400 gold and silver vessels. Sheshhbazzar brought all of them back when the exiles returned from Babylon to Jerusalem" (Ezra 1:9–11). A gesture, perhaps minor on the part of an empire, is reconceived as a way of using empire against itself. For the Judahites, the return of the temple vessels is an assertion of identity. It is not an insurrection that would likely fail but a workaround that has a chance of success.

The languages employed by the Judahites demonstrate accommodation and resistance to empire. In a time when the language used by official and commoner alike was Aramaic, using Hebrew was an affirmation of identity and nationality.[41] Persisting in Hebrew was problematic: the

---

41. Israel Eph'al, *Archaeology of the Land of the Bible*, vol. 2, *The Assyrian, Babylonian, and Persian Periods (732–333 BCE)* (New York: Doubleday, 2001), 360–66; Joseph Naveh and Jonas Greenfield, "Hebrew and Aramaic in the Persian Period," in *The Cambridge History of Judaism*, vol. 1, *Introduction: The Persian Period*, ed. William D. Davies and Louis Finkelstein (Cambridge: Cambridge University Press, 1984), 115–29; Joachim Schaper, "Hebrew and Its Study in the Persian Period," in *Hebrew Study from Ezra to Ben-Yehuda*, ed. William Horbury (Edinburgh: T&T Clark, 1999), 15–26; William M. Schniedewind, *A Social History of Hebrew: Its Origins through the Rabbinic Period*, ABRL (New Haven: Yale University Press, 2013), 140–42. That Hebrew had become suffused by Aramaic is documented in the Aramaic ostraca from Beersheba and Arad and in the coins, seals, and seal impressions from the region.

The continuing scholarly publication of Aramaic texts from Idumea demonstrates how Aramaic had become the dominant language of everyday life in the general area of the Persian province of Yehud. See Israel Eph'al and Joseph Naveh, *Aramaic Ostraca of the Fourth Century BC from Idumea* (Jerusalem: Israel Exploration Society, 1996); Bezalel Porten and Ada Yardeni, *Textbook of Aramaic Ostraca from Idumea*, 4 vols. (Winona Lake, IN: Eisenbrauns, 2014–2020).

At the same time, Hebrew authors transferred Aramaic writing patterns into Hebrew. See Mark Leuchter, "The Aramaic Transition and the Redaction of the Pentateuch," *JBL* 136 (2017): 249–68.

public reading of Scripture in Neh 8 requires translation. The people who have gathered cannot understand Hebrew and require its restatement into Aramaic. The complaint about the children of the Judahites who married non-Judahite women is that their children cannot speak Hebrew (Neh 13:23–25). Hebrew was not widely understood, and yet historiography in Hebrew asserts its central place in Judahite culture and the self-identity of those who use it, read it, and transmit texts in it in an ocean of Aramaic.

Yet at the same time, Aramaic is acknowledged as the language of the imperial overlord. The letters to and from the Persian kings are in Aramaic (Ezra 4:8–22; 5:6–17; 6:3–12). The framing narrative is also in Aramaic and could easily have been in Hebrew.[42] The letters evoke the voice of Persian officials. Trepidation aroused by the complaint to the emperor is resolved by the reply of the emperor, a reply that affirms Judahite rights without question. The use of Aramaic confirms the official approval for the Judahites' actions.[43]

Titles can also signal resistance. Sheshbazzar was the leader of the return of the exiles.[44] Most likely he was a Babylonian, yet in Ezra 1:7, he is termed with the Hebrew title נשיא rather than פחה, "governor," because the former title is a native Israelite one, in contrast to his imperial title of governor.

Arranging the Judahites according to an internal structure in Ezra 2 is another form of resistance against imperial order. The patterning of the returnees accentuates their self-identity. The specifics of the names, their link to the original exiles, the detailed numbers of family members, and their internal status, whether Levites, temple singers, gatekeepers, and more, serve to challenge external rule.

---

42. Ezra 4:24, for example, is a repetition of Ezra 4:4, a Hebrew verse.

43. For further analysis of the use of Aramaic in the Hebrew Bible, see Joshua Berman, "The Narrational Voice of the Scribes of Samaria: Ezra 4:8–6:18 Reconsidered," *VT* 56 (2006): 313–26; Berman, "The Narratological Purpose of Aramaic Prose in Ezra 4:4–6:18," *AS* 5.2 (2007): 1–27; Diana Edelman, "Identities within a Central and Peripheral Perspective: The Use of Aramaic in the Hebrew Bible," in *Centres and Peripheries in the Early Second Temple Period*, ed. Ehud Ben Zvi and Christoph Levin, FAT 109 (Tübingen: Mohr Siebeck, 2016), 109–31.

44. Scholars have speculated that he may have been Shenazzar, the fourth son of Jehoiachin. See Sara Japhet, "Sheshbazzar and Zerubbabel against the Background of the Historical and Religious Tendencies of Ezra-Nehemiah: Part 1," in *From the Rivers of Babylon to the Highlands of Judah: Collected Studies on the Restoration Period* (Winona Lake, IN: Eisenbrauns, 2006), 77–83.

The population categories that are included and omitted from the lists of returnees are striking. The laypeople are listed at the beginning by ancestor or geographic origin in the land of Israel. Nothing else distinguishes them, a striking contrast to Neh 3, where the names of lay leaders and their professions are specified. Missing from the list of returnees are descendants of the northern tribes: they are not included among the returnees. The structure of the listing manifests the idea that a united people will return: no tribal divisions are listed in Ezra 2, nor is their division into two kingdoms reestablished. The returnees are not styled as Judahites, nor are the two tribes, Judah and Benjamin, that constituted the southern kingdom mentioned. The people are termed "Israel" in various permutations in the lists, עם ישראל (Ezra 2:2 = Neh 7:7), בני ישראל (Ezra 2:70 = Neh 7:72; and ישראל in Neh 11:3, 20). Outside the lists, the returnees are identified as Judahites (עם יהודה, Ezra 4:4), as inhabitants of Judah (ישבי יהודה, Ezra 4:6), as a collective Judah (Neh 4:4), while their enemies are called צרי יהודה ובנימן (Ezra 4:1). They are the bearers of national identity.

The rest of the people in the lists are arranged in categories of cultic personnel. The priests are mentioned, then an elaborate listing of other cultic personnel is offered. The list includes 3,042 priests, in contrast to 74 Levites, 128 Levitical singers, and 139 (presumably Levitical) gatekeepers. The priests are catalogued in a single verse according to ancestry.[45] The number of Levites is small in comparison to the large number of priests. Yet they are accorded greater space, mirroring a focus on Levites internal to a number of Second Temple texts. Who is who in the community shapes the self-identity of the community, and arranging persons and families according to an internal structure contests overlordship. The self-perception of the community is expressed through the enumeration of the returnees, demonstrating the interrelationship between genealogy and cultural memory. The identity of those who constitute the group is at stake.

Imperial submission and asserting national identity are not a binary in conflict.[46] A subject group can create a self-identity that negotiates

---

45. Certain priests were disqualified because of missing genealogical records. The one disqualifying them is noted not by name but his Persian title (Ezra 2:63). It may be speculated that disqualification prompted hard feelings best directed at an outsider.

46. An issue that cannot be explored here is whether the emphasis on written documentation by Persian officials had an influence on the development of written Torah. See Elsie Stern, "Royal Letters and Torah Scrolls: The Place of Ezra-Nehemiah in Scholarly Narratives of Scripturalization," in *Contextualizing Israel's Sacred*

between the two. The Judahites interpreted imperial acts through their conceptual lens: the Edict of Cyrus, a singular example of this practice, is refracted though Judahite terminology and concepts. The return of temple vessels, perhaps a minor gesture on the part of the imperial bureaucracy, is highlighted as a significant act of restoration. Employing Hebrew in an ocean of Aramaic signals Judahite cultural identity through resistance from the point of view of a subject people. Arraying themselves in their native rankings resists the leveling impulse of imperial hierarchy of ruler and ruled. Yet at the same time, the Judahites have to submit to imperial authority: a return can happen only through imperial license, and privileges can only be affirmed through an appeal couched literally in imperial language.

Conclusion

Every act of memory is a reconstruction. The ordering of events into a narrative creates a sense of coherence and religious value.[47] The reasoning, whether implicit or explicit, of cause and effect and the ideological stance of the narrator inform the message the historical narrative conveys. Unpacking the choices, conscious or unconscious, of the writers and editors shows how they came to terms with the situation in which they lived.

This is undoubtedly so for the period we are examining. The Judahites who composed and maintained the historical narratives about the return shaped and were shaped by the social identity and literary culture of their community. The narratives had a social impact: they addressed and forged the implied community's memory and identity. The Judahites defined themselves in opposition to, and in integration with, the empire that subjugated them. They shaped the past to help them assess their status and prepare themselves to prevail and succeed in their own time.[48]

Texts produced under Persian auspices are informed by the needs of imperial propaganda, but the Judahites reshaped the Edict of Cyrus in Hebrew idiom and according to a Judahite viewpoint. It manifests the nuanced relationship between imperial overlord and subordinate people:

Writings: Ancient Literacy, Orality, and Literary Production, ed. Brian B. Schmidt, AIL (Atlanta: SBL Press, 2015), 239–62.

47. Hayden White, *The Practical Past* (Evanston, IL: Northwestern University Press, 2014), 94.

48. White, *Practical Past*, xiii.

the Judahites must rely on imperial favor yet can create a fictive correlation between imperial action and their own deity. The Judahite authors create an imaginative world in which an imperial authority is subject to a higher authority to which they have an independent relationship.

The restoration for the Judahites is incomplete. Exile abides. Its deleterious effects are not healed. The returnees live in a situation that falls short of the hopes the exiles had. They are still subjugated to Persia, and the monarchy was not restored. The temple was rebuilt, but the city is not completely rebuilt. And when the walls of the city are rebuilt, they are still subjugated. At the same time, imperial authority has to allow latitude to subject people because an imperial polity lacks a unified identity: merging multiple territorial populations, self-identified groups, and other assemblages under an imperial aegis requires an empire to assert authority and grant leeway. The accomplishments of the Judahites are therefore presented as equivocal, both successful and unsuccessful, triumphant and ineffective.

But more than their accomplishments, or lack thereof, characterize their self-perception. Exile and return comprise the two sides of Judahite cultural identity. Exile's other face is return, and both are fundamental to historical consciousness of the Judahite community. Return interprets and reshapes exile. Return is the lens through which exile is construed. The identity based on exile is reconceived through return, the remedy, if not the antithesis, of exile. Return was highlighted as a formative experience.[49] It was perceived to be a historical event of lasting significance, meant to reshape memory. The narrative was shaped so that the focus is on the returnees, not those who never left, not those who never returned. Return became formative.

Return exuded into the consciousness of the Judahites because the historical narratives on which we have focused do not disclose their authors or editors.[50] The settings in which they lived or the dates during which they wrote are not indicated. The anonymity of their third-person narratives produced accounts that appear unmediated and universal; the narratives seem to be not restricted by the particulars of their authors. The past

---

49. Martien Halvorson-Taylor analyzes how exile was reshaped as a formative experience in *Enduring Exile: The Metaphorization of Exile in the Hebrew Bible*, VTSup 141 (Leiden: Brill, 2011), 165–98.

50. See Daniel D. Pioske, *Memory in a Time of Prose: Studies in Epistemology, Hebrew Scribalism, and the Biblical Past* (Oxford: Oxford University Press, 2018), 1–9.

belongs to everyone. Cultural memory is an inheritance accessible to all and immersing all.

The Art of Control: Iconography of the Early Achaemenid Empire

Ryan P. Bonfiglio

The reign of Cyrus II (559–530 BCE) ushered in a new world order in ancient Near Eastern geopolitics. In contrast to most of his Neo-Babylonian and Neo-Assyrian predecessors, Cyrus instituted a kinder, gentler approach to imperial control. Under his rule, divine statues and other cultic paraphernalia were restored, temples were rebuilt, and formerly displaced people groups were permitted to return to their lands. While it is debatable whether the famous Edict of Cyrus was truly a humanitarian document, as is sometimes suggested, there is no doubt that Cyrus showed a more conciliatory approach to foreign affairs.

Yet, Cyrus and the series of Achaemenid kings that followed him were no less concerned about asserting control over their sprawling empire. This is especially evident in the reign of Darius the Great. After the mysterious death of Cambyses II, Cyrus's successor, Darius, rose to power in 522. Within the first year of his reign, Darius successfully defeated a rival claimant to the throne and quelled a series of rebellions throughout the land. In the years that followed, Darius ushered in what could be called a Pax Persica—a period of peace, prosperity, and stability in which the world of Achaemenid Persia was under the control of a powerful but benevolent king.

One of the chief means by which Darius expressed, maintained, and deployed his vision of empire was through a carefully designed and curated program of art. The official iconography produced by the Achaemenid Empire in the late sixth century was envisioned under the close scrutiny of the king and sought to mobilize a particular message about kingship and the nature of royal control.[1] By deliberately borrowing and adapting prominent iconographic motifs from ancient Mesopotamia, the king was able to convey how his vision of empire differed from earlier Neo-Assyrian and Neo-Babylonian rulers.

The purpose of this study is to examine prominent motifs in early Achaemenid art with an eye toward how they further inform an understanding of key political and ideological conceptualities that emerged during the closing decades of the sixth century. In turning to iconography as a primary source in the study of ancient cultures, this study intentionally follows a growing trend in biblical research.[2] The underlying presumption of this and other studies interested in ancient iconography is that visual materials, along with and as much as textual materials, have the capacity to reflect the beliefs, values, and ideologies operative within a given historical and cultural setting. While early Achaemenid iconography does not provide us with straightforward and unmediated access to specific historical events or personages, it can further illuminate the particular royal ideologies that Darius and his successors wished to convey.

I will proceed by first examining the three most prominent motifs in early Achaemenid iconography: the king on high, the heroic encounter, and the tribute procession. In each case, I not only analyze their formal features and artistic antecedents but also describe the royal ideologies each motif was meant to convey. In the final section, I take up questions surrounding whether and how early Achaemenid art might have come to influence postexilic biblical literature. Of particular interest are instances in which biblical imagery describing YHWH's future control over earthly empires exhibits thematic congruencies with the above-mentioned iconographic motifs.

---

1. While the term "Persian art" refers to visual materials produced in all regions under Persian control during the sixth through fourth centuries, the term "Achaemenid art" refers more specifically to the official program of art that was produced in service of the imperial state under Darius and his successors and that was localized in the administrative heartland of the empire. The latter is the focus of this study.

2. This trend can be traced to Othmar Keel's pioneering study, *The Symbolism of the Biblical World: Ancient Near Eastern Iconography and the Book of Psalms*, repr. ed. (Winona Lake, IN: Eisenbrauns, 1997). This method of interpreting imagery in the Hebrew Bible in light of ancient Near Eastern art, known as iconographic exegesis, has been subsequently refined by Keel and a loose network of his students and colleagues. For a helpful survey of pertinent developments, see Ryan P. Bonfiglio, *Reading Images, Seeing Texts: Towards a Visual Hermeneutics for Biblical Studies*, OBO 280 (Fribourg: Academic Press; Göttingen: Vandenhoeck & Ruprecht, 2016).

Sources of Achaemenid Art

Before turning to the iconographic motifs themselves, it will be helpful to briefly outline the principal sources of early Achaemenid art. While it is likely that Achaemenid visual culture originally included a wide variety of image-bearing objects, such as papyrus documents, wooden reliefs, embroidered wall hangings, shields, and bronze statuary, a good portion of this material is no longer extant in the archaeological record. Fortunately, three well-preserved sources remain.

One source consists of monumental reliefs. These large-scale images are preserved in numerous places, including a massive tableau carved into a vertical rock face at Bisitun, the tomb of Darius and his successors at Naqsh-i Rustam, and various wall reliefs found on buildings at Persepolis and Pasargadae. Arguably the most magnificent examples of Achaemenid monumental reliefs are the football field–length displays on the north and east stairways of the Apadana at Persepolis. Several freestanding statues also are extant, including the statue of Darius from Susa and the canal stela of Darius. The artistic motifs on these monumental reliefs are well documented.[3]

Another important source of Achaemenid art is the official coinage initiated during the reign of Darius. Minted in gold and silver, this series consists of four main coin types, each of which depicts a crowned archer dressed in pleated, full-sleeved court robe in various combat poses.[4] It is widely believed that the figure on the coin is the king, though the coins do not so much offer a portrait of Darius as they do a dynastic image of the glory and concept of Achaemenid kingship. Previous studies suggest that these so-called archer coins, or darics, did not play a significant role in the internal economy of Achaemenid Persia. Instead, they primarily functioned as a form of mobile media, circulating a carefully curated image of the king and his role as royal archer and protector.[5]

The most plentiful source of Achaemenid art comes in the form of two massive archives of seal impressions found at the imperial capital

---

3. The seminal study of Achaemenid monumental art is Margaret Cool Root's *The King and Kingship in Achaemenid Art: Essays on the Creation of an Iconography of Empire*, Acta Iranica 19, TM 9 (Leiden: Brill, 1979).

4. For an overview of this series of coins, see David Stronach, "Early Achaemenid Coinage: Perspectives from the Homeland," *IrAnt* 24 (1989): 255–83.

5. Cindy L. Nimchuk, "Darius I and the Formation of the Achaemenid Empire: Communicating the Creation of an Empire" (PhD diss., University of Toronto, 2001).

at Persepolis. The first archive is found on the Persepolis treasury tablets, a set of administrative documents dealing with royal transactions between the years 492 and 459 BCE. This archive contains 77 distinct seal designs, 43 of which are from cylinder seals and 34 from stamp seals or signet rings. The second archive is found on the Persepolis fortification tablets, which date from 509 to 494. This collection contains 1,174 distinct seal designs, many of which are still being published in a multi-volume catalogue by Mark Garrison and Margaret Cool Root.[6] The seal designs being published by Garrison and Root represent only the tip of the iconographic iceberg, since this collection consists only of seals found on the 2,087 tablets examined in Richard Hallock's original study of the Persepolis fortification archive.[7] It has been estimated that the full archive consists of closer to 30,000 tablets, the vast majority of which bear seal impressions.[8]

Motifs in Achaemenid Art

Since space prohibits an exhaustive survey of early Achaemenid art, in what follows I examine the three most prominent motifs in the imperial iconography of the late sixth and early fifth centuries.

---

6. To date, only the first volume of the Persepolis fortification seals has been published: Mark B. Garrison and Margaret Cool Root, *Seals on the Persepolis Fortification Tablets, Images of Heroic Encounter*, OIP 117 (Chicago: Oriental Institute of the University of Chicago, 2001). For an introduction to the archive as a whole, see Mark B. Garrison and Margaret Cool Root, *Persepolis Seal Studies: An Introduction with Provisional Concordances of Seal Numbers and Associated Documents on Fortification Tablets 1–2087*, AH 9 (Leiden: Nederlands Instituut voor het Nabije Oosten, 1998). See also Mark B. Garrison, "Archers at Persepolis: The Emergence of Royal Ideology at the Heart of the Empire," in *The World of Achaemenid Persia: History, Art and Society in Iran and the Ancient Near East*, ed. John Curtis and St. John Simpson (New York: I. B. Tauris, 2010), 337–59.

7. Richard T. Hallock, *The Persepolis Fortification Tablets*, OIP 92 (Chicago: Oriental Institute of the University of Chicago, 1969).

8. Mark B. Garrison, "Achaemenid Iconography as Evidenced by Glyptic Art: Subject Matter, Social Function, Audience and Diffusion," in *Images as Media: Sources for the Cultural History of the Near East and the Eastern Mediterranean (First Millennium BCE)*, ed. Christoph Uehlinger, OBO 175 (Fribourg: University Press; Göttingen: Vandenhoeck & Ruprecht, 2000), 115–63.

The King on High

The king-on-high motif is one in which a royal figure is represented aloft or above symbolic representations of the people groups he controls. Variations on this motif recur in a number of Achaemenid monuments, including the statue of Darius from Susa, the tomb facades at Naqsh-i Rustam, the Bisitun relief, and several doorjambs from Persepolis. The king-on-high motif is rare in the minor arts in part because the complex formal features of this design would be difficult to execute on the tiny carving surfaces available on seals and coins.

This motif is best understood as a visual expression, or metaphor, of a particular relationship between the king and the people he controlled.[9] As Root points out, in Achaemenid art this relationship is "consistently expressed as a cooperative effort of voluntary support of the king by his subject people."[10] That this is the intended message comes into focus when one examines how the Achaemenid motif of the king on high rejects, or at least significantly reworks, the stereotypical manner in which the king is depicted in relationship to his people elsewhere in ancient Near Eastern art. Almost without exception, these antecedents emphasize forced subjugation.[11]

One such example comes in the form of Mesopotamian scenes of "pious subjugation." In these images the king is pictured standing above, and sometimes on top of, defeated and often naked and mutilated enemies. An early example comes from the famous victory stela of Naram-sin, which shows the king standing on top of two tiers of conquered foes (fig. 3.1).[12] As he tramples over one of his fallen enemies, others beg for mercy.

Neo-Assyrian prototypes of the pious subjugation scene are also attested, though less commonly in sculptures in the round. Instead, one finds narratives of military conquest in which the images of defeated enemies are carved into the vertical surfaces of what structurally function as platforms or struts for the king's throne. In the compositional arrangement of these prototypes, the person of the king takes the place of the image of the king. Thus, from the perspective of the viewer, it is the king

---

9. For further discussion of how the Persian Empire portrayed mental representations of kingship to subject people, see Mark W. Hamilton's essay in this volume.

10. Root, *King and Kingship*, 131.

11. For a fuller discussion of the king on high motif and its ancient Near Eastern antecedents, see Root, *King and Kingship*, 131–61.

12. See the figure credits (xv–xvii) for the sources of the figures in this essay.

Figs. 3.1–3.3. Left (3.1): Close-up of the victory stela of Naram-sin, twenty-third century BCE. Center (3.2): Sphinx of Thutmose III reclining on the nine bows, fifteenth century BCE. Right (3.3): Close-up of one of nine bound captives, Ramesses II's temple at Abydos, thirteenth century BCE.

himself, seated upon his throne, who appears on high above images of defeated, killed, or otherwise subjugated people.

Perhaps even more revealing are antecedents from Egypt that display what is known as the "nine bows" symbolism. In the most basic and perhaps original iterations of this theme, one finds nine archer bows under the feet of representations of Pharaoh or his sphinx (fig. 3.2). In these scenes, the bows function as metaphors, or more precisely, metonyms, of the military might of specific people groups. Depicting Pharaoh standing atop these bows thus symbolizes the subjugation of his enemies. This theme is on display in artifacts in which the nine bows are found on the inside of Pharaoh's footwear, such as is the case with the royal slippers of Tutankhamun. As is the case in the Neo-Assyrian throne platforms, in this artifact it is the actual person of the king who stands above—and literally on top of—the symbolic representation of subject people.

An important variation of this symbolism is found on Egyptian images in which the bows are replaced by nine human figures (fig. 3.3). In these cases, great attention is given to differentiating the people groups depicted through distinct clothing, physical characteristics, or an accompanying inscription. While such imagery goes back at least to the predynastic period, it is in the Eighteenth Dynasty that we find prototypes in which the subjugated people are depicted on structural elements, such as throne supports or statue bases, that physically uplift the king.[13] In these situations, the people are always shown as subjugated captives, often with arms bound behind the back and tethered at the neck and elbows.

---

13. Root, *King and Kingship*, 138–40.

The forced subjugation implied in these Mesopotamian and Egyptian antecedents stands in sharp contrast to what we find in Achaemenid art. For instance, the Bisitun relief (fig. 3.4) shows King Darius on the left, accompanied by two weapon bearers. To the right is a row of nine captives, each with distinctive dress, symbolizing the nine rebellions Darius subdued in the first year of his reign. Under Darius's elevated left foot lies the defeated usurper Gaumata. Auramazda, in the form of an anthropomorphic deity emerging from a winged disk, hovers above. Here the king is quite literally on high—the image appears on a rock face elevated some 500 feet above the roadway beneath (and 300 ft from the nearest vantage point). The presence of nine subjugated rebels seems to allude to the Egyptian nine-bows symbolism. Though fettered, the captives walk upright, only slightly bent at the waist. Aside from Gaumata, the captives are not found beneath the feet of the king but rather on the same compositional register.

Figs. 3.4–3.6. Top left (3.4): Bisitun relief, near the modern-day city of Kermanshah in western Iran, late sixth century BCE. Bottom left (3.5): Detail of the base of the statue of Darius, Susa, late sixth century BCE. Right (3.6): Relief of the king's throne, south door of the Hundred Column Hall at Persepolis, late sixth century BCE.

An even more pronounced contrast is found in the Egyptianized canal stela of Darius I. On the front is a row of twenty-four cartouches inscribed with the names of the different lands of the Persian Empire, on top of each of which is a small kneeling figure. These figures appear unbound and uninjured, in marked contrast to Mesopotamian and Egyptian antecedents. Also significant is the hand gestures of these figures. In each case, their hands are raised, palms facing forward and directed toward the cartouche of the king. As in Middle Egyptian hieroglyphic script, this gesture iconographically signifies an attitude of praise.[14]

A similar scene is found on the statue of Darius from Susa (fig. 3.5). On both long sides of the base are twelve name rings with kneeling figures on top, once again unfettered and unharmed. As in the canal stela, the arms of the people are raised, but instead of their palms facing forward they are upturned. This gesture conveys the idea of symbolic support. A similar image appears in hieroglyphics as a determinative for presenting an offering of support.[15] In both the canal stela and statue of Darius, one thus sees a deliberate effort to reconfigure an existing paradigm for representing the king's relationship to his people. Rather than being crushed by the king, the Achaemenids' subjects are shown offering their voluntary support.

One final image type is worth discussion. In various places, including the tomb facades of Naqsh-i Rustam, as well as the central building and throne hall at Persepolis, one finds an iteration of the king-on-high motif in which subject people are depicted in what is known as the atlas posture. In these scenes, the people are shown bearing aloft the throne of the king with arms raised, bent slightly at the elbows (fig. 3.6). That the throne can be born on the fingertips of the people suggests that the king's rule places little burden on his subjects. Antecedents of the atlas posture are known from both Mesopotamian and Egyptian art. However, in these contexts, this posture is only assumed by mythical beings who lift up the image of a god in the form of a winged disk or by cosmic creatures or kings enacting rituals of symbolic support.[16] In light of this observation, it is possible to conclude with Root that "the Achaemenids clearly adapted a pose previously found almost exclusively in ritual/cosmic contexts for a decidedly

---

14. Alan H. Gardiner, *Egyptian Grammar*, 3rd rev. ed. (London: Oxford University Press, 1957), 32.

15. Gardiner, *Egyptian Grammar*, 454.

16. Root, *King and Kingship*, 147–49.

political representation."¹⁷ The overall effect is to highlight the burden-less quality of the king's rule and to underscore the notion that the people who found themselves under Achaemenid rule willingly and even joyously offered their support to the king.

This is not so say that violence, coercion, and subjugation were altogether absent from the reign of the early Achaemenid kings. From the texts on the Bisitun relief, we know that Darius brutally put down rebellions at the outset of his reign, killing and mutilating rebels and a rival claimant to the throne. Nevertheless, the *vision* of kingship that Darius wished to convey was one that made a concerted effort to present a profoundly different image of royal control than that which is found among most of his Mesopotamian and Egyptian counterparts.¹⁸ In rejecting the Mesopotamian and Egyptian imagery of violent subjugation, Darius sought to convey a vision of Achaemenid kingship that stressed not only that the king was in control, but that such control was not achieved by coercive measures but by the voluntary and joyful support of his people.

The Heroic Encounter

While the heroic encounter scene is discernable in some monumental reliefs, it is the dominant motif in the minor arts of the early Achaemenid period. This motif is evident in all four major types of the archer series coins, and it is the most commonly occurring design in the two previously mentioned seal archives from Persepolis. Heroic encounter scenes can be classified into two subvarieties: (1) the heroic *control* scene, where a hero grasps with extended arms an animal or hybrid creature on either side of his body; and (2) the heroic *combat* scene, in which a hero is pictured in

---

17. Root, *King and Kingship*, 153.

18. The image of Darius's actions on the Behistun relief is noticeably less violent than the description of Darius's actions in the accompanying inscriptions (Nimchuk, "Darius I and the Formation, 14). For instance, in the main narrative the captives are said to be impaled, mutilated, and killed, but no such violence is depicted in the relief, with the exception of Gaumata. That the image presents a less violent picture of the king is perhaps not surprising given that the image would have been far more decipherable to most viewers than the text. Not only were textual literacy rates exceedingly low, but from the nearest vantage point, some 300 ft beneath the relief, the text itself would hardly have been legible to any passersby. This suggests that the king was well aware of what media was best suited for conveying his intended image of kingship.

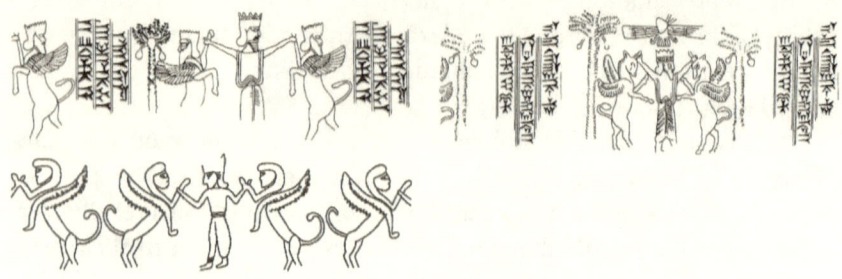

Figs. 3.7–3.9. Top left (3.7): PFS 0113*, court style. Top right (3.8): PFS 0007*, court style. Bottom left (3.9): PFS 0034, fortification style.

a more explicit battle pose, with a weapon and fighting against an animal or hybrid creature.

A classic heroic control scene is on display in Persepolis fortification seal 0113* (fig. 3.7).[19] The style of the carving, known as the court style, shows clear parallels with monumental reliefs and is closely tied to the royal iconographic program of Darius and his successors.[20] In this seal, the hero appears in profile, in characteristic royal garb, including a crenulated crown and full, pleated Persian robe. The bearded hero has arms fully extended, with each hand grasping the raised limb of a composite creature. The creatures, who face away from the royal hero, have the body of a winged bull and the head of a human. The trilingual paneled inscription names Darius, though it is not necessarily the case that this was the seal of the king himself.

Another example of the heroic control scene comes in the form of Persepolis fortification seal 0007*, also in court style (fig. 3.8). This seal likewise shows a crowned and bearded figure in a pleated robe, with arms extended. He grasps the horns of two rampant winged bulls. Two date palms frame the scene. The paneled trilingual inscription reads, "I am

---

19. Here and elsewhere, a raised asterisk after the catalogue number (PFS 0113*) indicates that the seal is inscribed. Fewer than 10 percent of the seals in the Persepolis fortification archive are inscribed.

20. The term "court style" originated with John Boardman as a way of categorizing a particular class of Achaemenid seals that featured elaborate detail, a sense of symmetry and verticality, and shared stylistic elements with Achaemenid reliefs. See Boardman, *Greek Gems and Finger Rings* (New York: Abrams, 1970), 305. That there is a similarity between the court-style seals and wall reliefs suggests that they both were conceived of and commissioned as part of the same royal iconographic program.

Darius, the Great King." One feature of this seal not included on Persepolis fortification seal 0113* is the winged disk hovering directly over the head of the hero and likely representing Auramazda. A similar figure is shown in the same formal relationship to the hero in the Bisitun relief. The formal features of Persepolis fortification seal 0034 (fig. 3.9) are quite similar to Persepolis fortification seals 0007* and 0113* insofar as the hero is pictured in profile, flanked by two rampant composite creatures. Here the arms are not fully extended, and the figure faces left instead of right. Rather than being executed in the court style, Persepolis fortification seal 0034 reflects what is known as the fortification style, a classification peculiar to this archive and that exhibits simple lines, a general lack of detail, and somewhat attenuated figures.[21]

In these and other iterations of the heroic control scene, the presence of the crenulated crown and full pleated royal Persian robe make it likely that viewers would have identified the figure as the king himself, or at least as embodying the concept of Achaemenid kingship. Iconographically, the composite creatures represent forces of chaos that must be mastered. The royal hero holds these forces at bay with outstretched arms. That the hero lacks weaponry seems to underscore the fact that control of the kingdom, quite literally, is in the hands of the king. The presence of Auramazda in Persepolis fortification seal 0007* indicates that the reign of the king is exercised under divine authorization and guidance. The prevalence of this motif in glyptic art effectively miniaturizes and mobilizes the iconographic message writ large on the Bisitun relief and in its accompanying inscriptions: The king, figured as a royal hero, has brought peace, stability, and order to the world of Achaemenid Persia. In this way, the heroic control scene functions as a powerful visual metaphor of the Pax Persica.

The second variety of the heroic encounter motif, the combat scene, is even more prolific in Achaemenid glyptics. A prominent example is Persepolis fortification seal 0009*, carved in the fortification style (fig. 3.10). The hero is dressed in the Persian court robe, facing left, with an extended arm that grasps an ostrich-like bird at the neck. While this seal design shows similarities with aspects of the heroic control scene, what distinguishes it as the combat variety is the presence of a weapon in the hero's left hand. The hero seems poised to use the weapon against the bird or the rampant horned creature to his right.

---

21. Garrison, "Achaemenid Iconography," 131.

Figs. 3.10–3.13. Top left (3.10): PFS 0009*, court style. Top right (3.11): PFS 0057*, fortification style. Bottom left (3.12): PFS 0182, court style. Bottom right (3.13): PFS 0118, fortification style.

Another example of heroic combat is found in Persepolis fortification seal 0057*, this time in the local fortification style (fig. 3.11). The hero wears a knee-length skirt with elaborate fringe. With one leg raised, the hero places his foot on the back of a composite creature's lower leg. In his one hand the hero carries an ax, and in the other he appears to take hold of the creature's wing. The creature in question is a composite animal with wings, double horns on the nose, and a spiky mane. An Elamite inscription fills the terminal field. Both Persepolis fortification seals 0009* and 0057* allude to earlier Neo-Assyrian royal seal types in which the king grasps a rampant lion by the top of its mane while plunging a dagger into its upper chest or neck.

While there are many variations of this motif in early Achaemenid glyptics, by far the most commonly occurring type is one in which the royal hero appears as an armed archer.[22] In a significant portion (44 percent) of the archer scenes in the Persepolis fortification seal archive, the archer is depicted in a kneeing position. This is evident in Persepolis fortification seal 0182 (fig. 3.12), which shows a dynamic protection scene where the kneeling archer aims his arrow over the head of a stag and in the direction of a winged and horned lion, whose raised front limbs are stretched out toward its would-be prey. The stag twists its neck and head back toward the archer, seemingly in anticipation of help. As an interesting variation, the archer is sometimes pictured as a composite creature. Though the details vary, the composite creatures always have the head,

---

22. Within the Persepolis fortification archive, 31 percent of the seals that depict human or humanoid activity feature archers.

Figs. 3.14–3.16. Archer series coins, type II (left, 3.14), type III (center, 3.15), and type IV (right, 3.16).

arms, and torso (waist up) of a human, but the lower body (often winged) of an animal. An example is found in Persepolis fortification seal 0118, where the archer emerges out of the back of a bull body, with scorpion's tale, taking aim at a rampant lion (fig. 3.13).

The theme of the royal archer in combat is even more pronounced in Achaemenid coins, especially types II–IV (figs. 3.14–16). In the type II coin, the king appears in kneeling position, his sleeves are pushed back, the lower hem of his robe is pulled up, the bow is extended out with his left hand, and his right hand is drawing back the string of the bow in a ready-to-fire position. An arrow is loaded on the string. The royal archer wears a quiver on his back with three additional arrows. The archer is poised for action. The type III and type IV coins are often understood as typological relatives of the type II coin, though they are dated to after Darius's reign. In these coins, the figure still appears in a kneeling position and ready for combat. However, instead of bearing a drawn bow, the hero grasps a spear (type III) or a dagger (type IV). In both cases, an undrawn bow is held in the opposite hand.

In Achaemenid depictions of the kneeling archer, the images of hunter and military protector have merged in the person of the king. The king is depicted as both an aggressor against his enemies (symbolized by the rampant composite creatures in Persepolis fortification seals 0196 and 0057*) and a protector of those in need (symbolized by the stag in Persepolis fortification seal 0182). In contrast to the heroic-control scenes, the direct, military intervention of the king is foregrounded. This iconographic feature effectively translates into visual form Darius's efforts to violently subdue rebellions and secure his claim to the throne in the year following his rise to power. The subsequent viability of the kingdom rested on the ongoing efforts of Darius's successors to likewise repel threats and provide protection for those loyal to their reign.

In the case of the archer coins, the rhetorical force of this message is heightened by the function of the medium itself. Among other things, the archer coins were used as gifts, given by the king to confer favor, status, and wealth on the recipient. Those who were recipients of these coins were reminded that their prosperity (represented by the coin's economic value) was made possible by the military accomplishments of the powerful king (represented by the heroic-combat scene depicted on the coin). At the same time, by displaying himself in an aggressive, hunting pose, the king can be seen as aiming his bow at anyone who should happen to possess an archer coin. Thus, the coins are both gift and threat: the bent bow of the king promises both to protect those loyal to the throne and to punish those who threaten the stability of the empire. The Pax Persica was a two-sided coin.

The Tribute Procession

The tribute-procession motif is not as widely disseminated as either the king-on-high or heroic-encounter motifs. Yet, its presence looms large in early Achaemenid iconography if for no other reason than the sheer size of its most well-known exemplar. On both the north and east stairways of the Apadana (or audience hall) at Persepolis, there appear three-hundred-foot-long reliefs that, though not exactly identical, each depict a procession of dignitaries bringing tribute to the king. These reliefs were commissioned in the latter years of Darius's reign but were not completed until the time of his successor, Artaxerxes I. Both the scale and elaborate detail of these reliefs make for a complex visual tableau, only the basic features of which can be summarized here.

The focal point of each relief is a central panel that depicts an image of the enthroned king receiving a Persian official holding a spear in one hand (fig. 3.17).[23] The official's other hand is raised in a gesture of greeting, perhaps suggesting that he is announcing the arrival of the tribute procession. Two large incense burners are positioned between this official and the seated king. Behind the king are three figures, the first of which likely represents the crown prince. Of the two other figures, both rendered

---

23. This figure has been variously understood as a worshiper, the head bodyguard of the king, the king's chief treasurer, or as the grand marshal who announces the arrival of the tribute procession (Root, *King and Kingship*, 238).

Figs. 3.17–3.19. Top (3.17): Original central panel of the Apadana (north stairway), Persepolis. Bottom (3.18): Detail from Wing B of the Apadana (east stairway). Right (3.19): Detail of hand-holding gesture from Wing B of the Apadana (east stairway).

in smaller scale, one holds an ax and bow case, while the other is adorned with an elaborate headdress and holds a towel or scarf. It is important to note that while the scene described above was almost certainly original to the Apadana reliefs, the panels on which they appear were, at some point, removed and stored in the adjacent treasury building, perhaps for safekeeping.[24] The replacement panels depict two sets of Persian soldiers, all bearing long spears, facing toward one another. A large empty space separates the two groups. The design of the original central panels makes more sense of the overall theme of the reliefs than the replacement panels, which are still found in situ.

In each relief, the central panel is flanked on both sides by a procession of smaller figures facing the king and organized in three parallel registers. Horizontal bands of rosettes divide the registers. The procession of figures who approach from behind the king (Wing A) consists of an assortment of Persian court officials, guards, and dignitaries, as well as a number of horses and chariots. The procession of figures who approach the king from his front side (Wing B) consists of twenty-three foreign delegations bringing various forms of tribute. Each group is differentiated by dress

---

24. Root, *King and Kingship*, 94.

and physical characteristics (fig. 3.18).[25] A Persian marshal grasps the hand of the first figure in each delegation, ushering the group toward the king. Above the central panel is a frieze that depicts the winged sun disk, Auramazda, flanked on the left and right by a composite creature with the head of a human and the body of a winged bull.

Taken together, these reliefs compress into one complex visual frame a carefully crafted message about the scope and nature of the king's power. On the one hand, the tribute brought to the king may have functioned as a regular tax required of subject nations in exchange for ongoing protection. Both the quantity and diversity of tribute bearers represented in Wing B make obvious to any visitor to the Apadana the far reach of the king's imperial control. In this sense, the tribute procession motif is a vehicle for expressing "the universality of the imperial domain, of the all-encompassing nature of the king's ability to conquer, to control or to command respect and homage."[26] Indeed, such a message is echoed in other early Achaemenid reliefs and inscriptions, including those writings in which Darius boasts of the many people groups he had subjugated and the peace and stability he had brought to the land.[27]

On the other hand, tribute can also function as a type of gift voluntarily provided as an expression of gratitude and allegiance. While the giving of such gifts might well have been politically expedient for the subject people, the design of the Apadana relief underscores that such offerings were not made under compulsion but rather were offered voluntarily. This point is suggested by two iconographic details. First, the foreign delegates in Wing B are unbound, and a number of them are shown bearing arms. This manner of representation suggest that the delegates should be "understood as non-belligerent, willing participants in the ceremony shown to be taking place."[28] The second iconographic detail that suggests voluntary, and perhaps even joyful, participation in the tribute

---

25. While these iconographic distinctions clearly are meant to indicate different people groups, it remains to be seen whether the intended ethnicity or nationality of the groups can be determined with precision (Root, *King and Kingship*, 235).

26. Root, *King and Kingship*, 247.

27. For further discussion, see Brent A. Strawn, "'A World under Control': Isaiah 60 and the Apadana Reliefs from Persepolis," in *Approaching Yehud: New Approaches to the Study of the Persian Period*, ed. Jon L. Berquist, SemeiaSt 50 (Atlanta: Society of Biblical Literature, 2007), 96.

28. Root, *King and Kingship*, 235.

procession is the appearance of the Persian marshal who ushers each delegation toward the king. The marshal is shown as grasping the slightly outstretched hand of the lead figure in each delegation (fig. 3.19). A similar gesture is found in earlier Mesopotamian art. In these "presentation scenes," a minor deity grasps the slightly extended hand (or wrist) of a supplicant as he is led toward a supreme deity, who is seated on a throne. The iconographic resonance between these scenes is intentional. By alluding to this ancient presentation scene, the designers of the Apadana reliefs transformed the tribute-procession motif into a scene of pious reverence in which foreign delegates, portrayed in the manner of would-be worshipers, are led into the presence of the deity/king.[29]

That the intended message of the Apadana's tribute procession scene is one of joyous and pious cooperation comes into even sharper focus when compared with Mesopotamian antecedents. One example is the Black Obelisk, a nearly seven-foot-tall stone that depicts the reception of tribute by Shalmaneser III. As in the Apadana reliefs, an entourage of attendants is located behind the king, who is greeted by an official. Parallel registers depict the arrival of tribute-bearing foreign delegations. A winged sun disk is also present. However, on the Black Obelisk the tribute is clearly forced. Each delegate is shown slightly bent at the waist, as if weighed down by the weight of the burden of the tribute, or subjugation more broadly.[30] In addition, several of the delegates are pictured with clenched fists raised near their faces, a gesture that Root understands as one of submission.[31] Particularly striking is the portrayal of the tribute bearers who approach the king. The tribute bearers are on their hands and knees, with bent backs and faces toward the ground, a posture likely meant to suggest they were kissing the king's feet.[32]

While other Neo-Assyrian prototypes of this motif, such as those found in Sargon's palace at Khorsabad, significantly downplay the forced nature of the tribute, there are no examples from this time period that explicitly portray tribute procession in terms of voluntary gift giving, as

---

29. Root, *King and Kingship*, 284.
30. Root, *King and Kingship*, 255.
31. Root, *King and Kingship*, 255.
32. While the tribute procession motif is far less frequent in Egyptian imperial iconography, examples of this theme from the tombs of Eighteenth Dynasty court officials likewise emphasize the compulsory nature of the tribute (see Root, *Kings and Kingship*, 240–50).

seems to be the case in the Apadana reliefs.[33] Thus, the contrast presented between the Apadana relief and the Black Obelisk is indicative of the way in which early Achaemenid iconography reworks older artistic traditions in service of new royal ideologies. Namely, the use of the hand-holding gesture by the Persian marshals in place of any posture of submission—represented by clenched fists, bent backs, and feet-kissing gestures—suggests that the Achaemenid kings wanted to present the tribute procession not as a forced tax but rather as a form of voluntary encomium, offered as a "symbolic gift of praise" to the king himself.[34]

It is important to note that, despite the clear differences between how this motif was rendered in and through their imperial iconographies, Neo-Assyrian and Achaemenid literary sources tend to describe tribute procession in a similar manner. For instance, Sargon's Cyprus stela inscription and the Cyrus Cylinder both refer to foreign delegates bringing tribute to the king and kissing his feet.[35] If this common literary description suggests the presence of similar protocols for how tribute-procession ceremonies were actually carried out, then the rhetorical force of the Achaemenid artistic program is all the more striking. It would suggest that Darius and his successors wished to convey an image of tribute procession that deliberately masked actual court practice. In other words, the difference between Achaemenid and Neo-Assyrian kings is found less in their actions and more in the public image they wished to maintain.

Achaemenid Art as Visual Rhetoric

Having considered the iconographic features and intended messages of the king-on-high, heroic-encounter, and tribute-procession motifs, I turn now to the question of their function: What can be concluded about the intended purpose of these iconographic motifs? The argument of this chapter is that the program of Achaemenid imperial iconography is best understood as a form of visual rhetoric—a calculated, intentionally planned vehicle of communication that was designed to disseminate political and ideological messages central to the Achaemenid vision of kingship.[36] By

---

33. Root, *King and Kingship*, 284.
34. Root, *King and Kingship*, 278.
35. Root, *King and Kingship*, 266.
36. For further discussion of the way in which mental representations of political

describing Achaemenid iconography in terms of visual rhetoric, I aim to highlight two important points about its design and diffusion.

As to the former issue, the commonly held position in the scholarly literature prior to the late 1970s was that the nationality of the artisans who were responsible for executing Achaemenid iconography was the primary factor in determining its design. In this view, the reason that the eyes, hair, and drapery of some Achaemenid statuary resembled Greek statuary was simply that these statues were made by Greek sculptors.[37] This line of reasoning was bolstered by the discovery of a foundation charter from Darius's palace at Susa that described the construction process, including the national origins of the workers involved in the project. Of particular interest was a reference to "stone cutters" from Ionia and Sardis. This reference seemed to cinch any question about whence the design of Achaemenid art came.[38]

However, as Root convincingly demonstrated in her 1979 study, *The King and Kingship in Achaemenid Art*, this artisan-oriented explanation is beset with a number of problems. First, foundation charters such as the one found at Susa are rhetorical documents in their own right, often more interested in demonstrating the vast extent of the imperial reign (symbolically expressed through the diverse nationalities of those who built the palace) than they are in providing an accurate report of the national origins of each artisan.[39] Second, and even more to the point, the artisan-oriented explanation unnecessarily assumes that image makers are the only ones responsible for the resulting appearance of an art object. This view minimizes the creative role of those who conceive of and commission art in the first place—in the case of this study, the king himself. On this point, I follow Root in concluding that the design of the iconographic motifs discussed above reflects a coherent artistic program that was carried out under the close supervision of Darius and his successors.

There is ample evidence from other ancient Near Eastern contexts that rulers, in fact, took on an active role in crafting an iconographic program that would convey an image of kingship that reflected their specific vision

---

and social realities are constructed and disseminated, see the essay by Caralie Cooke in this volume.

37. See, e.g., Marcel Dieulafoy, *L'art antique de la Perse: Achéménides, Parthes, Sassanides* (Paris: Librairie central d'architecture, etc., 1884–1885).

38. For the translation of the Susa foundation charter see Pierre Lecoq, *Les inscriptions de la Perse achéménide* (Paris: Gallimard, 1997).

39. Root, *King and Kingship*, 8.

of empire. At times, this process involved the creation of new artistic forms, but more frequently it involved adapting artistic motifs from other regions and time periods in a conscious effort to allude to, and adjust, the connotations those earlier motifs were already known to convey. This latter strategy, which is especially pronounced with the king-on-high and tribute-procession motifs, puts into sharp relief the fact that the Achaemenid iconographic program was "the product of a creative process of informed selection and adaptation of very specific traditional ideas and formal prototypes for the portrayal ... of a new vision of hierarchical order and kingship."[40]

In describing Achaemenid art as a form of visual rhetoric, I also aim to highlight several observations about its diffusion. There is little doubt that this artistic program was meant to be seen and "read" by an audience that stretched far beyond the king's court. For instance, the Apadana reliefs would have been viewed by large crowds from across the empire that visited Darius's royal palace. It is plausible that, upon returning home, these audiences would have reported on what they had seen, including the messages about kingship those reliefs conveyed. But this is not the only, nor even the primary, means by which the message of Achaemenid art was disseminated. Due to their ease of production and compactness of size, Achaemenid minor art in the form of seals and coins was readily disseminated across vast territories and through various segments of society. As a form of mass or mobile media, the coins and seals discussed above were particularly adept at bringing royal ideology to the far reaches of the empire.

The wide diffusion of Achaemenid iconography is especially evident in the case of the archer coins. These coins were circulated in Greece and Asia Minor and, as a result, in these regions archer imagery became intrinsically connected to notions of the Achaemenid king.[41] Herodotus (*Hist.* 7.28), for instance, refers to the Achaemenid coins as "darics," while Plutarch (*Art.* 20.4; *Ages.* 15.6) calls them "archers." Aeschylus (*Pers.* 556) calls Darius the "chief archer" (τόξαρχος). In addition, a seal

---

40. Root, *King and Kingship*, 161.

41. For a fuller discussion of the circulation patterns of darics and sigloi, see Ian Carradice, "The 'Regal' Coinage of the Persian Empire," in *Coinage and Administration in the Athenian and Persian Empires: The Ninth Oxford Symposium on Coinage and Monetary History*, ed. Ian Carradice, BARIS 343 (Oxford: British Archaeological Reports, 1987), 73–95.

from Thebes, Egypt, known as the seal of Darius, shows the king riding on the back of chariot, Auramazda overhead, drawing back a bow. While other examples could also be cited, these observations about the archer coins suggest not only that Achaemenid minor arts were widely circulated but also that the message they intended to convey—in this case, the king as a heroic protector—was effectively transmitted to the peripheries of the empire.[42]

Nevertheless, not all art produced in Persia in the late sixth and early fifth centuries was part of the official Achaemenid program. Alongside the iconography designed and commissioned by Darius and his successors is found other iconographic styles, produced by local workshops and circulated within a given area.[43] These localized iconographic materials, often in the form of cylinder or stamp seals, occasionally show thematic similarities with official Achaemenid art but more often than not were distinct in terms of their motifs and formal features. As such, despite the wide diffusion patterns of Achaemenid art, the iconographic repertoire of many satrapies expressed a visual vocabulary that was distinct from that which was found in Persepolis, Pasargadae, or other royal cities in the heartland of the empire. That these local iconographic styles existed side-by-side with official Achaemenid art suggests that the Achaemenid policy of not compelling standardization of local political, social, and religious institutions applied to visual culture as well.

This diffusion of Achaemenid art in sixth- and fifth-century Palestine offers a representative case study in the coexistence of local and official iconographic styles. In his analysis of Palestinian glyptic art of the Persian period, Christoph Uehlinger notes the presence of "persianisms" (i.e., motifs that explicitly reference official Achaemenid art) in heroic-encounter scenes found on some Palestinian seals and coins, especially those from Samaria.[44] For instance, in several seals a

---

42. For further discussion of the relationship between the core and periphery of ancient empires, see the chapter by Mark W. Hamilton in this volume.

43. For a discussion of the diffusion of Achaemenid seals, see Garrison, "Achaemenid Iconography," 155–56. For a broader discussion of the topic, see Margaret Cool Root, "From the Heart: Powerful Persianisms in the Art of the Western Empire," in *Asia Minor and Egypt: Old Cultures in a New Empire; Proceedings of the Groningen 1988 Achaemenid History Workshop*, ed. Heleen Sancisi-Weerdenburg and Amélie Kuhrt, AH 6 (Leiden: Nederlands Instituut voor het Nabije Oosten, 1991), 1–29.

44. Christoph Uehlinger, "'Powerful Persianisms' in Glyptic Iconography of Persian Period Palestine," in *The Crisis of Israelite Religion: Transformation of Religious*

royal figure is depicted with pleated robe and crenulated crown (both of which are distinct features of the Achaemenid artistic tradition) in combat with an animal or composite creature. Although Uehlinger admits that such persianisms occur less frequently in the glyptic art of Palestine than in that of Asia Minor, he nevertheless concludes that "as far as miniature media are concerned, the image of the Persian royal hero—which western provincials would easily identify either with the king or with Achaemenid kingship in general—must have been the most powerful and renowned among the visual expressions of Persian imperial ideology in Palestine."[45]

In another work, Uehlinger (with Othmar Keel) notes that portrayals of the king as an armed (though not always with bow and arrow) "royal hero" suddenly emerge in Palestinian glyptic art near the end of the sixth century—precisely at the time when the archer coins would have been in circulation.[46] Martin Klingbeil makes a similar observation in his study of Palestinian glyptic art of the Persian period.[47] He describes a seal of the Herakles figure, kneeling and in profile, with a bow in his left hand and with his right hand raised as if holding a club or spear. A quiver is attached at his waist. By alluding to the royal archer imagery of the Achaemenid program, Palestinian representations of Herakles, the prototypical Greek hero, came to be assimilated into notions about the Persian king. Thus, whether or not a postexilic biblical author had ever visited Persepolis or possessed an archer coin, the political and ideological conceptualities conveyed by official Achaemenid art penetrated into Palestine even as other iconographic styles were still being locally produced and disseminated.

The Bible and Achaemenid Art

Given the rhetorical function and wide diffusion of Achaemenid art, it remains to be considered whether and how the iconography of Darius and

---

Tradition in Exilic and Post-exilic Times, ed. Bob Becking and Marjo C. A. Korpel, OtSt 42 (Leiden: Brill, 1999), 172.

45. Uehlinger, "Powerful Persianisms," 60.

46. Othmar Keel and Christoph Uehlinger, *Gods, Goddesses, and Images of God in Ancient Israel,* rev. ed., trans. Thomas H. Trapp (Minneapolis: Fortress, 1998), 376.

47. Martin G. Klingbeil, "Syro-Palestinian Stamp Seals from the Persian Period: The Iconographic Evidence," *JNSL* 18 (1992): 95–124.

his successors might have come to influence postexilic biblical literature. By way of conclusion, I will briefly highlight several instances in which biblical imagery describing YHWH's future control over earthly empires exhibits thematic congruencies with the above-mentioned iconographic motifs.

One such congruency is found between the king-on-high motif and the imagery of Ps 22:3 [Heb. 22:4]: "Yet you are holy, enthroned on the praises of Israel" (NRSV).[48] Root herself notes the "parallel conceptualizations of the relationship of king to subjects" found between the poetic language of Ps 22 and the iconographic representations of Darius's throne from the south door of the Hundred Column Hall at Persepolis.[49] In both art and text, the king's reign, symbolized by his throne, has a burden-less quality. In the case of the relief, Darius is easily born aloft on the fingertips (atlas posture) of fourteen subject people. Psalm 22 develops this visual metaphor one step further, specifying that the king in question, YHWH, is borne on the praises (תהלות) of Israel.

Observing this image-text congruency can potentially help resolve what are difficult text-critical issues in this verse. While space prohibits a fuller discussion, some commentators render the unusual construction ואתה קדוש יושב as "you sit upon the holy throne," thus reading the adjective קדוש as a metonymy for the throne itself.[50] This reading is not unwarranted in light of similar imagery in Ps 114:2. However, the placement of the athnakh in the MT under קדוש and the above-mentioned image-text correspondence both suggest that it is better to read יושב as a participle expressing what YHWH is doing (sitting, or being enthroned) on the תהלות ישראל.

The heroic-encounter motif, especially in the combat variety, finds resonance in the theophany of Zech 9:13–17.[51] The description of YHWH bending Judah as a bow and loading Ephraim as its arrow (9:13) calls to mind a battle pose that is quite similar to that which is depicted in the type

---

48. Postexilic dating for this psalm is far from certain. However, the clear thematic similarity between this psalm and sixth century Achaemenid iconography should be considered as one important datum in the discussion.

49. Root, *King and Kingship*, 160.

50. See Mitchell Dahood, *Psalms*, AB 16–17A (Garden City, NY: Doubleday, 1965–1970), 1:136–38.

51. For further discussion, see Ryan P. Bonfiglio, "Divine Warrior or Persian King? The Archer Metaphor in Zechariah 9," in *Iconographic Exegesis of the Hebrew Bible/Old Testament*, ed. Izaak J. de Hulster, Brent A. Strawn, and Ryan P. Bonfiglio (Göttingen: Vandenhoeck & Ruprecht, 2015), 227–42.

II archer coins. In both image and text, the archer bears a drawn bow in a ready-for-combat posture. Likewise, the larger context of Zech 9:13–17 might be read as a type of heroic-combat scene in ways that are analogous to that which is found in many Persepolis fortification seals in which an archer protects an animal threatened by a predator. Specifically, verses 15–16 describe YHWH as protecting (*hiphil* of פנן) and saving (*hiphil* of ישע) from danger "the flock of his people." Just as the royal archer fells the rearing lion in figure 3.13, so too does YHWH subdue (כבש) Israel's enemies with a bow in Zechariah's theophany. Thus, the literary description of YHWH in Zech 9 mirrors in many respects the iconographic profile of the royal archer in Achaemenid iconography.

As in the case of Ps 22:3, the presence of this image-text congruence can help shed light on an important textual issue. Many earlier commentators have suggested that the imagery of Zech 9:13–17 draws on divine-warrior imagery by means of intertextual references to early Israelite victory hymns and/or thirteenth-century Ugaritic myths.[52] Such a connection is certainly not implausible, since biblical literature and Canaanite myths both describe the divine warrior in terms of a storm god marching in battle and shooting forth arrows as lightning. However, at least in the biblical tradition, the divine warrior is rarely described as explicitly wielding a bow. In fact, the only other time outside Zech 9:13 that the divine warrior is said to bend the bow is in Lam 2:4, though in this latter case YHWH aims his bow at Zion as a form of punishment, not protection. Thus, while the bent bow is surely implied by the divine-warrior motif, it is more specifically and frequently a feature of the Achaemenid royal archer, a motif widely disseminated at the time Zech 9 was likely written. Thus, I contend that it is no longer tenable to assert that the presence of the archer metaphor in Zech 9:13–14 *solely* reflects a recapitulation of the divine-warrior motif from ancient literary traditions. While some degree of textual dependency is possible, Achaemenid royal archer imagery provides an equally relevant comparative context for understanding the meaning and background of this metaphor.

Finally, as detailed in a study by Brent Strawn, the Achaemenid tribute-procession motif finds strong points of contact with the description of tribute from the nations streaming toward Jerusalem in Isa 60.[53] A

---

52. See, e.g., Carol L. Meyers and Eric M. Meyers, *Zechariah 9–14: A New Translation with Introduction and Commentary*, AB 25C (New York: Doubleday, 1993), 15.

53. Strawn, "World under Control," 85–116; Izaak J. de Hulster and Brent A.

number of points of similarity can be noted. The solar imagery in verses 1–3 and 19–20 frames the chapter in a manner that recalls the presence of Auramazda, depicted as a winged sun disk, hovering over the original central panels at the Apadana. Isaiah 60:6 mentions a "multitude of camels," and at least five camels are present in the Apadana relief. References to nations bringing their wealth and kings being "led" in procession (60:11) are suggestive of the formal composition of Wing B, in which twenty-three foreign delegates, shown bearing various types of tribute, are led toward the king. The description of the nations bowing down (*hishtaphel* of חוה), which is the characteristic verb of worship in the Hebrew Bible, might even recall the presentation-scene motif that is alluded to by the wrist/hand-grasping gesture of the Persian marshal. Most strikingly, the tribute procession in Isa 60 is decidedly unforced and indeed peaceful (see 60:17–18).[54]

To what extent can one conclude that the imagery of Isa 60 distinctly reflects themes in Achaemenid iconography? Strawn notes that one can find examples of much of the imagery in Isa 60 in textual and iconographic sources prior to the Achaemenid period.[55] This is true especially of solar imagery and theophany motifs, which are well-documented in the Hebrew Bible, and the tribute-procession scene, which is found in Mesopotamian art, including the previously discussed Black Obelisk. While individual motifs in Isa 60 are traceable to a variety of non-Achaemenid sources, what Strawn demonstrates is that the entire "constellation of motifs" found in this postexilic biblical text is not found in any textual or iconographic antecedent other than the Apadana reliefs.[56] This specificity of correspondence need not imply direct, genetic dependence of the biblical imagery on Achaemenid iconography or even Achaemenid literature that reiterates similar concepts. Yet, it remains possible to conclude with Strawn that Isa 60 and the Apadana reliefs represent "reflexes, one textual and one artistic, of Persian imperial propaganda" about the joyful,

---

Strawn, "The Power of Images: Isaiah 60, Jerusalem, and Persian Imperial Propaganda," in de Hulster, Strawn, and Bonfiglio, *Iconographic Exegesis of the Hebrew Bible*, 197–216.

54. For further discussion of Isa 60, see the chapter by Mark W. Hamilton in this volume.

55. Strawn, "World under Control," esp. 104–10.

56. Strawn, "World under Control," 108.

even pious participation of the people in bringing tribute to the powerful and benevolent deity/king.[57]

These three examples outlined above are just the tip of the iceberg when it comes to exploring the value of Achaemenid iconography when studying the imagery of postexilic biblical imagery. Indeed, one of the most promising developments in biblical studies, and religio-historical research more broadly, in recent years is the realization that iconographic materials provide at least as valuable a source for understanding ancient cultures as literary texts and inscriptions. This is no less true of the sixth century. Images, especially in the form of the three motifs discussed above, provide a window into the thought world behind the dominant imperial ideologies of the early Achaemenid dynasty. By studying these iconographic sources, we thus come face to face with a compelling witness to the political history of the sixth century and, along with it, the vision of kingship that Darius and his successors wished to convey.

---

57. Strawn, "World under Control," 114.

Controlling the Narrative:
The Babylonian Exile as Chosen Trauma

Caralie Cooke

Who controls the narrative in the event of an exile? The Bible seems to grapple with this question following the exile of a small group of elites from Jerusalem to Babylon in 587/597.[1] Despite the fact that this exile only included a small number of elites in Jerusalem, biblical trauma scholarship ignores or rejects the scholarship suggesting a limited exile. Instead, it points to an exile that looms large in the biblical texts.[2] Indeed, David Carr, the scholar who arguably has done the most work on how the Babylonian exile affected the biblical text, claims that the Bible was written by exiles, for exiles.[3] Further consideration must be given to the gap that remains between the comprehensive and universal trauma of the exile as presented

---

1. On the limited extent of the exile, see, e.g., Hans M. Barstad, *The Myth of the Empty Land: A Study in the History and Archaeology of Judah during the "Exilic" Period* (Oslo: Scandinavian University Press, 1996); J. Maxwell Miller and John H. Hayes, *A History of Ancient Israel and Judah*, 2nd ed. (Louisville: Westminster John Knox, 2006).

2. See recent volumes of collected essays by Eve-Marie Becker, Jan Dochhorn, and Else Kragelund Holt, eds., *Trauma and Traumatization in Individual and Collective Dimensions: Insights from Biblical Studies and Beyond*, SAN (Göttingen: Vandenhoeck & Ruprecht, 2014); Elizabeth Boase and Christopher G. Frechette, eds., *Bible through the Lens of Trauma*, SemeiaSt 86 (Atlanta: SBL Press, 2016). See also David Janzen, *The Violent Gift: Trauma's Subversion of the Deuteronomistic History's Narrative*, LHBOTS 531 (New York: T&T Clark, 2012); Kathleen M. O'Connor, *Jeremiah: Pain and Promise* (Minneapolis: Fortress, 2011); O'Connor, *Lamentations and the Tears of the World* (Maryknoll, NY: Orbis, 2002).

3. David Carr, *The Formation of the Hebrew Bible* (New York: Oxford University Press, 2011), 226. See both Carr, *Formation of the Hebrew Bible*; and Carr, *Holy Resilience: The Bible's Traumatic Origins* (New Haven: Yale University Press, 2014).

in the biblical text and the current scholarship suggesting that the majority of Judahites were not exiled after the fall of Jerusalem. Therefore, in this essay, I argue that the trauma narrative in the Bible is constructed. That is, the Bible presents a trauma narrative that is misleading, at least on the factual level. Not everyone in Jerusalem was exiled. Further, I draw from the theory of collective memory and address the way traumatic experiences affect the formation of collective memory. Finally, from this analysis I ask and give one possible explanation for why all of the Judahite people, despite their different experiences during the exilic period, accepted these texts as normative. Thus, my argument is that the Babylonian exile should be understood as a chosen trauma, a "shared mental representation" of the exile.[4] As such the exile becomes the lens through which subsequent generations of even nonexiled Judahites viewed their history.

In order to make this argument, I will first offer a brief discussion of the concept of chosen trauma. Then I will describe literate cultural producers who created the Hebrew Bible. I will then turn to questions about the transmission of the biblical text in order to demonstrate that the nonexilic community in Persian-period Yehud adopted this narrative as their own. Finally, I will attempt to answer the question of why the nonexilic community accepted the biblical texts as normative in spite of their different experiences of exile.

Chosen Trauma

Vamik Volkan defines chosen trauma as "the collective memory of a calamity that once befell a group's ancestors. It is, of course, more than a simple recollection; it is a shared mental representation of the event, which includes realistic information, fantasized expectations, intense feelings, and defenses against unacceptable thoughts."[5] In chosen traumas, the collective retains a memory of a traumatic event that occurred to previous generations. The group, particularly in times of threat, adopts their ancestors' trauma narrative. They then create and transmit a collective memory—the socially constructed memory that a group of individuals creates and remembers—of their ancestors' trauma.[6] Chosen trauma

---

4. Vamik D. Volkan, *Bloodlines: From Ethnic Pride to Ethnic Terrorism* (Boulder, CO: Westview, 1998), 48.

5. Volkan, *Bloodlines*, 48.

6. Lewis A. Coser, introduction to *On Collective Memory*, by Maurice Halbwachs,

operates as a way to bind together a group and their collective memory through a shared narrative.

The principle of chosen trauma provides an avenue for explaining why the biblical text became the dominant narrative, even among nonexiles. Before I can further explore this topic, I must first address how scholars have so far addressed the creation and transmission of biblical texts. Of course, the creation and transmission of biblical texts has been a large piece of the agenda of biblical scholarship for centuries. Here I draw only from a small corner of this discussion. I utilize the work of several scholars, including Carr, Karel van der Toorn, and Jan Assmann in order to address the impossibly large question of the creation of the biblical text.

Literate Cultural Producers

Stanley Stowers uses the terminology of "literate cultural producers" to designate the 2 percent or less of the population that produced written texts in the ancient world, specifically the ancient Mediterranean.[7] The language of the religion of literate cultural producers explains the role of the scribes who wrote down, edited, compiled, and redacted the Hebrew Bible during the exilic and postexilic periods. Regarding literate cultural producers, Stowers states: "Although small in number in any one location, they formed a large network due to the mobility and endurance of written texts across time and place."[8] In other words, the impact of literate cultural producers far surpassed their number because they were the ones who controlled the sacred texts and had the ability to keep a record in writing. The language of literate cultural producers offers a vocabulary pertinent to the Babylonian exile. Though the Babylonians exiled only a small portion of the population of Judah and its surrounding towns, the people they took into exile were those associated with the monarchy and the temple.[9] In a

---

ed. Lewis A. Coser (Chicago: University of Chicago Press, 1992), 22; Volkan, *Bloodlines*, 48.

7. Stanley K. Stowers, "The Religion of Plant and Animal Offerings versus the Religion of Meanings, Essences, and Textual Mysteries," in *Ancient Mediterranean Sacrifice*, ed. Jennifer Wright Knust and Zsuzsanna Várhelyi (New York: Oxford University Press, 2011), 41.

8. Stowers, "Religion of Plant and Animal Offerings," 41.

9. Megan Bishop Moore and Brad E. Kelle, *Biblical History and Israel's Past* (Grand Rapids: Eerdmans, 2011), 374.

largely illiterate culture, the exiled population contained a high percentage of Judah's literate cultural producers.[10] It was these literate cultural producers who were responsible for the creation of the biblical text.

Creation of the Biblical Text: A Bible from the Few for Everyone

According to Carr, this exiled population produced or redacted the majority of biblical texts while in exile or in the years immediately following the return.[11] Specifically, he argues that the Bible "was shaped by and for the community of returnees from exile, returnees who seem to have defined themselves as the true heirs of Israel, while defining those who remained as foreign 'peoples of the land.'"[12] In essence, according to Carr, the Bible largely tells the story of only a small group of the population over against everyone else's stories. Carr explains: "Thus, the category of 'exile' is not just a scholarly imposition on the data, but a major category in the Hebrew Bible itself.... The Hebrew Bible is a 'Bible for exiles.'"[13] These exiles experienced the traumatic event of the destruction of their society and subsequent removal from the land to dwell in a foreign place. They forged an identity there, focusing on remembering the traditions of their people and putting them together in a way representative to their stories. As Carr suggests, the experience of refugees "produces a need for reproduction (e.g., replicated neighborhoods, clan groups, etc.) and the retrieval of those rituals from home that can be practiced in the new circumstances."[14] Scribes focused on creating traditions and beginning to compile scriptures, which provided an avenue for reestablishing themselves and their religion after their return. Carr does not, however, address why the biblical text written by exiles for exiles became the source of authority in Yehud after the return from exile in 538 BCE. In other words, what role did the illiterate laypeople play in the creation of the biblical text? Again, I provide only a sampling of theories of a very complicated issue that possesses contradicting data. Many of the theories overlap or disagree, so I continue to focus on Carr and Van der Toorn in order to preserve some continuity in the discussion.

---

10. Moore and Kelle, *Biblical History and Israel's Past*, 376.
11. Carr, *Formation of the Hebrew Bible*, 226.
12. Carr, *Formation of the Hebrew Bible*, 226.
13. Carr, *Formation of the Hebrew Bible*, 226.
14. Carr, *Formation of the Hebrew Bible*, 229.

The majority of the population of Persian-period Yehud—90 percent or more—was not literate, at least not to the extent that they would have been able to read or produce biblical texts.[15] Because the majority of the population could not read, and certainly could not write, the scribes used writing in order to "support an oral performance."[16] Van der Toorn argues that scribes connected to the Jerusalem temple in the Second Temple period (500–200 BCE) created the Hebrew Bible in their scribal workshops.[17] These scribes were part of a class that was connected to but not part of the royal palace, and yet more than just men who copied texts.[18] Because of their connection to the monarchy, the Babylonians exiled these scribes after the fall of Jerusalem.[19] The basis for his argument that these scribes were connected to the temple stems from biblical evidence that the temple served as a location for legal material, an archive for the storage of written oracles, and a place for education and scholarship.[20] Therefore, Van der Toorn argues, "The Bible is a repository of tradition, accumulated over time, that was preserved and studied by a small body of specialists."[21] These specialists served as the people who produced texts in a largely illiterate society. The literate specialists also played the role of mediators to the texts for people who could not read. In essence, Van der Toorn argues that the majority of people did not have access to the scriptural texts without mediation and oral recitation by these specialists. According to Van der Toorn, in a time when the Torah served as the center of life and a guide

---

15. Susan Niditch, *Oral World and Written Word* (Louisville: Westminster John Knox, 1996), 39; Karel van der Toorn, *Scribal Culture and the Making of the Hebrew Bible* (Cambridge: Harvard University Press, 2007), 10. Literacy can mean different things: it can mean a person possesses the ability to read or write significant words, such as names or phrases important to business; it can also mean the ability to read complex texts; and it can mean the ability to produce these texts. Niditch describes this varying literacy as a sliding scale between oral and literate mentalities (*Oral World and Written Word*, 133). Here I use *literacy* to describe the ability to read as well as write complex texts such as the Bible. The literate cultural producers demonstrate an advanced type of literacy: the ability to produce these texts. I have chosen to describe this advanced ability to read complex texts because it is the level of literacy required for laypeople to engage with written texts.

16. Van der Toorn, *Scribal Culture*, 12.
17. Van der Toorn, *Scribal Culture*, 2.
18. Van der Toorn, *Scribal Culture*, 105.
19. Van der Toorn, *Scribal Culture*, 167.
20. Van der Toorn, *Scribal Culture*, 86.
21. Van der Toorn, *Scribal Culture*, 5.

for society, this mediation was essential. Indeed, Van der Toorn goes on to claim, "The scribes held the key to the symbolic capital of the nation." The scribes' ability to interpret these texts gave them their power in society.[22]

Apart from his discussion about the scribal class who produced texts, Van der Toorn also provides a way to think about the transmission of biblical texts, particularly in addressing why people would adopt an exilic narrative when they themselves experienced the destruction of Jerusalem but were not themselves exiled from the land. He states: "The Hebrew Bible is the product of the scribal culture of its time; its status as divine revelation is a construct of the Hebrew scribes as well. Though the scribes did not invent the notion of revelation as such, the framing of the books as Holy Writ was their doing."[23] In other words, the scribes were the ones who took the religion of the literate cultural producers and helped to establish or reestablish a state religion. According to Van der Toorn, the scribes became mediators between the written holy text and the people, or put another way, between the people and the divine.[24] Van der Toorn explains that with the rise of written texts, the role of scribes changed.[25] No longer was access to the sacred a part of oral tradition, but rather it became part of the written texts themselves.[26]

Both of these scholars' positions on the composition of biblical texts fit their larger arguments; however, seen as a whole, Van der Toorn mentions but does not give high importance to the impact of the Babylonian

---

22. Van der Toorn, *Scribal Culture*, 106, 108.

23. Van der Toorn, *Scribal Culture*, 205.

24. Here Van der Toorn deviates into an unhelpful place. He states: "Once the written tradition supplanted oral knowledge, it needed an authority that did not derive from those who transmitted it. The problem facing the scribes was legitimacy rather than credibility. Once the written texts came to serve as the standard of tradition, the tradition could not derive its authority from the experts who used the texts. The scribes found their new source of authority in the concept of divine revelation" (*Scribal Culture*, 219). So, here he argues that with the rise of written texts as the main source of tradition, scribes needed a way to infuse the tradition with authority that came from someone other than themselves. Thus, they applied divine revelation to the texts and then served as the ones who mediated between people and the tradition. This argument assumes the scribes had both the inclination and the power to change society and manipulate the laypeople without their consent. This argument does not work when considered alongside collective memory, which necessitates the support and consent of the community as a whole.

25. Van der Toorn, *Scribal Culture*, 219.

26. Van der Toorn, *Scribal Culture*, 219.

exile on the creation of the biblical text. Carr, on the other hand, frames his argument around the Babylonian exile. Van der Toorn's argument regarding the role of scribes in the transmission of biblical texts helps to fill in gaps in Carr's argument. Carr situates the composition of the biblical text alongside trauma theory. He argues that after their return from exile, scribes composed or redacted the biblical text both to make sense of their experiences and to ensure they remembered their traditions and who they were.[27] They brought the beginnings of these texts back from exile and continued to write about their experiences.[28] Yet Carr never explains how these texts became scripture, nor how or why the laypeople who remained in Judah came to accept this story as their own.[29] Van der Toorn, however, argues that these scribes who experienced exile returned, and with the development of scribal schools in the newly rebuilt temple, created what came to be the Hebrew Bible.[30] The oral recitation of texts and traditions was not new to Judahite society, but the idea that tradition lay within the texts as texts themselves was.[31] More to the point, I argue that the tradition embedded in texts begins to explain why the people as a whole adopted a narrative that contained familiar traditions; even if the texts were written from an exilic perspective, the texts were still familiar to the nonexiles.[32]

While Van der Toorn does address the question of the transmission of biblical texts, he places so much importance on scribes that the role of the laypeople fades into the background. Without the laypeople to adopt the biblical narrative as their own, the Bible could not have prevailed. For a

---

27. Carr, *Formation of the Hebrew Bible*, 226, 229.

28. Carr, *Formation of the Hebrew Bible*, 226, 229.

29. Carr does move toward this argument in saying that the Pentateuch is a collection of older materials to the end that the returnee community would find it agreeable. However, he does not mention the people who remained in the land. Instead, creating the Pentateuch and seeking Persian sponsorship was a bid for power and authority in Yehud (see Carr, *Formation of the Hebrew Bible*, 219).

30. Van der Toorn, *Scribal Culture*, 5, 86.

31. Van der Toorn, *Scribal Culture*, 107–8.

32. There is no way to know with any certainty that the returning exiles wrote their own story without incorporating the views of the nonexiles. However, if we accept Carr's argument that the Bible was written by exiles and for exiles, this argument is one way to explain how the exiles convinced the nonexiles to accept the biblical narrative as normative. Even if Carr is wrong and the exiles did take into consideration the perspective of the nonexiles, it was ultimately the scribes returning from exile who controlled whose voices to record.

complete understanding of the effects of the Babylonian exile on the transmission of the biblical text, I must look outside the field of Hebrew Bible to the field of collective memory studies. Specifically, I will address what happens to collective memory when crisis strikes a society.

Crisis and Collective Memory

Just as there are many different types of groups in a society, so too are there an equal number of collective memories.[33] That is, as Lewis Coser states in the introduction to his translation of Maurice Halbwach's *The Collective Memory*, "Social classes, families, associations, corporations, armies, and trade unions all have distinctive memories that their members have constructed, often over long periods of time."[34] Theories of collective memory, then, help to explain how and why memories become codified as part of a communal narrative. For my purposes, collective memory explains both the means of transmission of the biblical text and why the Yehudite and eventually the Jewish laypeople accepted the Hebrew Bible as their own communal narrative despite the fact that the texts were composed or redacted by literate cultural producers.[35]

When a society faces a crisis, one response is to form a type of nationalism, something Assmann refers to as "limitic upgrading."[36] He points to Josiah's reforms in Judah following the Assyrian destruction of Israel and in the face of impending domination by the growing Babylonian threat.[37] Here, all of the people of Judah are involved in the Deuteronomic turn that includes the finding of the lost book of the law and focuses on separation from other gods and societies.[38] In this movement, religion and ethnicity work together. Following the Babylonian exile and return, the people who remained in Jerusalem during the exile committed to this new/old identity that tied ethnic identity to religious identity.[39] The commitment of

---

33. Coser, introduction, 22.
34. Coser, introduction, 22.
35. For more on the discussion of the Bible and collective memory, see the chapter by Pamela Barmash in this volume.
36. Jan Assmann, *Cultural Memory and Early Civilization: Writing, Remembrance, and Political Imagination* (New York: Cambridge University Press, 2011), 137.
37. Assmann, *Cultural Memory and Early Civilization*, 137.
38. For examples in the ancient Near East outside the Hebrew Bible of kings who sought to legitimize their rule, see Matt Waters's essay in this volume.
39. Assmann, *Cultural Memory and Early Civilization*, 138–39.

the people in the land and the returnees to this new identity is an oddity, according to Assmann.[40] By all rights, they should have lost their identity the way all the other exiled people did, and the way the Israelites did during the Assyrian exile in 722.[41] Assmann claims, however, the exiles and those remaining in the land did not forget because "the exiled community in Babylon clung with all its might to the memory of the normative, formative self-image that had come down through the generations and had formed the foundations of its ethnic identity."[42] Ultimately, Assmann's explanation here explains the power of collective memory for a group to maintain their identity.

When crisis strikes, the collective memory is threatened. Assmann identifies the concept of shifting mythologies as a "mythomotor," which refers to a myth that is remembered and which moves a society in a new direction.[43] Essentially, it is a myth with a force like a motor that moves society.[44] These myths often occur in narratives with either a foundational function or a "contrapresent" one. The foundational function "makes the present into something meaningful, divinely inspired, necessary, and unchangeable." As an example of this foundational function, he points to the exodus story for Israel. For example, as Assmann says, Jews even today tell and to some extent reenact the escape from Egypt during Passover and the Seder.[45] This story serves as a foundational narrative that forms the identity of Jews and formed the identity of the Israelites in the Hebrew Bible.

The contrapresent function of the mythomotor occurs in myths when the present is less than ideal, and the people remember a "heroic age," a time

---

40. Assmann, *Cultural Memory and Early Civilization*, 137.
41. Assmann, *Cultural Memory and Early Civilization*, 137–38.
42. Assmann, *Cultural Memory and Early Civilization*, 138.
43. Assmann, *Cultural Memory and Early Civilization*, 62.
44. Specifically, Assmann states: "In cases of extreme deficiency, a contrapresent mythomotor may become subversive, for instance under foreign rule or oppression. Then traditional memories no longer support the existing situation but on the contrary throw it into question and call for total change. The past to which they refer appears not as an irrevocably lost heroic age but as a social and political Utopia toward which one can direct one's life and work. Thus memory turns into expectation, and they 'mythomotored' time takes on a different character. The circle of eternal recurrence now becomes a straight line leading to a distant goal" (*Cultural Memory and Early Civilization*, 62–63).
45. Assmann, *Cultural Memory and Early Civilization*, 73.

when things were better than they are now and explain why things went wrong.⁴⁶ In this approach to understanding the past, people acknowledge that there was a break between then and now. Often, narratives and myths that used to drive the society become irrelevant, or worse, harmful to the population. In the case of the Hebrew Bible, the myths, stories, and practices that defined the religion and society of the literate cultural producers of Judah lost their significance in the wake of the destruction of the first temple and the loss of the monarchy. Before the exile occurred, the literate cultural producers attempted to forestall the destruction of Jerusalem by instituting reforms, but they remained a fringe group and never garnered the support of the laypeople. After the exile occurred, the scribes' role shifted. They adopted the responsibility to explain why the exile happened and record the memories and myths of the people so that their society would continue if and when they returned to Jerusalem. When they did return to Jerusalem, they had the ability to record texts in order to shape the new society.⁴⁷ Assmann's theory of collective memory offers a different explanation from Carr and Van der Toorn for how the Hebrew Bible came to be, indeed, one that addresses both the composition and transmission.

The outline I have sketched of Assmann's composition history of the Hebrew Bible aligns with Halbwachs's concept of the importance of collective beliefs: the exiles impressed the importance of communal memory on each other in Babylon as well as in the postexilic period after the return. According to Assmann, Deuteronomy is a clear instance of the insistence on collective memory because of its preoccupation with remembrance.⁴⁸ The insistence in Deuteronomy that the community guard the law and remember it daily and nightly points to an anxiety for what would happen to the community if they forgot it.⁴⁹ Presumably, it would mean the end of their society; no collective memory would have been picked up by the laypeople who remained in the land. Moreover, the focus on recitation in Deuteronomy creates a way for the Yehudite

---

46. Assmann, *Cultural Memory and Early Civilization*, 59–63, 73.
47. Assmann, *Cultural Memory and Early Civilization*, 185–87.
48. Assmann, *Cultural Memory and Early Civilization*, 193. See also Georg Braulik on this point in "Deuteronomy and the Commemorative Culture of Israel: Redactio-historical Observations of the Use of למד," in *The Theology of Deuteronomy: Collected Essays of Georg Braulik, O.S.B.*, trans. Ulrika Lindblad (North Richland Hills, TX: BIBAL, 1994), 183–98.
49. Carr, *Formation of the Hebrew Bible*, 254–55.

people as a whole to adopt or recommit to this new communal set of beliefs.[50] When changes in society occur, memories tend to be forgotten, but this becomes less of a fear if the memories are written down, though texts can lose parts of their original meanings and require ongoing reinterpretation. Additionally, this fear of forgetting in the wake of societal changes, Assmann says, appears clearly in Deuteronomy. Not only did the exilic scribes write down their cultural memory, but they also inserted the command to keep, guard, and remember.[51]

Transmission of the Biblical Text: Why the Narrative Prevailed

Already I have addressed one possible narrative of how and why many of the biblical texts were created or redacted: literate cultural producers in exile in Babylon sought to explain, understand, and pass on their experiences. I have also asked: Why did the Yehudite people adopt these exilic-flavored texts as their own, despite the fact that they had never experienced the life of exiles? While I have begun to answer this question, throughout this section, I will attempt to answer this question in three parts. First, I will address the importance of laypeople who were not literate cultural producers and of memory and continuity with the past. Second, I will treat the role symbols play in codifying traumatic events. Finally, I will present the theory of constructed and chosen traumas and discuss how they apply to the Babylonian exile.[52]

Without a laypeople, a religion cannot survive.[53] After the Babylonian exile, scribal culture maintained the responsibility for upholding and transmitting religious traditions and memories.[54] The scribes, along with other high-ranking members of society close to the kingship, were the ones the Babylonians exiled and the ones who told and adapted the stories of their people and religion while in exile.[55] They also were the class that brought these traditions back to Jerusalem from exile and recorded them

---

50. See n. 48.

51. Assmann, *Cultural Memory and Early Civilization*, 49, 229, 193.

52. For a discussion of the effects of empire on the biblical text, see Mark Hamilton's essay in this volume.

53. Maurice Halbwachs, *On Collective Memory*, trans. Lewis A. Coser (Chicago: University of Chicago Press, 1992), 86.

54. Van der Toorn, *Scribal Culture*, 104–5.

55. Carr, *Formation of the Hebrew Bible*, 225–26.

during the Persian period.⁵⁶ The new religion that these scribes created shifted from the Yahwistic monarchism that dominated in Judah before its fall. The scribes were responsible for not only creating these stories and traditions, but also making them connect to the past so that the laypeople would be convinced to accept them as their own. They needed to allow room in the collective memory of their religion for the rebuilding of a temple when the Davidic line had been broken. Because both exiles and nonexiles now lived under the control of an imperial power, the loss of the monarchy was a shared collective memory.

In order for the laypeople to accept and adopt changes in myth and memory, the changes had to either be minor or cohere with the old collective memory. In particular, Halbwachs discusses society as the driving body that both changes and effects the change in the collective memory. A society cannot change everything about itself at once, but instead, in adapting its religion, it must keep its connection to the past in order to convince members of society to embody and enact the changes. Moreover, the society has to ensure that it presents the changes not as something new but as something that was part of the religion all along, though it might have been forgotten.⁵⁷

For a biblical example that illustrates the importance of collective memory, let me return to Josiah's reform in 2 Kgs 22–23, an example Van der Toorn and Assmann also point to.⁵⁸ Their discussions as well as my own fall more or less in line with Frank Moore Cross's double-redaction theory, though I have reframed his argument in light of the theory of collective memory.⁵⁹ In 2 Kgs 22–23, a book of the law is found during renovations of the temple, and Josiah discovers that the Judahite people had not been following many of the tenets laid out in the book of the law (2 Kgs 22:8–13). So Josiah details a series of reforms in order that the people will follow the law (23:2–3). For example, one change he makes is reinstituting the Passover celebration, which had not been celebrated in hundreds of years (23:21–23). While these reforms very well might have taken place in history as well as in the text, there is an element of convenience to the

---

56. Carr, *Formation of the Hebrew Bible*, 206.
57. Halbwachs, *On Collective Memory*, 86.
58. Van der Toorn, *Scribal Culture*, 93, 143–44; Assmann, *Cultural Memory and Early Civilization*, 194.
59. Frank Moore Cross, *Canaanite Myth and Hebrew Epic: Essays in the History of the Religion of Israel* (Cambridge: Harvard University Press, 1973), 289.

story: Josiah's regime finds a book of the law that allowed him to make changes. If, in fact, the historical Josiah did not find a book of the law, but instead enacted a series of reforms for whatever purpose, the Bible details the process in such a way consistent with the facets of communal memory. The Josiah in the Bible did not say he was going to create a new set of laws that the people had to follow, but instead invoked the past and the legal lineage that had come before him. He was merely reminding the people of the law that had been forgotten but that was inside them and their worldviews all along. In essence, this account of Josiah paints a picture of a king who instituted reforms by invoking the past and framing this new thing as something that was actually a part of tradition all along.[60]

Further, Josiah's reform began to shift society toward a religion connected to ethnicism. The cultural limitic upgrading became solidified in the Babylonian exile. The scribes in exile ensured that the memories were recorded, and once they returned from exile, that they were passed onto the people, much the way described in 2 Kings during Josiah's reform. They brought the temple-less religion they followed during the Babylonian exile back to Judah after the exile. This religion was a move away from monarchic Yahwism. The loss of the king was a narrative shared by both exiles and nonexiles that became a part of the shared collective memory. Moreover, this religion was based on separating the Judahite people from other groups in terms of practices and appearance.[61] In order to transmit this religion, the people were brought together, and the law was read and interpreted for the people (Neh 8:1–9). The stories that were always theirs became part of the newly written-down texts and reflected the experience of exile and set-apart religion and ethnicity. Indeed, these stories and texts, particularly the Torah, written originally by and for the exiles, became powerful symbols of identity for all of Persian-period Yehud and beyond.

Symbolizing traumatic events allows people to be able to interpret, understand, and remember these events. Often, these symbols encoded through narrative, and often war or in this case exile, can become such a way to remember an event. Regarding the symbolization of war, Kali Tal states: "Only in memory or in narrative can war be elevated to the level of symbol. Narratives are generated in order to explain, rationalize, and

---

60. For a discussion of the motif of book finding, see Thomas Römer, "Transformations in Deuteronomistic and Biblical Historiography: On 'Book-Finding' and Other Literary Strategies," *ZAW* 109.5 (1997): 1–11.

61. Assmann, *Cultural Memory and Early Civilization*, 175.

define events. The symbols which these narrators create are born out of the traumatic events of wartime."[62] These symbols help to shape social reality. This phenomenon helps to explain why, for example, the Babylonian exile and return became the narrative around which the canon was shaped.

Tal also addresses the issue of power and who controls the narrative. She states: "If survivors can retain control over the interpretation of their trauma, they can sometimes force a shift in the social and political structure.... If not, the penalty for repression is repetition."[63] As I have demonstrated throughout, the literate cultural producers maintained control over the collective memory in the Hebrew Bible. They caused a shift in religion and the political structure by ensuring that the new narratives meshed with the narratives of the larger community, as well as in deciding which of the larger community's oral narratives became canonized. Ultimately, these texts led to the group accepting a narrative that contained elements of familiar stories, but which scribes changed as a result of their experience of exile.

Further, if these symbols resulting from a traumatic event remain affectively charged, the emotion combined with the symbols enables the group to construct meaning in the aftermath of the trauma.[64] That is, the symbols evoke emotions associated with the traumatic event. Jeffrey Alexander argues that "events are not inherently traumatic"; a traumatic event does not even necessarily need to occur for it to be traumatic.[65] Instead, he states: "The truth of a cultural script depends not on its empirical accuracy, but on its symbolic power and enactment. Yet, while the trauma process is not rational, it is intentional. It is people who make traumatic meanings, in circumstances they have not themselves created and which they do not fully comprehend."[66] These events that traumatize that did not actually occur are no less traumatizing than events that did occur.[67] In essence, if the symbols are strong enough to create a collective imagination, the event that did not occur can still traumatize a group. Put in terms of the Hebrew Bible, though the exile may not have affected everyone in Judah the same

---

62. Kali Tal, *Worlds of Hurt: Reading Literatures of Trauma* (Cambridge: Cambridge University Press, 1996), 76.
63. Tal, *Worlds of Hurt*, 7.
64. Jeffrey Alexander, *Trauma: A Social Theory* (Cambridge: Polity, 2012), 2.
65. Alexander, *Trauma*, 13.
66. Alexander, *Trauma*, 5.
67. Alexander, *Trauma*, 13.

way, because the narrative symbols were so strong, the exile eventually became a communal narrative, indicating that everyone experienced the results of this traumatic event.

Finally, it is helpful to return to Volkan's concept of chosen trauma as defined in the beginning of this essay. Often a group will adopt a chosen trauma as their narrative if, as in collective memory, it contains the narrative of their ancestors. So, while the newly codified biblical texts primarily told the story of exile, even the people who did not experience exile adopted the exilic narrative because (1) the stories remained similar enough to the ones they already knew[68] and (2) they still lived under an imperial rule. Under Persian and Hellenistic rule, texts such as Daniel indicated that they were still in exile, metaphorically at least.[69] In other words, the scribes drew from the experiences of exile in order to create new literature. They adapted the trauma of their ancestors and claimed it as their own. In doing so, they adjusted it to fit a situation that the entire community was still enduring in some ways.

Conclusion

Throughout this essay I have attempted to piece together different elements of the scholarly understanding of the impact the Babylonian exile had on the biblical text. The scholars represented in this essay who work on the Bible and trauma agree that the Babylonian exile affect the biblical text.[70] Yet, this scholarship fails to address the fact that the majority of people were not exiled. Why would the nonexiled people adopt a narrative that was written by and for exiles? That is the primary question at stake in this paper. The Babylonian exile was indeed traumatic, but the exile in particular was traumatic mainly just for the small group of people whom it directly affected: the elites who served as the literate cultural producers. Through the writing and editing of biblical texts, these exiles created a narrative from older traditions to make sense of their traumatic experiences. Because they were the literate cultural producers and con-

---

68. Halbwachs, *On Collective Memory*, 86.

69. Daniel Smith-Christopher, *A Biblical Theology of Exile*, OBT (Minneapolis: Fortress, 2002), 65.

70. Every work in biblical trauma scholarship that addresses the text in its ancient context addresses the importance of the Babylonian exile on texts that originated both before and after the exile. For a sampling, see n. 2

trolled the narrative, they controlled their own story and passed it on to the rest of the population. The rest of the population, over time, came to accept it as their chosen trauma, despite the fact that it was not particularly traumatic for them. One possible explanation for the adoption of this chosen trauma is that in the aftermath of the return, the people needed a shared narrative to bind them together. The group identity was shaped and defined by the Babylonian exile because the leaders professed the exile as the common narrative; and because they were the ones controlling the written texts and group story, it was the narrative and ritual thread passed on through generations.

Bury Me with My Fathers:
A Voluntary or a Forced Return Migration?

Lisbeth S. Fried

As the tablets from Al Yahudu and other sites in Babylon make clear, the Judeans apparently lived a normal life in exile in Babylon.[1] They had children, property, and the rights to bequeath their property to their children. They had male and female servants. They served as royal tax collectors and inspectors; they were active in commerce and business, and engaged in various crafts. They bought and sold, rented and rented out. They served as prosecutors in law courts; they brought suits and served as witnesses in suits. They bought, sold, and leased land—from the crown, from the temple, and from private individuals as well. The image of the Jewish exiles in Babylon derived from the archives is consistent with the words of Jeremiah:

---

1. Francis Joannès and André Lemaire, "Trois Tablettes Cunéiformes à Onomastique Ouest-Sémitique (Collection Sh. Moussaïeff)," *Transeu* 17 (1999): 17–34, pls 1–2; Laurie E. Pearce and Cornelia Wunsch, *Documents of Judean Exiles and West Semites in Babylonia in the Collection of David Sofer*, CUSAS 28 (Bethesda, MD: CDL, 2014); Pearce, "New Evidence for Judeans in Babylonia," in *Judah and the Judeans in the Persian Period*, ed. Oded Lipschits and Manfred Oeming (Winona Lake, IN: Eisenbrauns, 2006), 399–411; Pearce, " 'Judean': A Special Status in Neo-Babylonian and Achaemenid Babylonia?," in *Judah and the Judeans in the Achaemenid Period: Negotiating Identity in an International Context*, ed. Gary N. Knoppers, Oded Lipschits, and Manfred Oeming (Winona Lake, IN: Eisenbrauns, 2011), 267–77; Cornelia Wunsch and Laurie Pearce, *Judeans by the Waters of Babylon: New Historical Evidence in Cuneiform Sources from Rural Babylonia in the Schøyen Collection*, BabAr 6 (Dresden: ISLET-Verlag, forthcoming); Bustenay Oded, "Daily Life of the Exiles in Babylon (6th–5th C BCE) in the Bible and in the Documents Which Have Appeared Recently" [Hebrew], *Bet Mikra* 63 (2018): 64–91.

> Thus says YHWH of hosts, the God of Israel, to all the exiles whom I have sent into exile from Jerusalem to Babylon:
>> Build houses and live in them; plant gardens and eat what they produce. Take wives and have sons and daughters; take wives for your sons, and give your daughters in marriage, that they may bear sons and daughters; multiply there, and do not decrease. Seek the welfare of the city where I have sent you into exile, and pray to YHWH on its behalf, for in its welfare you will find your welfare. (Jer 29:4–7)[2]

Why a Return to Judah?

If life was so normal, so placid, in Babylon, as it appears from the tablets, why then did the Judeans leave it to make the arduous trek across the empire to Judah, a walk that according to Ezra took five months (Ezra 7:9)? One theory, the so-called new economics of labor migration, considers return migration to be the result of a successful experience abroad during which migrants met their economic goals.[3] According to this model, typical migrants go abroad with positive expectations and with the intention of returning as soon as their economic goals are met or as soon as possible. The Judeans who appear in the cuneiform tablets certainly appear to have met their economic goals and may have gone to Babylon with the expectation of returning quickly. Data show that emigrating with the intention to return increases the level of work efforts of migrants, the amount of resources saved, and also the level of language acquisition and socialization in the host country. Further, the greater the self-identification with the homeland, the more likely that the eventual return will occur when the opportunity arises. Indeed, recently discovered documents from Babylon reveal some evidence that the exiles did hope to return to Judah. Names such as Yāšub-ṣidiqu ("the righteous will return") and Ia-a-šu-bu ("they will return") express this longing.[4]

Recent data on return migration show, however, that when migrants do actually return to the land of their origin, it is not when they have been

---

2. Unless otherwise stated, all biblical translations are modified from the NRSV.

3. Oded Stark and David Bloom, "The New Economics of Labor Migration," *AER* 75 (1985): 173–78.

4. Ran Zadok, *The Earliest Diaspora: Israelites and Judeans in Pre-Hellenistic Mesopotamia*, PDRI 151 (Tel Aviv: Diaspora Research Institute, Tel Aviv University, 2002); Pearce and Wunsch, *Documents of Judean Exiles*; Oded, "Daily Life of the Exiles."

successful, but rather it is most often a consequence of a failure abroad.[5] Recent economic data of immigration to the United States during 2005–2007 from a wide variety of countries show that within ten years 40 percent had returned to their home country, with the majority returning in the first two years.[6] Those who returned to their homeland were not those who prospered, but rather those who experienced downward earnings mobility in their host country. Indeed, this downward turn occurred in the two- to three-year period prior to their return home and likely precipitated it. Thus, these recent data contradict the expectations of the so-called new economic model, as it is not the successful who return but the economic failures. It may be, therefore, that those who returned to Judah were not the successful ones who appear in the cuneiform tablets and not the ones experiencing economic success. If it was the poor who returned, who paid for their journey? A five-month trip across the desert or through the mountains is considerably expensive. Rashi supposes that the ones who left were supported by the ones staying behind who, being wealthy, were loath to go.[7] It was more likely the Persians themselves, however, who had the ability and the desire to organize and pay for the return of the Judeans to Yehud.

One Fear: Dying in a Foreign Land

Whether it was the prosperous or the impoverished who returned, besides the positive perception of the homeland and the self-identification with it that the social-scientific data suggest, perhaps, as the biblical text implies, it was also the need to be buried in the grave of one's ancestors that motivated the returnees. The Hebrew Bible idealizes the family tomb.[8] A good death

---

5. Jean-Pierre Cassarino, "Theorizing Return Migration: A Revisited Conceptual Approach to Return Migrants," in *EUI Working Papers* (San Domenico di Fiesole, Italy: European University Institute Badia Fiesolana, 2004), 3; Amélie Constant and Douglas S. Massey, "Return Migration by German Guest-Workers: Neoclassical versus New Economic Theories," *IM* 40 (2002): 5–38.

6. Randall Akee and Maggie R. Jones, "Immigrants' Earnings Growth and Return Migration from the U.S.: Examining Their Determinants Using Linked Survey and Administrative Data," NBER Working Paper Series, 2019, # 25639.

7. Rashi, ad loc. Ezra 1:4; Lisbeth S. Fried, *Ezra, a Commentary*, SPCCS (Sheffield: Sheffield Phoenix, 2015), 60–62.

8. Matthew J. Suriano, *A History of Death in the Hebrew Bible* (Oxford: Oxford University Press, 2018), 2.

meant being "gathered to one's people"; a bad death was dying in isolation.⁹ Indeed, one implication of exile may have been that of dying in an isolated grave, separate from that of one's ancestors, while return presumably meant burial in the ancestral tomb, one's bones gathered together with the bones of one's forebears. This cliché is evident throughout the Tanak:

וימת אברהם ... ויאסף אל־עמיו
Abraham died ... and was gathered to his people. (Gen 25:8)

ישמעאל ... וימת ויאסף אל־עמיו
Ishmael ... died and was gathered to his people. (Gen 25:17)

ויגוע יצחק וימת ויאסף אל־עמיו
Isaac breathed his last, died, and was gathered to his people. (Gen 35:29)

יעקב ... ויאסף אל־עמיו
Jacob ... was gathered to his people. (Gen 49:33)

לכן הנני אספך על־אבתיך ונאספת אל־קברתיך בשלום
Therefore, see, I will gather you to your fathers and you will be gathered to your [fathers'] graves in peace. (2 Kgs 22:20)

Presumably being "gathered to one's fathers" or "to one's people" meant being buried in the family tomb, the burial cave of one's people—whether with one's ancestors, or, as in the case of Abraham and Joseph, with one's descendants.[10] Joseph, for example, makes the Israelites promise to bring his bones back to Israel and bury them there, even though it was not in the ancestral tomb. The book of Joshua affirms that they did so:

> Then Joseph said to his brothers, "I am about to die; but God will surely come to you, and bring you up out of this land to the land that he swore to Abraham, to Isaac, and to Jacob." So Joseph made the Israelites swear, saying, "When God comes to you, you shall carry up my bones from here." And Joseph died, being one hundred ten years old; he was embalmed and placed in a coffin in Egypt. (Gen 50:24–26)

---

9. Saul M. Olyan, "Some Neglected Aspects of Israelite Interment Ideology," *JBL* 124 (2005): 601–16.

10. Elizabeth Bloch-Smith, *Judahite Burial Practices and Beliefs about the Dead*, JSOT-Sup 123 (Sheffield: Sheffield Academic, 1992), 110; Olyan, "Some Neglected Aspects."

> The bones of Joseph, which the Israelites had brought up from Egypt, were buried at Shechem, in the portion of ground that Jacob had bought from the children of Hamor, the father of Shechem, for one hundred *qesiṭah*; it became an inheritance of the descendants of Joseph. (Josh 24:32)

Joseph is not buried with his fathers but with his descendants. If this fictional story of Joseph was indeed written in Judah in the sixth–fifth centuries, as Donald Redford suggests,[11] then these verses may be expressing the desire of an author living in Jerusalem in the fifth century BCE to repatriate his missing family members still in Babylon. It is interesting to note that only of Joseph is it not said that he was "gathered to his peoples," and he alone of the patriarchs was not buried with his fathers in the Cave of Machpelah.[12]

The importance of burial with one's family in a family tomb is expressed most poignantly, however, in Jacob's repeated attempt to ensure that he will not be buried in Egypt but in Judah.[13] Jacob pleads twice with Joseph, his son, not to bury him in Egypt but to bring him back to the land of his ancestors:

> Jacob lived in the land of Egypt seventeen years; so, the days of Jacob, the years of his life, were one hundred forty-seven years.
> When the time of Israel's death drew near, he called his son Joseph and said to him, "If I have found favor with you, put your hand under my thigh and promise to deal loyally and truly with me. Do not bury me in Egypt.
> "I will lie down with my ancestors, so carry me out of Egypt and bury me in their burial place." He answered, "I will do as you have said."
> And he said, "Swear to me"; and he swore to him. Then Israel [Jacob] bowed against the head of his bed. (Gen 47:28–31)

> Then he charged them, saying to them, "I am about to be gathered to my people. Bury me with my fathers—in the cave in the field of Ephron the Hittite, in the cave in the field at Machpelah, near Mamre, in the land of Canaan, in the field that Abraham bought from Ephron the Hittite as a burial site. There Abraham and his wife Sarah were buried; there Isaac

---

11. Donald B. Redford, *A Study of the Biblical Story of Joseph (Genesis 37-50)* (Leiden: Brill, 1970), esp. 250.

12. Suriano, *History of Death*, 29.

13. Joshua Berman, "The Narratorial Voice of the Scribes of Samaria: Ezra 4:8- 6:18 Reconsidered," *VT* 56 (2006): 313-26.

and his wife Rebekah were buried; and there I buried Leah. The field and the cave that is in it were purchased from the Hittites."

When Jacob ended his charge to his sons, he drew up his feet into the bed, breathed his last, and was gathered to his people. (Gen 49:29–33)

The strong desire not to be buried on foreign soil but in a family tomb is apparent in this story of Jacob. The biblical ideology of death can be described as reunion with dead kin inside a communal or family tomb, where the bones of the deceased can eventually be mingled with those of one's ancestors and one's descendants.[14]

Not only the biblical text but also the archaeology of Israel and Judah reveals family tombs that were used for many generations of an extended family, stressing not only generational continuity but also the permanent nature of the family itself.[15] Some of these tombs include dozens of individuals, in one case reaching almost a hundred.[16] The tombs were symbols of kinship and links to one's ancestors, so that all family members expected their bones to be gathered there to be mingled with those of their fathers.[17]

Correspondingly, exile seems to have meant being buried far from home, far from the family burial cave, perhaps even far from God, as described in Ezek 37:1–14. The deserved punishment for the evil priest

---

14. Robert E. Cooley and Gary D. Pratico, "Gathered to His People: An Archaeological Illustration from Tell Dothan's Western Cemetery," in *Scripture and Other Artifacts: Essays on the Bible and Archaeology in Honor of Philip J. King*, ed. Michael D. Coogan, J. Cheryl Exum, and Lawrence E. Stager (Louisville: John Knox, 1994), 70–92; Suriano, *History of Death*, 29.

15. Gabriel Barkay, "Burial Caves and Burial Practices in Judah in the Iron Age" [Hebrew], in *Graves and Burial Practices in Israel in the Ancient Period* [Hebrew], ed. Itamar Singer (Jerusalem: Yad Yitzhak ben Avi, 1994), 96–164; Barkay, "Burial Caves and Dwellings in Judah during the Iron Age II: Sociological Aspects" [Hebrew], in *Material Culture, Society and Ideology: New Directions in the Archaeology of the Land of Israel* [Hebrew], ed. Aren M. Maeir and Avi Faust (Ramat-Gan: Bar-Ilan University Press, 1999), 96–102; Bloch-Smith, *Judahite Burial Practices*; Avraham Faust and Shlomo Bunimovitz, "The Judahite Rock-Cut Tomb: Family Response at a Time of Change," *IEJ* 58 (2008): 150–70.

16. Barkay, "Burial Caves and Dwellings," 97; Gabriel Barkay, "The Necropoli of Jerusalem in the First Temple Period" [Hebrew], in *The History of Jerusalem: The Biblical Period*, ed. Shmuel Aḥituv and Amichai Mazar (Jerusalem: Yad Yitzhak ben Zvi, 2000), 268.

17. Faust and Bunimovitz, "Judahite Rock-Cut Tomb," 154; Suriano, *History of Death*, 40.

Jason, high priest and collaborator under Antiochus III, was death in Egypt, in exile with no funeral and without his bones being gathered into the tomb of his fathers:

> Finally he [Jason] met a miserable end. Accused before Aretas the ruler of the Arabs, fleeing from city to city, pursued by everyone, hated as a rebel against the laws, and abhorred as the executioner of his country and his compatriots, he was cast ashore in Egypt. There he who had driven many from their own country into exile died in exile, having embarked to go to the Lacedaemonians in hope of finding protection because of their kinship. He who had cast out many to lie unburied had no one to mourn for him; he had no funeral of any sort and *no place in the tomb of his fathers.* (2 Macc 5:8–10)

Safety, then, seems to imply burial in one's native land; danger and abandonment mean burial abroad. This assumes, of course, that the graves themselves would be protected and known and visited, but this eventuality could not be guaranteed. Nehemiah begs permission of King Artaxerxes to be sent to Judah because the city of the graves of his ancestors lays waste, its gates consumed by fire.

> I said to the king, "May the king live forever! Why should my face not be sad, when the city, the place of my fathers' graves, lies waste, and its gates destroyed by fire?" Then the king said to me, "What do you request?" So I prayed to the God of heaven.
> Then I said to the king, "If it pleases the king, and if your servant has found favor with you, I ask that you send me to Judah, to the city of my ancestors' graves, so that I may rebuild it." (Neh 2:3–5)

We do not know whether Nehemiah intended to return to Susa or whether this was a ruse to enable him to leave the king's employ, but it was definitely a plea the king understood. No matter how long Nehemiah or his family had been in exile, even if it had been generations, the attachment to his ancestors' graves in Judah was palpable. The pain of exile thus seems to include living and being buried far from the grave of one's fathers. If so, the return from exile to Judah under the Persians may have been prompted by the need to be able to live near and to tend the family burial caves, and ultimately to be interred with within them, not in far-off Babylon. This may have been one reason for the return to Judah from Babylonian exile.

Was the Return Voluntary?

Besides the desire to return to Judah in order to live near and tend the graves of one's ancestors, and besides the desire to return in order to be buried within them oneself, another possibility that must be considered is that the return to Judah may not have been voluntary. Did Cyrus, upon his accession to the throne of Babylon, simply permit the Judeans who wanted to return to the land of their fathers, or did he command them to? As the text is usually translated, Cyrus permitted the Judeans to return to Judah in the first year of his ascendancy to the throne of Babylon, implying that those returning returned voluntarily.

מי־בכם מכל־עמו יהי אלהיו עמו ויעל לירושלם אשר ביהודה ויבן את־בית יהוה
אלהי ישראל הוא האלהים אשר בירושלם:

Whoever of you among all his people, let his god be with him, let him go up to Jerusalem which is in Judah and let him build the temple of YHWH the god of Israel, he is the god who is in Jerusalem. (Ezra 1:3)

The tense used, however, is the jussive, and one may question whether the words connote a command rather than a permission. The hypothesis of a voluntary return can be tested. If it were a voluntary return following Cyrus's permission, then logically the return would have been to the towns and villages from which the exiles had come, the places where their ancestors had been buried. It the return was a result of a command, however, and if the command gave them no choice in the place to which they had to settle, then it would not necessarily have been to the places where their fathers had died and were interred. A third possibility also exists, that the choice of returning to Judah might have been voluntary, but with the precise place within Judah where they were to reside being determined by the Achaemenid rulers.

Judah during the Babylonian Exile

As the archaeology of Judah has confirmed, there was indeed an exile in the sixth century BCE. While once doubted,[18] it is doubted no more.

---

18. E.g., Charles C. Torrey, *Ezra Studies* (repr., New York: Ktav, 1970), 285–300; Hans M. Barstad, *The Myth of the Empty Land: A Study in the History and Archaeology of Judah during the "Exilic" Period* (Oslo: Scandinavian University Press, 1996);

Archaeological evidence from Jerusalem and the city of David shows that the Babylonian destruction was complete and devastating.[19] Destruction at the end of the Iron Age has been found in every part of the city.[20] There is no doubt that the temple in Jerusalem was destroyed, its vessels carried off to Babylon, its priests put to death or deported, and—one month later—the city razed to the ground.[21] The emptying of the city was, of course, not entirely due to death in battle or the deportation of the citizens. Many fled, while others died from famine in the besieged city, or from disease.[22]

Barstad, "After the 'Myth of the Empty Land': Major Challenges in the Study of Neo-Babylonian Judah," in *Judah and the Judeans in the Neo-Babylonian Period*, ed. Oded Lipschits and Joseph Blenkinsopp (Winona Lake, IN: Eisenbrauns, 2003), 3–20; Robert P. Carroll, "Exile! What Exile? Deportation and the Discourses of Diaspora," in *Leading Captivity Captive: "The Exile" as History and Ideology*, ed. Lester L. Grabbe, JSOTSup 278, ESHM 2 (Sheffield: Sheffield Academic, 1998), 62–79; Lester L. Grabbe, review of *The Templeless Age: An Introduction to the History, Literature, and Theology of the Exile*, by Jill Middlemas, *RBL* (July 2008): https://www.sblcentral.org/home/bookDetails/6072.

19. Avraham Faust, "Deportation and Demography in Sixth Century B.C.E. Judah," in *Interpreting Exile: Interdisciplinary Studies of Displacement and Deportation in Biblical and Modern Contexts*, ed. Brad E. Kelle, Frank R. Ames, and Jacob L. Wright (Atlanta: Society of Biblical Literature, 2011), 91–103; Faust, *Judah in the Neo-Babylonian Period: The Archaeology of Desolation*, ABS 18 (Atlanta: Society of Biblical Literature, 2012), 23–24, 140–43; Israel Finkelstein, "Jerusalem in the Persian (and Early Hellenistic) Period and the Wall of Nehemiah," *JSOT* 32 (2008): 501–20; Finkelstein, "Archaeology and the List of Returnees in the Books of Ezra and Nehemiah," *PEQ* 140 (2008): 7–16; Finkelstein, "Persian Period Jerusalem and Yehud: A Rejoinder," *JHebS* 9 (2009): article 24; Oded Lipschits, "Judah, Jerusalem and the Temple (586–539 B.C.)," *Transeu* 22 (2001): 129–42; Lipschits, "Demographic Changes in Judah between the Seventh and the Fifth Centuries B.C.E.," in *Judah and the Judeans in the Neo-Babylonian Period*, ed. Lipschits (Winona Lake, IN: Eisenbrauns, 2003), 323–76; Lipschits, *The Fall and Rise of Jerusalem* (Winona Lake, IN: Eisenbrauns, 2005), 210–18; Lipschits, "Shedding New Light on the Dark Years of the 'Exilic Period': New Studies, Further Elucidation, and Some Questions Regarding the Archaeology of Judah as an 'Empty Land,'" in Kelle, Ames, and Wright, *Interpreting Exile*, 57.

20. Lipschits, *Fall and Rise of Jerusalem*, 211.

21. Oded Lipschits, "Achaemenid Imperial Policy, Settlement Processes in Palestine, and the Status of Jerusalem in the Middle of the Fifth Century B.C.E," in Lipschits and Oeming, *Judah and the Judeans*, 19–52.

22. Israel Eph'al, *The City Besieged: Siege and Its Manifestations in the Ancient Near East* (Boston: Brill, 2009); Faust, "Deportation and Demography"; Faust, *Judah in the Neo-Babylonian Period*, 140–43.

The picture from the Judean hills is the same—almost complete destruction, followed by collapse. Ephraim Stern provides a long list of excavated cities of the Judean hill country that were destroyed or abandoned as a result of the Babylonian onslaught and that recovered only in the Persian or Hellenistic period, if at all.[23] The southern Judean hills and the Shephelah suffered a similar fate of almost complete destruction and were almost completely deserted.[24] The same is true of the Negev. Cities all the way to Beersheba were utterly destroyed or abandoned, and not rebuilt until the mid-fourth century BCE, if at all.[25]

This devastation was apparent not only in the cities; rural areas were also destroyed or abandoned.[26] Excavations and surveys revealed hundreds of rural sites in Judah and Benjamin from the Iron Age, but none from the Babylonian period; they had all been destroyed or abandoned when the cities collapsed. The land was virtually empty after the Babylonian destruction. The population of Judah and Benjamin had either been killed, died from famine in the siege of the cities, had fled, or was exiled, and the majority of those exiled were exiled to Babylon. The situation was as described in Jer 44:1-2:

> The word that came to Jeremiah for all the Judeans [who had fled to] the land of Egypt, and were living at Migdol, at Tahpanhes, at Memphis, and in the land of Pathros. Thus says YHWH of hosts, the God of Israel: You yourselves have seen all the disaster that I have brought on Jerusalem and on all the towns of Judah. Look at them; today they are a desolation, without an inhabitant in them.

---

23. Ephraim Stern, *Archaeology of the Land of the Bible*, ed. David Noel Freedman, ABRL 2 (New York: Doubleday, 2001), 323–24; Eph'al, *City Besieged*; Faust, "Deportation and Demography"; Faust, *Judah in the Neo-Babylonian Period*, 140–43.

24. Oded Lipschits, "Nebuchadnezzar's Policy in 'Hattu-Land' and the Fate of the Kingdom of Judah," *UF* 30 (1998): 467–87.

25. Ruth Amiran and Ze'ev Herzog, *Arad* (Tel Aviv: Tel Aviv University Press, 1997), 239, 242.

26. Avraham Faust, "Judah in the Sixth Century B.C.E.: A Rural Perspective," *PEQ* 135 (2003): 37–53; Faust, "Social and Cultural Changes in Judah during the Sixth Century BCE and Their Implications for Our Understanding of the Nature of the Neo-Babylonian Period," *UF* 36 (2004): 157–76; Faust, *Israel's Ethnogenesis: Settlement, Interaction, Expansion, and Resistance* (London: Equinox, 2006); Faust, *Judah in the Neo-Babylonian Period*, 33–72; Yitzhak Magen and Israel Finkelstein, eds., *Archaeological Survey of the Hill Country of Benjamin* (Jerusalem: Israel Antiquities Authority, 1993).

This makes the return all the more bewildering. Why would Judeans return voluntarily to such a desolate place—and where did they return to?

To Where Did the Judeans Return? The Archaeology of Persian Yehud

The Cities

Archaeology shows, in fact, that the Judeans did not return to the towns or villages that were inhabited in the Iron Age, or to the burial sites where their ancestors were interred. For the most part those towns and villages either no longer existed or were not in Yehud.[27] Even Jerusalem itself was still small and thinly populated by the end of the Persian period, with no more than several hundred inhabitants.[28]

The boundaries of Persian-period Yehud have been drawn based on the existence of Yehud seals and coins.[29] The most southerly point on the west from which a Persian Yehud coin was found is Beth-Zur (Khirbet et-Tubeiqah, about 30 km south of Jerusalem and 6 km north of Hebron).[30] ʿEin-Gedi (Tel Goren), 800 meters west of the Dead Sea, is the most southern site where *yehud* seals were found.[31] There is scant evidence of either Yehud coins or seal impressions south of the border from Beth-Zur to ʿEin-Gedi. The major preexilic cities of Lachish, Hebron, and Beersheba were all south of this border and were now part of the Arab kingdom of Qedar, home to Arabs and Idumeans.

---

27. Avraham Faust, "Forts or Agricultural Estates? Persian Period Settlement in the Territories of the Former Kingdom of Judah," *PEQ* 150 (2018): 34–59.

28. Faust, *Judah in the Neo-Babylonian Period*; Finkelstein, "Jerusalem in the Persian Period"; Lipschits, "Demographic Changes," 323–76; Lipschits, *Fall and Rise of Jerusalem*; Lipschits, "Achaemenid Imperial Policy," 19–52.

29. Oded Lipschits and David S. Vanderhooft, *The Yehud Stamp Impressions: A Corpus of Inscribed Impressions from the Persian and Hellenistic Periods in Judah* (Winona Lake, IN: Eisenbrauns, 2011).

30. André Lemaire, "Populations et Territoires de Palestine À l'Époque Perse," *Transeu* 3 (1990): 31–74; Robert W. Funk, "Beth-Zur," *NEAEHL* 1 (1993): 259–61; Charles E. Carter, *The Emergence of Yehud in the Persian Period: A Social and Demographic Study* (Sheffield: Sheffield Academic, 1999), 153; Ephraim Stern, *Material Culture of the Land of the Bible in the Persian Period, 538–332 B.C.* (Jerusalem: Israel Exploration Society, 1982), 36; Lisbeth S. Fried, "A Silver Coin of Yoḥanan Hakkôhen," *Transeu* 26 (2003): 65–85, pls. II–V; Lipschits, *Fall and Rise of Jerusalem*, 140.

31. Carter, *Emergence of Yehud*, 158–89; Lipschits and Vanderhooft, *Yehud Stamp Impressions*, 27–28.

Jericho and Tell en-Naṣbeh (identified as biblical Mispah) are the northernmost cities in which Persian-period seals or coins have been found.[32] Cities north of this line, most notably Bethel and Ai, were now part of Samaria and home to Samaritans. Towns west of the Tell en-Nasbeh–Beth-Zur line belonged now to Phoenicia and were home to Phoenicians; Judeans did not go back to those cities. The area east of the Jericho to ʿEin-Gedi line sloped down to the Jordan River and was largely desert. These boundaries (Beth-Zur to Mispah to Jericho to ʿEin-Gedi) delimit a very small Yehud. Besides Jerusalem, the major cities of preexilic Judah had been Jericho, Bethel, Beersheba, Lachish, Gezer, Hebron, and Bethlehem. Of these, all but Bethlehem and Jericho were beyond the borders of Persian-period Yehud.

The list of towns provided in Ezra 2 has often been used as the list of towns of Judah from which the exiles had come and to which they returned. The towns within Judah that are listed in Ezra 2 are Gibeon, Bethel, Hadid, Jericho, Bethlehem, Netophah, Anathoth, Azmaveth, Kiriath-jearim, Chephira, Beʾeroth, Ha-Ramah, Geba, Michmas, and Ai. They were all strongly inhabited both in the late Iron Age and again in the Hellenistic period, but there is little evidence for occupation under the Persians in most of these sites.[33] Of the fifteen Judean sites listed in Ezra 2, only three—Azmaveth, Michmas, and Jericho—exhibit occupation in both the Iron Age and the Persian periods. Although not included in the town lists of either Ezra 2 or Neh 7, Persian-period Yehud-type seal impressions indicate Persian-period occupation in four additional sites: Ramat Raḥel, Nebi Samuel, Mispah, and ʿEin-Gedi. Ramat Raḥel, however, was an administrative center in the Iron Age and likely a governor's mansion during the Persian period and so was apparently not occupied by normal Judeans.[34] Nebi Samuel, 7 kilometers northwest of Jerusalem, seems to have been occupied during the Iron II and the Persian period, as shown by both Iron

---

32. Carter, *Emergence of Yehud*, 162; Lipschits and Vanderhooft, *Yehud Stamp Impressions*, 27.

33. Finkelstein, "Archaeology and the List"; Israel Finkelstein, "The Territorial Extent and Demography of Yehud/Judea in the Persian and Early Hellenistic Periods," *RB* 117 (2010): 39–54.

34. Oded Lipschits et al., "The 2006 and 2007 Excavation Seasons at Ramat Raḥel: Preliminary Report," *IEJ* 59 (2009): 1–20; Oded Lipschits, Yuval Gadot, and Dafna Langgut, "The Riddle of Ramat Raḥel: The Archaeology of a Royal Persian Period Edifice," *Transeu* 41 (2012): 57–79.

Age and Persian-period finds in the fills of the Hellenistic quarter of the site.³⁵ ʿEin-Gedi, on the southern tip of the Dead Sea, was occupied both in the Iron Age and in the Persian period, but Persian-period occupation appears to have begun only in the fifth century. If so, a return under Cyrus or Darius is unlikely. Of these four additional sites, then, only of Jerusalem, Mispah, identified with Tel en-Naṣbeh, and perhaps Nebi Samuel, can it be confirmed that there was normal Judean occupation during both the Iron Age and early Persian periods. These five sites with some Persian-period occupation (Jerusalem, Mispah, Azmaveth, Michmas, and Jericho) cannot prevent our conclusion: the Judean exiles who returned, by and large, did not return to the cities from which they or their fathers had been exiled. If the list of towns in Ezra 2 (= Neh 7) has any legitimacy at all, it must be a list of all the towns from which these Judeans had been exiled, rather than a list of towns to which they returned. Indeed, all the towns identified in this list were occupied during the Iron Age.

Rural Sites

If the Judeans generally did not return to the towns or cities in Yehud from which they were exiled, what about the rural areas? Perhaps the returnees were not from towns at all but were simply descendants of farmers from the rural areas of Judah. Unfortunately, what was said above regarding the towns is also true of the rural areas in Judah. Rural sites in Judah that had been inhabited in the Iron Age were generally not inhabited under the Persians.³⁶ Continuity of rural settlements between the Iron Age and the Persian period was negligible. Of the Persian-period rural sites excavated in Judah and Benjamin, the vast majority did not exist in the Iron Age at all. Further, of the forty-five late Iron Age farmsteads excavated, only seven also showed habitation in the Persian period, and this was probably simply due to coincidence. The unavoidable conclusion is that Judeans in Persian-period Yehud did not go back either to the rural homesteads from which their families had been deported or to their towns.³⁷

---

35. Yitzhak Magen, "Nebi Samwil," *NEAEHL* 5 (2008): 1972–76.
36. Faust, *Judah in the Neo-Babylonian Period*, 56.
37. Kenneth G. Hogland, "The Achaemenid Context," in *Second Temple Studies*, vol. 1, *The Persian Period*, ed. Philip R. Davies, JSOTSup 117 (Sheffield: Sheffield Academic, 1991), 54–72.

The Burial Caves

Neither did the Judeans return to the burial caves of their fathers. Burial caves of the Iron Age were not in use during the Persian period.[38] Out of hundreds of Iron Age tombs, few exhibit any use under the Persians. It must be concluded either that the goal of the Judeans' return from exile was not to be buried in the graves of their ancestors, or even to care for them, as Nehemiah had stated he wanted to do. Yet, if it was not from a desire to return to the places where their fathers had been buried, what, then, was the reason for the return? Why did they leave their pleasant and normal life in Babylon for the five-month trek to Judah?

Life Back in Judah

The *Ilku*

The lack of correspondence between Iron Age and Persian-period cities and rural sites, and the lack of correspondence between Iron Age graves and Persian-period graves, suggests either a voluntary return to any random location that was suitable for farming and for making a living, or that whether the return was voluntary or not, Persian officials had simply assigned land to the returnees irrespective of their place of origin and irrespective of their desires.

Texts from the Murašu archive, from the Egyptian Arsames archive, and from the newly translated archive from Bactria confirm what was already clear from the Greek historians—that conquered land throughout the empire was confiscated and held by the Persian king or members of the royal family and parceled out by them as fiefs.[39] These fiefs were allocated

---

38. Faust, "Social and Cultural Changes."
39. Guillaume Cardasçia, *Les Archives des Murašû, une Famille d'Hommes d'Affaires À l'Époque Perse (455–503 Av. J.-C.)* (Paris: Impr. nationale, 1951); Gerhard Ries, *Die Neubabylonischen Bodenpachtformulare*, MUS 16 (Berlin: Schweitzer, 1976); Muhammad A. Dandamayev, "Die Lehnsbeziehungen in Babylonien unter den ersten Achämeniden," in *Festschrift für Wilhelm Eilers: Ein Dokument der Internationalen Forschung zum 27. September 1967*, ed. Gernot Wiessner and Wilhelm Eilers (Wiesbaden: Harrassowitz, 1967), 37–42; Dandamayev, "The Domain-Lands of Achaemenes in Babylonia," *AoF* 1 (1974): 123–27; Matthew W. Stolper, *Entrepreneurs and Empire: The Murašû Archive, the Murašû Firm, and Persian Rule in Babylonia* (Leiden: Nederlands Instituut voor het Nabije Oosten, 1985); Govert van Driel, "The

to communities of agnatic families of the conquered peoples in a land-for-service scheme. The service required from the people assigned to a fief was either military or corvée labor in imperial building projects—or both.

In Nippur, for example, agnatic families of the conquered peoples deported to Babylon were each assigned to a *ḫaṭru*, headed by a foreman. This foreman was responsible for allocating fiefs or shares within the *ḫaṭru* to members of the extended family, for assuring that the land was productive, for collecting the taxes on the land, and for ensuring that the members living on the land performed the service obligations incumbent on them—military or otherwise. This service obligation was called the *ilku* in Akkadian.[40] The *ḫaṭru* was thus a means for ensuring cultivation of confiscated or vacant land, and for providing both a military reserve and cadres of state-controlled workers accountable ultimately to the king. The use of foreigners on these lands also enabled the integration of deportees into the economy.[41] Michael Jursa suggests that land around Nippur had been "singularly depopulated" and that in the sixth and early fifth centuries Nippur was "rather isolated and self-contained and detached from the main axis of communication along the Euphrates River," uniquely enabling foreign workers to be settled in the area and assigned land in exchange for service.[42] The conquered peoples who were moved onto the land were not slaves, in that they could not be bought or sold, but rather serfs who could not be alienated from the land they were assigned and could not leave it. Tied to the land, they were serfs with military and service obligations. This unique service obligation, called the *ilku* in Akkadian, was called the *halak* in Aramaic.

A good example of this *ilku*-service appears in a text drawn from the Murašu archive:

Murašus in Context," *JESHO* 32 (1989): 203–29; Van Driel, *Elusive Silver: In Search for a Market in an Agrarian Environment; Aspects of Mesopotamia's Society*, UNINO 9 (Leiden: Nederlands Instituut voor het Nabije Oosten, 2002); Michael Jursa, *Aspects of the Economic History of Babylonia in the First Millennium BC*, AOAT 377 (Münster: Ugarit-Verlag, 2010), 198–203; Lisbeth S. Fried, "The Exploitation of Depopulated Land in Achaemenid Judah," in *The Economy of Ancient Judah in Its Historical Context*, ed. Marvin L. Miller, Ehud Ben Zvi, and Gary N. Knoppers (Winona Lake, IN: Eisenbrauns, 2015), 149–62; Joseph Naveh and Shaul Shaked, *Aramaic Documents from Ancient Bactria (Fourth Century BCE)* (London: Khalili Family Trust, 2012), 30.

40. Stolper, *Entrepreneurs and Empire*, 70.
41. Van Driel, *Elusive Silver*, 227–28.
42. Jursa, *Economic History of Babylonia*, 406.

> In the joy of his heart, Gedaliah son of Rahim-ili speaks thus to Rimut-Ninurta son of Murašu:
>> "You hold the land both planted and in stubble, the horse-land [*bît-sisî*] of Rahim-ili, the whole part of Barik-ili, because in adopting Rahim-ili, your uncle Ellil-šum-iddin has received it. Give me one horse with his *ḫušuku* and the harness, a DI of leather, an iron caparison, an iron helmet, a body-suit of *ḫattu* leather, a shield for my torso, 120 (heavy) impact and flying (light) arrows, an iron *rebû* for the shield, two iron swords, and one mina of silver for my supplies on the order of the king in view of my mission to Uruk and I will fulfill the *ilku*-service incumbent upon the horse-land [*bît-sisî*], all of it."
>
> Then Rimut-Ninurta agreed to it and gave me one horse and all the accessories of combat, conforming to what is written above, plus one mina of silver for my supplies on the order of the king in view of the mission to Uruk which is incumbent (as the *ilku* service) upon the said horse-land [*bît-sisî*]. Gedaliah carries the responsibility if he does not present what has been entrusted to him. Gedaliah will draw up the receipt coming from Sabin, head of the army paymasters, and will give it to Rimut-Ninurta.
>
> Names of nine witnesses and of the scribe, Nippur, 18th day of the ninth month, the second year of Darius II.[43]

This text concerns an agreement in which the Judean Gedaliah son of Rahim-ili promises to fulfill the *ilku*-service that his father owes on his horse-fief (*bît sîsî*). Rimut-Ninurta son of Murašu agrees to provide all the equipment necessary for Gedaliah to fulfill his service obligation, primarily a horse and tackle. It is clear that the *ilku*-service here is military.

According to this text, Ellil-šum-iddin of the house of Murašu has adopted Rahim-ili and in so doing received complete control of the usufruct of Rahim-ili's property. In fact, Rahim-ili was adopted only in order to enable the Murašu firm to take control of the produce from the land, the usufruct, since the land itself was inalienable. The adoption was thus a necessary legal fiction. The *ilku*-service owed by Rahim-ili was now owed by the Murašu family, but still fulfilled by Rahim-ili's son, now part of the Murašu family by adoption. It is also clear that although his fief was in Nippur, Gedaliah was ordered south to Uruk to fulfill his *ilku*-service there.

---

43. Cardasçia, *Les Archives Des Murašû*, 179–82, my translation of the French original.

While we do not know what he was being sent to Uruk to do, his *ilku*-service might not have been completely military. We see from Persian-period letters from Bactria that soldiers were routinely used for ordinary building projects, such as building city walls. We also know from Darius's many inscriptions that conquered peoples were brought from all over his empire to participate in building his palace in Susa, for example, among other installations.

As seen in the Aramaic documents from Egypt and Bactria, the Aramaic word for *ilku* is *halak*.[44] That the Judeans in Yehud were also obligated by this *ilku* tax is clear from Ezra 4:13:

כען ידיע להוא למלכא די הן קריתא דך תתבנא ושוריה ישתכללון מנדה־בלו
והלך לא ינתנון

Now, let it be known to the king that if this city wall be built and her walls completed, neither rent, tribute, nor corvée [הלך] will be paid.

Here Reḥum expresses the fear that if a wall around Jerusalem were to be built, the Judeans would no longer pay their *ilku* or *halak* tax. Further evidence of the obligation of Judeans for the *ilku* or *halak* service tax is found in Ezra 7:24, when Ezra, in the seventh year of Artaxerxes II, releases the priesthood from this obligation:

ולכם מהודעין די כל־כהניא ולויא זמריא תרעיא נתיניא ופלחי בית אלהא דנה
מנדה בלו והלך לא שליט למרמא עליהם:

We inform you [pl.] regarding all … [temple personnel] of the house of this god neither rent, tribute, nor corvée [*halak*] is authorized to impose upon them.

I have suggested recently that both of these texts are, at base, authentic.[45] If so, references to the *halāk* (*ilku*) in these Aramaic letters reveal Judeans in Yehud being obligated by the *ilku* service tax, living in *ḥaṭrus*, and on land

---

44. Jean Hoftijzer and Karel Jongeling, *Dictionary of the North-West Semitic Inscriptions* (Leiden: Brill, 1995), 283; van Driel, *Elusive Silver*, 254; André Lemaire, "Administration in Fourth-Century BCE Judah in Light of Epigraphy and Numismatics," in *Judah and the Judeans in the Fourth Century B.C.E.*, ed. Oded Lipschits, Gary N. Knoppers, and Rainer Albertz (Winona Lake, IN: Eisenbrauns, 2007), 63; Naveh and Shaked, *Aramaic Documents from Ancient Bactria*, 30.

45. Fried, *Ezra, a Commentary*, ad loc.

encumbered as fiefs. Although not using the word *halak,* the text in Neh 5:4–5 also suggests the conditions of this land-for-service scheme:

> ויש אשר אמרים לוינו כסף למדת המלך שדתינו וכרמינו ... ואין לאל ידנו
> ושדתינו וכרמינו לאחרים
>
> And there are those who say, "we have borrowed money for the king's rent for our fields and vineyards.... Our hands are powerless and our fields and vineyards belong to others."

The word translated "rent" here is *midda',* which also appears in Ezra 7:24. This passage clarifies that land that Judeans were living on in this land-for-service scheme belonged to the king.[46]

All of this suggests that the exiles were moved onto vacant land in Yehud, land from which neither they nor their fathers had been exiled and land for which they were obligated in a land-for-service scheme. The scheme in Yehud was the same land-for-service scheme that had obligated them when they lived in Babylon in and around Nippur. The Persians seem to have purposefully moved the exiled Judeans from Babylon onto vacant land in Yehud in order to populate and cultivate it, so that whether or not the return was voluntary, the place to which they were returned was not. Indeed, we know from Xenophon that the Persian king would not tolerate unpopulated and uncultivated land.

> As for the countryside [χώρα], he [the king] personally examines so much of it as he sees in the course of his progress through it; and he receives reports from his trusted agents on the territories that he does not see for himself. To those governors who are able to show him that their country is densely populated and that the land is in cultivation and well stocked with the trees of the district and with the crops, he assigns more territory and gives presents and rewards them with seats of honor. Those whose territory he finds uncultivated and thinly populated either through harsh administration or through contempt or through carelessness, he punishes, and appoints others to take their office. (Xenophon, *Oec.* 4.8 [Marchant and Todd])

A Persian compulsion to populate and cultivate vacant land is exhibited in the newly discovered temple to Osiris and Isis at the southern end of the Kharga oasis in Egypt, 120 kilometers away from the modern town

---

46. Fried, "Exploitation of Depopulated Land."

of Kharga.[47] The Egyptian site had been occupied from the end of the Paleolithic period until the end of the third millennium BCE, but at the end of the third millennium the springs dried up, and the site was abandoned. In the middle of the fifth century, in the reign of Artaxerxes I, a network of tunnels (*qanats*) was built, which allowed the underground water reservoir to be tapped. A settlement was built, which continued as long as the water lasted, until the first decades of the fourth century CE, although the temple was abandoned in the Roman period. This system of *qanats* enabled the desert to bloom. The excavators suppose that it took at least five years to build each of these *qanats*. The means necessary to build them and to establish a viable settlement in what had been an arid desert zone would have to have come from the satrap or the king himself—not from the people. The only reason for the construction of the site posited by the excavators was the king's compulsion to populate and cultivate empty land, as suggested by Xenophon. This compulsion to restore vacant land to cultivation throughout the empire would have been what motivated Cyrus or Darius to move Judean exiles from Babylon to Yehud: to repopulate and to cultivate the barren areas of Yehud.

The Ḥaṭru

It seems that the Persians moved Judeans onto vacant land in Yehud in the same way that those Egyptians were moved onto vacant land in Egypt and that the Persians built a temple there in Jerusalem for the Judeans in the same way that Artaxerxes I built a temple for Isis and Osiris for the Egyptians. That Judeans were being encumbered by the *ilku* or *halak* tax reveals that they had been moved onto land organized into the same system of estates called *ḥaṭrus* that we see in the Murašu archive.

The list of *ḥaṭrus* associated with the Murašu firm in Nippur is revealing. Matthew Stolper lists sixty-seven separate *ḥaṭrus* located in and around Nippur.[48] These agnatic holdings were each labeled, sometimes by ethnic group, sometimes by the town of origin, sometimes by profession,

---

47. Bernard Bousquet et. al., "Première Rapport Préliminaire des Travaux sur le Site de 'Ayn Manawir (Oasis de Kharga)," *BIFAO* 96 (1996): 385–451; Michel Wuttmann et. al., "Ayn Manawir (Oasis de Kharga)," *BIFAO* 98 (1998): 367–462; Wuttmann, Thierry Gonon, and Christophe Thiers, "The Qanats of 'Ayn-Manawir (Kharga Oasis, Egypt)," *JASR* 1 (2000): 162–69.

48. Stolper, *Entrepreneurs and Empire*, 72–79.

but all the labels were prefixed by either "men of" or by "sons of," exactly as we see in the list in Ezra 2. This suggests that the list in Ezra 2 may be a list of agnatic families organized into *ḥaṭrus*. The exiled Judeans of Babylon may have been moved from a system of serfdom in Babylon to the exact same system of serfdom in Yehud, and it may not have been voluntary.

Conclusion

Exiled Judeans did not return to the cities or farmlands of their fathers, nor did they use or even maintain their fathers' burial caves. Since they did not return to the land from which they had come, and since they did not return in order to tend the burial caves of their ancestors or even to be interred within them, what sparked their return? Data from present return migrations suggest that those who do not prosper in their host country are those who tend to return. These may have been those who do not appear in the cuneiform tablets from Babylon and who did not take part in the economic life there.

Once in Judah these returnees were obligated by the *ilku*-service tax, revealing that under the Achaemenids the Judeans in Judah participated in the same land-for-service scheme that they had participated in when in Babylon, a scheme that was in effect and common throughout the empire. All this suggests that the Judeans were assigned their land by the Persians and that the transfer from Babylon, whether or not it was voluntary, was part of an Achaemenid long-standing need to populate and cultivate vacant land within their empire. Whatever the desire to be buried in the tombs of their ancestors may have been, it was not fulfilled under the Persians.[49]

---

49. Coming to my attention too late to be incorporated here is Peter van der Veen, "Sixth Century Issues: The Fall of Jerusalem, the Exile and the Return," in *Ancient Israel's History: An Introduction to Issues and Sources*, ed. Bill T. Arnold and Richard S. Hess (Grand Rapids: Baker Academic, 2014), 383–405.

The Exiles of Empires in Prophetic Images of Restoration (and Micah 4:8–5:1 [ET 5:2])

Martien A. Halvorson-Taylor

The literary images of Israel and Judah's defeat are stirring, if not potent views onto the influences of empires and the theologizing of defeat. How these similes, metaphors, and exilic tropes developed, insofar as we can perceive this growth diachronically, reflects Judean thinking in response to the bearing down of empires, especially as that thought changed over time. It has been our habit to attempt to illuminate those changes by examining and comparing the redactional layers in the bundles of traditions that become associated with a named prophet. In cases where we can discern redaction, biblical scholars trace how images of coming and certain destruction were supplemented, extended, and perhaps even supplanted by images of restoration, often in the period of the Babylonian exile and following. We find this kind of reshaping of words of woe into more extended messages of hope, for example, in Jeremiah's Book of Consolation and in much of Second Isaiah. The image, to take just one, of the battered woman, a metaphor for the defeat of the Judeans, is transformed into the image of the woman restored. The image of a battered woman was not only potent but flexible because it could communicate the shame and violation of defeat but also offer hope through the transformation of the image of a woman healed, restored, and praised. These transformations, then, are a source for discerning thinking about exile, at least as it was interpreted by postexilic exegetes.

There are, roughly speaking, several different strategies that guide such a diachronic exercise. Based on language, allusions, the history of ideas, and sometimes the rare reference to specific events and places, scholars have made their cases for one or another approach to prophetic materials. Some will take both the materials on destruction and the materials on consolation as being of a piece and argue that both are preexilic, anticipating the events to come. The more common tendency, to which I referred above, is to argue that while the materials on destruction are late preexilic, the materials on consolation come from the other side of 586/587 BCE, in the exilic or even the postexilic period; the materials on consolation are a late updating of a tradition that circulated in the name of a prophet, and the two layers may indeed be separated by decades, straddling 586. Finally, then, there is a third approach: to regard both materials on destruction and consolation as coming after the destruction, perhaps even after the early decades of exile. This might be the case in the materials known as Third Isaiah. In any case, it is a literary strategy that develops throughout the Second Temple period and beyond, in which, long after the events of the sixth century, texts figure the speaker or Israel as "in exile."[1]

Of these approaches, the classical solution has been to treat materials about restoration as later layers or hopeful updating—even a disingenuous gloss. The treatment of Mic 4:1–5:14 is an excellent example of this tendency to differentiate. In this view, Micah is recalled as a prophet of judgment, a characterization borne out by the thrust of much of chapters 1–3, and also by the reminiscence in Jer 26:17–19, which makes the vivid images of restoration in Mic 4:1–5:14 to be essentially different in character. The chapters contrast the gloomy situation in which Jerusalem, the nation, and Jacob find themselves with future eschatological prospects. The former have been read to reflect the Babylonian destruction; not only do the thought world and the verbal patterns resemble those of later thinkers, particularly those responsible for the subsequent layers of Jeremiah and Second Isaiah, but also Babylon is mentioned (Mic 4:10). The latter, the hopeful visions, are seen as coming even later, so that the oracles are regarded as composite. Accordingly, the transitions from judgment to restoration within Mic 4–5 have been termed "often quite harsh," the units have been regarded as distinct entities that have been "welded together," "short poems" with "little obvious architecture," or units that are apparently "grouped together on a catchword principle"—"a most superficial organizing principle!"[2] Even scholars who argue for a development using

---

1. See Martien Halvorson-Taylor, *Enduring Exile: The Metaphorization of Exile in the Hebrew Bible*, VTSup 141 (Leiden: Brill, 2011).

2. Brevard Childs, "Micah," in *Introduction to the Old Testament as Scripture* (Philadelphia: Fortress, 1979), 432; Hugh G. M Williamson, "Micah," in *The Oxford*

more organic metaphors are guided by the notion of a conscious updating of the original material that is then "filled out and equipped with promises appropriate to the distress they express."[3]

There are a number of challenges to this approach in which restoration oracles are regarded as later and somewhat inconsistent accretions—challenges, indeed, that have the potential to yield more interesting methods and more interesting insights into the passages such as those in Mic 4–5. For one, in those chapters, like innumerable others, it is hard to posit with certainty whether the attachment of words of future hope to oracles of destruction actually happened in stages. Sometimes the seams between the two kinds of material may—or may not—reflect a later redaction and could, indeed, reflect the poet's prerogative to speak in a different register or even mood. Complete destruction-restoration images may have developed of a piece in the late exilic or early restoration period. As our notions of text, tradition, and scripture become ever suppler, too, the notion of material as fixed or static enough to host a later redaction becomes more fragile. In our field, we have tended toward metaphors of interpolation and graft for understanding these kinds of interpretive moves, and that is difficult to sustain in certain textual situations.

Even without the certainty that a destruction-restoration passage contains layers of composition (by which we could assert with confidence which materials came earlier and which later), the relationship between images of exile and images of restoration—even and especially when it appears organic—can provide fertile material for thinking about exile, for the perception of defeat. Even though these images do not themselves describe exile (and indeed comparatively fewer passages in the Hebrew Bible do), the manner by which these images describe return, restoration, and renewal sheds light on how ancient Israel conceived of their inverse—exile. Poetry about restoration necessarily reflects thinking about exile as the condition that needs to be remedied. It may not reflect thinking about the anticipation of exile or the immediate experience of exile. It may, rather, reflect exile as it is remembered. Its information may be less "historical," but it is no less culturally significant. In this perspective, these images of return, restoration, a hopeful future, no less than images of defeat, provide a chance to examine the gathering associations of the

---

Bible Commentary, ed. John Barton and John Muddiman (New York: Oxford University Press, 2001), 597; Delbert R. Hillers, "The Book of Micah," *ABD* 4:807.

3. James L. Mays, *Micah*, OTL (Philadelphia: Westminster, 1976), 26–27.

concept of exile.[4] The images that the author chooses, their placement alongside each other—all of these may yield important insight into the perception of exile as a tool of empires.

Micah

The book of Micah is, according to the superscription in 1:1, set in the eighth century when the Assyrian threat loomed: Micah appears to have been active from the fall of Samaria through perhaps the time of Sennacherib's invasion of Judah in 701 BCE. But the rest of the book is vague about this setting, loosely imagined. There are a few references to Assyria (e.g., 5:4–5, 7:12) and, of course, the one odd reference to Babylon (4:10). In place of a clear identifier, we have instead "the many nations" arrayed against Israel in 4:11, which is either generic or cumulative, such that it is difficult to accept that it reflects actual preexilic geopolitical forces. The phrase, indeed, has the ring of the supra-historical (see Zech 12), when the full force of nations rises up against Israel, setting the context somewhat beyond the specificity of Assyrian or even Babylonian domination. Since the metaphor for Israel in crisis seems to gather up older metaphors for Assyrian defeat and interweave images from the Babylonian crisis, the passages appear to cut tributaries across the boundaries of time.

Central to Mic 4:1–5:14 is a series of vivid images of coming destruction and restoration that gives insight into how exile was interpreted. The passage opens and closes in 4:8 and 5:1 (ET 5:2) with two אתה ("you," masc. sg.) statements, providing the upper and lower frame of the whole.[5] The body of the passage has been structured into three subunits that are headlined by the temporal indicators עתה ("now"; 4:9, 11, 14 [5:1]). Each

---

4. For a sensitive perspective on the relationship between past and future imaginings in prophetic literature—how exile represents past experience by which also "the future is remembered"—see Ian D. Wilson's essay in this volume.

5. Both of these "you" (masc. sg.) statements, in 4:8 and 5:1, have a similar structure: they begin with "but you," addressing a (male) personified place ("O, Migdal-Eder" and "O, Bethlehem"), qualified by a short description, followed (in the form of a prepositional phrase) by a prediction about the future leadership of Israel. Westermann argues these are adaptations of ancient tribe sayings (*Stammessprüche* on the model of Judg 5; Gen 49; Deut 33) that referred to a town. See Westermann, "Micha 5.1–3," in *Herr, tue meine Lippen auf*, vol. 5, *Die Altentestamentlichen Perikope*, ed. Georg Eichholz (Wuppartel-Barmen: Müller, 1964), 54–59.

of the עתה subunits addresses Daughter Zion, often in direct speech. And each moves from disaster to salvation.[6]

There is a literary artistry to the final form of the text, even beyond the clever use of homonyms in the אתה frame (4:8, 5:1) and the עתה subunits (4:9–10, 11–13, 14). This suggests that even though the passage has layers of composition, it was the final redaction of the passage that gave it its shape and thus the meaning that we inherit. This is no clumsy graft; the verbal ties extend across the imagery of destruction and the visions of salvation, cinching the whole. There is, for example, the way that the salvation of the third inner passage is found in the final אתה frame, giving the frame a double function. There are, moreover, verbal repetitions (4:9 and 4:12's "counselor" and "counsel," both forms of עצה), rhythmic repetitions (for example, כיולדה, "like a woman in labor," in 4:9–10), the double feminine imperatives that open the two salvation notes of verse 10 and verse 13, which pair them in the ear of the hearer (חולי וגחי, "writhe and push!" and קומי ודוש, "arise and thresh!").

Still, while they are tightly structured, these עתה passages contain layers of material. How we discern where the fault lines fall changes how we read these passages as reflecting on the exilic experience and what it can offer us. The typical solution for understanding the shifts in tone has been to sever the announcement of doom from the message of restoration, pushing restoration off as a later accretion. In the first passage, for example, the notice of the king is interpreted to refer to a human king, so that the questions, which point toward a dire situation, are either taken to refer to Sennacherib's invasion of 701 BCE or to the end of the monarchy in 586 BCE. Accordingly, the reference to Babylon is, in the first case, taken to be a later substitution for Assyria or in the second to be a marker of the time of the composition.[7]

If instead of presuming the seams between destruction and restoration materials within an עתה passage, we find that the seam comes between the two עתה passages, our insight into the ways in which redaction has and has not shaped the notion of exile shifts. Tracing similarities in language and structure, we can adumbrate the early kernel of the composition, which has all of its features in taut array: the passages making up the outer frame (4:8 and 5:1–4a), which resemble each other, and, in turn, the

---

6. In the case of the third, 4:14, the salvation is announced through the אתה frame of 5:1.

7. For an elucidating examination of this issue, see Mark Boda, "Babylon in the Book of the Twelve," *HBAI* 3 (2014): 225–48.

first עתה passage, verses 9–10, and the third, verse 14, which originally followed immediately after the first. This unit cuts across the fault lines of oracles of defeat and visions of restoration.[8] If we accept this as the earliest layer, then it becomes more apparent that a second עתה passage, 4:11–13, which reflects later themes and language, was inserted later—dividing the original unit of 4:9–10, 14.

Accepting the organic relationship between the first set of oracles of destruction and restoration (4:9–10) means that instead of having a restoration passage that supplants the language of destruction, the two are in more organic connection. The passage reports and even spins out the consequences of a certain way of thinking and then reverses itself. It appears, in other words, to overrule itself synchronically in the manner that some have read the relationship between oracles of destruction and consolation diachronically. Again, in this case, however, we do not have a literary seam with diachrony, but rather a theology articulated through a dialogue between doom and restoration. This pattern will again be repeated in the second—and later inserted—עתה passage, 4:11–13. Indeed, the description of doom presents one view onto the situation and then plays on that same language in the restoration vision to present another. Moreover, their juxtaposition as complete units also provides insight into the ways in which female Zion arrayed in defeat found redress.

Micah 4:9–10, the First עתה Passage

In its present arrangement, 4:9–10 is one of the literary subunits of the poem—most obviously because it opens with עתה and is followed by a second עתה that opens the second subunit, verses 11–13. The similarities between 4:9–10 and Jer 6:24–26 suggest, further, a literary prehistory in which Mic 4:9–10 may have originally been joined directly to verse 14—a

---

8. Jan A. Wagenaar has argued, based on similar language and theme, if we start with the bottom אתה frame, 5:1–4a, we can identify a number of parallels that allow us to imagine the early shape of the passage as a whole: 5:1 is structurally similar to 4:8, the upper אתה frame; 5:2, which uses the labor metaphors, is thematically similar to 4:9–10 in its use of the metaphor of painful labor for defeat with a reversal (and return from exile) associated with eventual birth; and finally, 5:3 resembles 4:14, which, as I will argue below, originally connected to 4:9–10 and shares a vision of the future ruler. See Wagenaar, *Judgement and Salvation: The Composition and Redaction of Micah 2–5*, VTSup 85 (Leiden: Brill, 2001), 292–94.

verse that is now delayed by verses 11–13, the second עתה passage.⁹ Furthermore, if, as is usually supposed, Mic 4:9–10 is dependent on Jer 6:24–26, another passage in which the people react to impending destruction, then this suggests an exilic or postexilic provenance for the unit as a whole. The reference to "as far as Babylon," if we take it to be original, further suggests this provenance.

The imagery that describes Zion's condition in verses 9–10 is multifarious, beginning in one register in verse 9 and then shifting to another by verse 10:

עתה למה תריעי רע
המלך אין בך אם יועצך אבד
כי החזיקך חיל כיולדה

Now why do you shout out?
Is there no king in you? Has your counselor perished,
that pangs have seized you like a woman in labor?"¹⁰

But, as we will see, this shift is not a sign of redaction but rather the enlarging of a certain semantic range that will allow the author to spin a theology of exile. Verse 9 opens with תריעי רע, an idiom that is largely associated with battle cries; in Exod 32:17, רע is characterized as "the noise of war," and in Isa 42:13 it is the sound that YHWH himself makes as he "goes forth like a soldier." תריעי רע is normally associated with male figures, although the passage here uses the rarer female form to apply to Woman Zion.¹¹ The following questions—"Is there no king in you? Has your counselor perished?"—also presume a political and military crisis.¹² The questions, indeed, appear to reflect the alarmed cries of the people.¹³

---

9. For a further overview of the similarities between the two passages, see Wagenaar, *Judgement and Salvation*, 278–80, 284–85.

10. Unless otherwise indicated, biblical translations are mine.

11. See Zeph 3:14, where it is associated with Woman Zion and shouts of joy, a less frequent use.

12. This is true whether or not they seek to chastise or to assure, whether and how they are rhetorical, whether they refer to a human king and counselor or (less likely) to YHWH.

13. In Jer 8:19, similar questions figure, also in a setting in which the city gives voice to its alarm at impending destruction: היהוה אין בציון אם מלכה אין בה. The questions there differ from our passage in Micah by specifying that at least the first is about YHWH, but, as in Micah, the questions express the alarm of the people, that indeed they are vulnerable—the credible panic of people on the verge of defeat.

This alarm in Mic 4:9 is further articulated by a common simile: in verse 9c, these expressions of panic, to the speaker, sound as if "pangs have seized you like a woman in labor." Some translators seek to smooth over the transition from sounds of war to sounds of labor pangs by rendering תריעי רע, as, for example, "crying out in distress," implying a laboring cry that will be made explicit by the end of the verse (so, for example, REB). But this is overharmonizing between the opening imagery and the closing. Moreover, the expression likening panicked warriors or a people in crisis to woman in labor is common enough for conveying public reaction to devastation, particularly in materials associated with the Babylonian exile.[14] If anything, it is common enough that it verges on a frozen metaphor. It is a gendered metaphor, to be sure, in the way that "crying hysterically" is a gendered metaphor in English, originally referring to a female condition associated with the womb.[15] And, even though frozen, it has the tinge of emasculation when applied to male Judeans.

From this dire language, the prophet pulls out a message of salvation and from a frozen metaphor conjures a productive metaphor to not only promise but explain restoration. The language of writhing labor in verse 9c might have been but a passing simile, a stock expression, as indeed it is in Isa 13:8, Jer 22:23; 30:6; 49:24; Ps 48:6. Micah 4:10, however, further extends dire political language into the semantic range of the laboring woman to read into the possibilities of a fuller field of associations: חולי וגחי בת ציון כיולדה, "Writhe and push, O Daughter Zion, like a woman in labor." Now Zion is not simply crying out "like a woman in labor," but she is to be "like a woman about to give birth" and thus is instructed to do all that labor requires. Labor pangs now signal the eventual dawning—birth, even—of a new period. These extended associations in verse 10 are such that a threshold has been crossed in the passage from one semantic realm to another—a crossing first mooted by the simile in verse 9c. This crossing is more notable, again, when compared to Jer 6:24–26, a passage that is otherwise quite similar to this one, but where the suggestive simile does not develop into an extended metaphor.

---

14. See especially Jer 6:24 for חיל כיולדה, and also the delightful inversion in 50:43; simply with 30:6, יולדה or חולה in 4:31. For כיולדה as associated with general crisis, beyond Israel and Babylon, see Isa 13:8; 21:3; Jer 22:23; 49:24; Ps 48:7.

15. The English word derives from the Latin *hystericus* and from Greek *hysterikos* ("of the womb").

The image and crossing transform the finality of the bad news in Mic 4:9, the anguish that seizes Judah, into a new frame for understanding what unfolds. The reference to a woman no longer simply describes anguish but is mined to prescribe, first, that Zion gird herself for the long haul: "writhe and push,[16] O Daughter Zion." This is counsel both that there will be suffering and that it is durative. It also provides, however, for the suffering as productive, like labor—something to be endured as terrifying as it is in the moment, pain that they must resolve themselves to with the hope of something that will both merit suffering and redeem it. The lack (signaled in the questions by אין, "is there no …" and אבד, "destroyed," in the pointed questions of v. 9b) that may have cast doubt on the efficacy of the labor pangs in verse 9c now yields to the urging to "writhe and push" in verse 10a. The referent for this notion of a period of labor (and stages within it) is provided by verse 10b-c in a series of geographical relocations, each associated with loss:

חולי וגחי בת ציון כיולדה
כי עתה תצאי מקריה ושכנת בשדה
ובאת עד בבל שם תנצלי
שם יגאלך יהוה מכף איביך

Writhe and push, O Daughter Zion, like a woman in labor.
For now you shall go forth from the city and settle[17] in the open country;[18]
you shall go as far as Babylon—there you will be saved.
There YHWH will redeem you from the hands of your enemies.

---

16. BDB (161) regards this as a *qal* transitive form of (a primarily intransitive) גיח, namely, "burst forth." Wagenaar takes it further to propose that the *qal* of גיח has a transitive sense of "*to cause* to burst out," i.e., "to push," which matches the idiom in English for delivering a child (*Judgement and Salvation*, 153). The verb has been used of men "bursting forth" in ambush (Judg 20:33 in the *hiphil*). It is here used in the sense of the bursting forth of the child at delivery, although there may be a clever double entendre at work that preserves the military sense as well as its associations with childbirth. Others translate the verb to mean "to groan," which is the meaning of the root in later Hebrew. The version are varied and do not clarify the original form or sense; a number of different emendations have been offered.

17. שכן indicates at least semipermanence, not the temporary sense of "camping."

18. In the parallel passage, Jer 6:24–25, Woman Zion is also addressed in the second-person feminine singular, but, by contrast, she is told *not* to go the open country (השדה), since she is under threat from "the word of the enemy, terror on every side." By contrast in Mic 4:10, she needs to leave the city, camp in the open country, and go "as far as" Babylon in order to be redeemed from "there." See Jer 40:7, 13; 41:8; Ezek 7:15.

There is the leaving of the city, dwelling in the open country, and the destination of Babylon—each a fresh pain but one that puts Zion eventually in the place for redemption. In this tightly structured explanation for why Zion should writhe and give herself over to her labor pangs, the end result, her redemption, is implicit already in the bad news that will bring them eventually to Babylon—for *there* they shall be saved (v. 10c), *there* (v. 10d) Zion will be redeemed by YHWH, who is her true King (see v. 9b). The repetition of שם discloses both the endpoint of the journey and the perspective of the speaker, who is not situated "there" but presumably in Jerusalem, putatively at the locus of the writhing and the outset of the labor pangs. Extending the image in this way contrasts other passages that simply leave the phrase to denote a city that is petrified or, more often, panicked male warriors emasculated "like a woman in labor." Verse 10 instead offers: Don't be fearful emasculated men in battle; be a woman about to bring forth a child.[19]

It is worth noting another vantage point onto the theological innovation of Mic 4:9–10 by returning again to its parallel passage, Jer 6:24–26. In that passage, Woman Zion is also addressed in the second-person feminine singular, but, by contrast, she is told *not* to go the open country (השדה). In that passage, she is under threat from "the word of the enemy, terror on every side," making such travel dangerous. By contrast, in Mic 4:10 she needs to stay in the open country, and then travel to Babylon in order to be redeemed from "there." If indeed Jeremiah is the base text, we see the deliberate transformations that the theologian of Mic 4:10 is fashioning. The expectations of an empty pain have been replaced by the urging to give herself over to productive labor; the open country, which Jeremiah warns against, has been made into a stop along the way to redemption.[20] Finally, the birth metaphor recedes, yielding to the language of redemption: "There you will be saved from the hands of your enemy." The language of redemption for the return from exile is familiar from Isaiah and a familiar metaphor for the return from the Babylonian exile, but it is also worth noting that it is an economic metaphor in the context of family law

---

19. The opening questions presume the absence of male leadership: המלך אין בך. As in Judg 4:20—in which Sisera instructs Jael as she puts him to bed, should anyone ask, היש פה איש, to answer, אין—the absence of "real" men leads to women (real and metaphorical) to take charge.

20. The reference to deportation, not found in the parallel passage of Jer 6:24–26, further suggests that the provenance of Micah is the Babylonian siege and deportations.

(versus, e.g., פדה); it is the familial relation that is leveraged for economic liberation. The semantic range of the metaphor has shifted, although perhaps, in the sense of the verb in Ruth 4, new birth is impressionistically associated with the activity of the kinsman-redeemer. The body of the woman in labor was particularly popular as an image of anxiety about anticipated defeat (Isa 13:8; 21:3; Jer 4:31; 6:24–26; 13:21; 30:6; 49:24; Ps 48:27); and the metaphor that 4:9–11 redeploys for gain. It is not simply a reversal but an extension. Exile is not simply overcome by restoration—indeed, restoration and return are born of exile.[21]

Micah 4:11–13, the Second עתה Passage

The second עתה passage was inserted into the passage as a whole in a second phase of redaction, separating 4:9–10 from verse 14. The passage is modeled on the first: like the first passage, the second is addressed to Woman Zion and builds the vision of restoration out of the opening language of defeat (v. 11). In both passages, these future modifications are not only similar in patterning but also are syntactically similar. Both announcements of restoration are structured as double imperatives addressed to Woman Zion: in verse 13, "Arise and thresh, O Daughter Zion, for I will make your horn iron," and in verse 10, "Writhe and push, O Daughter Zion, … for how you shall go forth from that city." Both the tone and timing of this passage are, however, palpably different—stressing restoration as a military reversal of fortune, a vindication, and pushing that moment into an eschatological future.[22] The vocabulary in both parts of the passage, as well as its motifs (prime among them, the *Völkerkampf* motif), strongly associate it with the postexilic period.[23]

---

21. In another impressionistic association, the exodus from Egypt is forecast by what the Hebrew midwives report as "the vigorous" and fast labors of the Hebrew women: כי חיות הנה בטרם תבוא אלהן המילדת (Exod 1:19). This, along with their prolific multiplying under oppression (1:12, כאשר יענו אתו כן ירבה וכן יפרץ), is another literary strategy to talk of "the birthing" (or rebirth) of the Israelite nation through the exodus—which also begins in toil and labor (in every sense of the word).

22. While consonant in eschatological timing, the tone of 4:11–13 contrasts with 4:1–5; those verses, too, envision "many nations" (גוים רבים) who come to Zion, though in that case their implements of war become plowshares and pruning hooks. It is a vision of demilitarized peace, not of military vindication.

23. The language that may signal its postexilic provenance includes the use of אסף with גוים and of חנף; see further Wagenaar, *Judgement and Salvation*, 289.

The second עתה passage opens, in 4:11, by describing the dire situation and providing the eventual vocabulary for reversal: "And now, many nations are gathered against you [fem. sg.]." The language of nations gathered in opposition suggests the mustering of foreign agents, although the precise identity of those mustering in this verse is not clear.[24] This is no problem since the verb אסף does not require a specified subject—indeed, there are instances where the verb is used to mean simply that troops or nations have mustered for battle without stipulating who is commanding the mustering.[25] This ambiguity will, however, allow for a dramatic turn in the later verses on restoration.

The dire depiction continues in verse 11b with those assembled mocking Zion: "They say, 'Let her be profaned, and let our eyes gloat over Zion.'" It cannot be known whether this was a foreign taunt that had a life of its own—or whether Micah has formulated it to capture the spirit of the times. In any case, חנף, "to be profaned or desecrated," interprets the foreign encroachments as "shaming" Zion. The language has a ritual and cultic dimension, but certainly in later literature of the Babylonian period, the connection between the violation or the infidelity of female Zion and the verb has been suggested (see, e.g., Jer 3:1, 9). In Micah, the danger and the shame of this gaze are intimated by the gendered identities of the (male) foreigners and the female personification of Zion. Further, as Daniel Smith-Christopher has argued based on the related noun, חרפה, the term reflects "a very personal phenomenon."[26] Daughter Zion is shamed by all the foreign nations who gaze upon her, "with gloating."

---

24. The notion of nations gathered against Israel is part of the Zion complex. It is worth noting, too, that the phrase (the combination of אסף with גוים) features most prominently in late exilic and postexilic texts—for example, Ezek 38:12; Zeph 3:8; Zech 12:3; 14:2—which, while it may not decide the provenance of this motif within the Zion complex, at least contributes to our understanding of the provenance of these verses (see above).

25. Francis I. Andersen and David Noel Freedman further suggest that though the *niphal* is here commonly taken as the passive (which leaves the agent unclear), it may however be by analogy with 1 Sam 17:1, in which it is clear that the nations have assembled themselves. They observe further, "These two meanings operate simultaneously. All that the nations know is that they have assembled for war; and that is true: they are free to do that." See Andersen and Freedman, *Micah*, AB 24E (New York: Doubleday, 2006), 451.

26. Daniel Smith-Christopher, *Micah*, OTL (Louisville: Westminster John Knox, 2015), 157.

Micah 4:12 makes of this dire situation something quite different, just as in the first עתה passage. It extends the language of the vulnerable female body and directs the ambiguities of the quoted taunt in verse 11 to promise restoration. So, for example, the ambiguity over *who* musters the nations in verse 11 yields to the certainty that YHWH oversees this, mustering the nations against Israel. This is both worse news than expected and better. In verse 12, Micah starts toward this, by saying that, in contradiction to this taunt, "*But* they [the nations who taunt Zion] do not know YHWH's thoughts, nor do they understand his plan"—that, indeed, YHWH has arrayed the nations as first step, by which power they, in turn, will be defeated. But to do so, the verse trades one image for another metaphor: the nations have not assembled, but in fact have been gathered (and here the verb is קבץ, instead of אסף) as "sheaves to the threshing floor" (see Zech 12:6).[27] This shift in semantic range is also possible because the image of nations mustered against Israel is associated with, if not regarded as a prelude to, YHWH's restoration (Zech 12:2–4). In the process, the coming defeat is but part of larger "plan," as Micah terms it, imperceptible to those nations. That is, even if Zion is under the male gaze, then the imperceptible thoughts of YHWH provide her cover. They think they know what they see, but in fact they do not know and do not understand. In verse 13, the metaphorical complex has been assembled so that Woman Zion is commanded to "thresh!" those whom YHWH has gathered to the threshing floor. In one final metaphorical turn, the threshing is enhanced and deepened by parallelism as "crushing" the foreign nations.

Much has been made of the metaphorical assemblage of Woman Zion with a horn of iron and hooves of bronze in verse 13. It is not simply the animal imagery ascribed to a female figure in human form, but the images of power that are now attached to that female figure, images that some argue are more commonly associated with male figures. Others say it is not simply discordant but troubling that the figure takes on more commonly male associations when she is restored. Rather than simply assume that the

---

27. There is another nuance to "the gathering of sheaves," if we again consider the book of the Ruth: Boaz's insistence that Ruth "stay with his young women" in his field and his reassurance that he has told his men "not to touch her" (2:18) adumbrates the reality that when women gather sheaves in the field, they are vulnerable. In the ancient world (and our modern world), when women work alone in the field or at the threshing floor, they are at risk of sexual assault. In Micah, this vulnerability is redirected to the nations when they are gathered "to the threshing floor."

woman is reimagined as male, we should note that the force of the verse comes from the very assemblage: metaphors remade into new metaphors that range over gender attributes. The power of the woman to give birth in the first passage mediates against the assertion of female weakness. The intentional slippage, between traditional imagery and new manifestations, male and female, the language of defeat-and-restoration imagery is part of the power of the composition. More to the point: the figure even with horns ("your horns," with fem. sg. suffix) and hooves ("your hooves," with fem. sg. suffix) retains it female identity: she is told that "you [fem. sg.] shall beat" (v. 13). Here she is like the heifer of Hos 10:11, "who loved to thresh" (also דוש). These are images of war, most of all. And if the conquerors are perceived as having "horns of iron and hooves of bronze," the drift of this imagery is to accessorize the conquered with these to frame them as transformed, new conquerors. Again, this picture of restoration reflects the experiences of destruction—the restoration is imagined through and by it.

Image and Time

Taken together, both of these passages (Mic 4:9-10, 11-13) begin with a description of defeat that trades in some sort of quotation—a stock image, perhaps even a popular taunt, but at the very least a way of interpreting no future beyond exile—the language of which is then, in a rhetorical reversal, refashioned into and redeployed as an image of restoration. That the two kinds of material are of a piece matters for understanding their meanings. For one, they are not redacted to envision restoration; restoration is already implicit in the language used to describe defeat. Along the way, in both, the meaning of foreign oppression and exile is interpreted not as a sign of defeat but as a step along the way to redemption. The vision of restoration does not override the description of defeat; rather, in both, how things appear to be is not how they will be. Indeed, the very images of defeat—Zion doubled over in pain or sexually shamed—were chosen because they could organically be transformed into images of restoration. In other words, the author, a poet-theologian, chose to describe the anguish of defeat using the known trope of a woman in labor with the narrative plan of bringing this metaphorical woman to the point of birth. The body of the woman in labor was particularly popular as an image of anxiety about anticipated defeat (Isa 13:8; 21:3; Jer 4:31; 6:24-26; 13:21; 30:6; 49:24; Ps 48:27); the metaphor is amenable to this extension. She provided a host of associate metaphors for thinking about restoration—so that Israel gripped by fear could be transformed into a woman birthing. While a positive vision was not in view in the semantic range of the opening verses, this is the kind of remarkable reversal that would capture the imagination, if not hopes of exiled Israel—so that simile urges toward metaphor, and stock images are upended into hopeful visions.

Supplementing the first passage with a second that follows the same pattern is not simple mimicry. The juxtaposition is productive. The addition of the second circles around and then deepens the themes of the first. First, verse 12, which comes between the description of Israel's dire situation (as a shamed woman, v. 11) and the imperatives that open the oracle of restoration in verse 13, is unmatched in the parallel form of the first passage; verse 12 provides a new perspective on the situation, namely, "the thoughts of YHWH." If exile is conceived of as a silence from YHWH or, more essentially, as YHWH having turned away from the people, then this verse on the inscrutable thoughts of YHWH offers an assurance: the remove the exiles perceive is actually YHWH deep in silent thought on their behalf. Israel is not passive in this; both metaphors require the Israelites to work through to their own redemption—they must push and thresh.

There is a second, related way in which these two passages redacted together reflect thinking about exile, and that is in their construction of time. In each case, the passage opens with a fairly dire and unresolvable description of the present situation, but in each case the extension of the language punches through the finality of the crisis situation, so that defeat and exile portend a new era of restoration. Again, the image of the laboring woman is perhaps the best example of this: an image of Woman Zion writhing is asserted as labor, and the terror becomes the promise of rebirth. In each case, this tantalizing vision is sketched out, but also posited as just beyond reach, in sight but not yet arrived. Taken as a whole, the two עתה passages both anchor in a "now" that reflects a descent into defeat, but the restoration visions of both passages, verse 10c–d and verse 13, orchestrate a layered future—the former presenting the liberation from Israel's enemies and the latter providing an eschatological scrim that suggests an even deeper future. Restoration and revenge are embedded from the start within the metaphors of labor to birth and threshing the gathered sheaves.

This is most evident in the use of עתה, "now," which is meaningfully repeated not only at the start of each of the passages but within. The *now* that opens the passage in verse 9a, serving as its headline, is temporally coordinated with another *now* in verse 10b, which lays out the restoration; again, a way of reading their future migrations implicit in the current suffering, but also, thereby, bringing the redemption at the conclusion of these into this "now." After this second *now* the verbs, which had been in the past, now adumbrate a future: "For now you *will* go forth, ... you *will* camp ... you will come ... you will be saved ... you will be redeemed." With the addition of the second passage, that *now* returns to the dire situation, Zion shamed; when that second passage, too, moves into its future verbs, in the visions of restoration, without an explicit *now*, the restoration has been pushed off into a more distant future.

Conclusion

Micah 4:8–5:5a does not give insight in the fashion of direct reportage that we might hope for and that, indeed, we rarely get in the Hebrew Bible.[28] The two עתה passages, however, both present two modes of thinking, the former of which the composition as a whole will override with the later: in both the sense of the dire situation, associated with exile and defeat, is expressed by a question or quotation that either expresses popular thinking or a popular taunt. In each, these materials are upended in the final vision. Indeed, both convey thinking *precisely* in the slippage—the interpretive chasm between exile and restoration. To read this slippage requires a certain literary sensitivity, especially if we allow that this process involves more than the substitution of a name (Babylon for Assyria) or tacking on additional materials. Scholarly descriptions of the process of redaction, which themselves draw on certain kinds of metaphors for the formation of biblical literature, miss the nuance, the multiple points of contact, possible extensions that allow for the transformation of a text. Further, they are predicated on diachrony. They presuppose, furthermore, a proto-canon that is stable enough that it can be redacted. But most of all, we may be missing *how* the very images of defeat before foreign empires, in the minds of ancient redactors, implied a message of salvation.[29] I would add that this distance is bridged rhetorically by redeploying the very language of defeat

---

28. For a nuanced treatment of the Bible's reticence from the perspective of Third Isaiah, see Mark W. Hamilton's essay in this volume.

29. Ehud Ben Zvi notes the motivation for this kind of redaction and its powerful effect when he writes, "[The] distance between the imagination and present reality ... provides the reading with rhetorical power." See Ben Zvi, *Micah*, FOTL 21B (Grand Rapids: Eerdmans, 2000), 95.

as language of restoration and, indeed, that the powerful effect of these verses comes from that careful redeployment. Indeed, if we look more closely at the heart of Mic 4–5, still allowing for redaction, we see that the book's images of restoration are in an organic if not intimate relationship with its images of exile. How better to depict an alternate reality than to borrow and bend the all-too-familiar language of defeat to a different purpose? These kinds of redirections and inversions are powerfully affecting for both acknowledging the current crisis and, simultaneously, indicating that it is not all that it seems—or, at least, not forever.

Micah's oracles, moreover, were redacted so as not to constrain its words to a particular historical moment. Whether or not the materials originally reflected on the looming threat of Assyria or Babylon or even beyond, the audience may well have been wise to the fact that there was a paradigmatic view of history at work here. The prophecies reflect, moreover, what their collectors wanted their current audience to think about their own time, rather than direct information about that past. The enduring meaning of these prophecies is evident in that it is never clear whether it is Assyria or Babylon that is in view or some other empire. The historical ties are loose, and there is no reason to imagine that the passage intended for its audience, living long beyond that imagined time, to constrain what they heard to a particular historical moment. Prophecy gives us thinking about exile that is temporally flexible with extended meaning. Indeed, the sense of time in these passages would make it possible for them to be prolonged ever further. In the process, the threat of the empires, be it Assyrian or Babylonian, is pushed into the present and into the future—surely a vivid if terrifying example of the long reach of the sixth-century losses.

This volume seeks to test the evidence and our preconceptions about the events of the sixth century and ask, What do we know about that period, and what, ultimately, can we not know? The semantic range of Judah's metaphors, and some of its shifts evident in redaction, may seem like tenuous evidence at best. But we are more aware than ever that how we perceive the world is as potent as what actually is going on around us; so that while sifting through these materials does not yield hard data, it nonetheless points to a perception of the world, as all metaphors do. Moreover, it points to a shift in the notion of history that will animate the prophet and his audience.

"Empire" as a Political Category and Reflections on It in Centers and Peripheries

Mark W. Hamilton

The study of the long sixth century BCE poses several problems for modern historians, not least the survival of empire as a political form less dependent on the charisma of individual rulers than on self-legitimating (masquerading, valorizing, naturalizing) power structures. Rulers of that and subsequent eras faced the great challenge of holding together often fragile connections among subjects with diverse histories and hopes. While multicultural states agglomerating previously independent polities had existed earlier, they had repeatedly given way to smaller states, even in the anomalous case of Egypt.[1] Expansion and collapse alternated in cycles long or short. For western Asia, however, this cycle all but stopped in the long sixth century as the disintegration of Assyria led to another empire and then others in a succession lasting, with few interruptions, into the mid-twentieth century. Empire established itself as a viable long-term solution to the problems of power and legitimacy. This shift exercised profound effects on the religious traditions now embedded in the Bible.

Several biblical texts that reflect on the experiences of the long sixth century concentrate on the nature of the imperial systems themselves and not just the experience of forced migration, not of course with the tools of modern social sciences but with a keen eye on the interplay of political structure, economics, religion, and both local and translocal traditions over time.[2]

---

1. On the relative lack of fragility of the centralized Egyptian state, see Ellen Morris, "Ancient Egyptian Exceptionalism: Fragility, Flexibility, and the Art of Not Collapsing," in *The Evolution of Fragility: Setting the Terms*, ed. Norman Yoffee (Cambridge: McDonald Institute for Archaeological Research, 2019), 61–87.

2. Without identifying the central importance of the dramatic movements of peoples, one must take a broader view than that pioneered by, e.g., Rainer Albertz, *Israel*

After making a few remarks on the study of empire in general, I survey a variety of Israelite/Judahite political reflections, identifying biblical texts that reflect on the long sixth century in various ways, and turn more fully to the Third Isaiah, a text slightly postdating our period but drawing on several generations of meditations on it. While modern empire studies have studied these polities from the top with an externally derived set of theories about their inner workings, a text such as Third Isaiah (or for that matter, most of the texts of the Hebrew Bible) consider the succession of ancient Near Eastern empires from the point of view of subaltern elites, who employ theological lenses to see political leaders and structures, and who must respond both to their imperial masters and to their own ethnic group. To shift the metaphor, the Israelite texts hold up a mirror to the imperial center as the leaders in it gaze, in turn, on the subject peoples, including Israelites. We have, then, one mirror facing another, with all the bending of images that such a setup must inevitably create.

Empire as Problem

Distinguishing reflections from realities poses both evidentiary and conceptual problems for students of empire, as evidenced by the explosion of publications not only on individual empires (from the Cambridge History of the British Empire, published 1929–1961, to recent studies of Assyria or Persia) but on the political category called empire itself.[3] The phenomenological approach to empire has given rise to such multidisciplinary conversations as the H-Empire online discussion board, or *The Journal of Empire Studies*, or, closer to home, studies of such diverse topics as taxation in the Achaemenid empire, business and social networks, relationships between

---

in Exile: *The History and Literature of the Sixth Century B.C.E.*, trans. David Green, SBLStBL 3 (Atlanta: Society of Biblical Literature, 2003). I regret that the excellent book by Jonathan Silverman on precisely these issues appeared as the present volume was being completed and therefore it was impossible to integrate his work fully into this study. See Jason M. Silverman, *Persian Royal-Judaean Elite Engagements in the Early Teispid and Achaemenid Empire: The King's Acolytes*, LHBOTS 690 (London: T&T Clark, 2020).

3. On Assyria, see Mario Liverani, *Assyria: The Imperial Mission* (Winona Lake, IN: Eisenbrauns, 2017); Daniel R. Miller, "Objectives and Consequences of the Neo-Assyrian Imperial Exercise," *R&T* 16 (2009): 124–49. On Persia, see Pierre Briant, *From Cyrus to Alexander: A History of the Persian Empire*, trans. Peter T. Daniels (Winona Lake, IN: Eisenbrauns, 2002).

center and periphery, and so on.[4] While such analysis has a long prehistory, tracing back not just to such nineteenth-century multivolume histories as Rawlinson's *Seven Great Monarchies of the Ancient Eastern World* or Eduard Meyer's *Geschichte des Altertums*, but even earlier to the foundations of the European empires after contact with the New World,[5] contemporary research assumes that in studying empires we are studying the past, a political structure no longer viable, because it is morally discreditable and economically unsustainable. Whether such a judgment will prove true remains to be seen.

Empire studies as a cluster of disciplines turns inside out the prevailing interest in postcolonial discourses without displacing them. Recognizing subordinate peoples as the creators of history, often in important ways, does not nullify the fact that their choices were often circumscribed by actors more powerful than they, even when those other actors must take account of the very subjects they thought themselves able to control. Considering

---

4. On taxation: e.g., Michael Jursa, "Agricultural Management, Tax Farming and Banking: Aspects of Entrepreneurial Activity—Babylonia in the Late Achaemenid and Hellenistic Periods," in *La transition entre l'empire achéménide et les royaumes hellénistiques (vers 350–300 avant J.-C.)*, ed. Pierre Briant and Francis Joannès, Persika 9 (Paris: de Boccard, 2006), 137–222; Rhyne King, "Taxing Achaemenid Arachosia: Evidence from Persepolis," *JNES* 78 (2019): 185–99. On business and social networks: Caroline Waerzeggers, *Marduk-rēmanni: Local Networks and Imperial Politics in Achaemenid Babylonia*, OLA 233 (Leuven: Peeters, 2014); Mark B. Garrison, Charles E. Jones, and Matthew W. Stolper, "Achaemenid Elamite Administrative Tablets, 4: BM 108963," *JNES* 77 (2018): 1–14. On relationships between center and periphery: Craig W. Tyson and Virginia R. Herrmann, eds., *Imperial Peripheries in the Neo-Assyrian Period* (Boulder: University Press of Colorado, 2018). Note, for example, the depiction of the empire's diverse topography in Neo-Assyrian art. See Allison Karmel Thomason, "Representations of the North Syrian Landscape in Neo-Assyrian Art," *BASOR* 323 (2001): 63–96. On perceptions of wetlands in Assyrian inscriptions, see Sebastian Borkowski, "'Of Marshes, Kings and Rebels': On the Perception and Representation of Southern Mesopotamian Wetlands at the Neo-Assyrian Royal Court," in *Text and Image: Proceedings of the 61ᵉ Rencontre Assyriologique Internationale, Geneva and Bern, 22–26 June 2015*, ed. Pascal Attinger et al., OBO.SA 40 (Leuven: Peeters, 2018), 103–15.

5. George Rawlinson, *The Seven Great Monarchies of the Ancient Eastern World: History, Geography, and Antiquities of Chaldaea, Assyria, Babylon, Media, Persia, Parthia, and Sassanian, or New Persian Empire*, 3 vols. (New York: Alden, 1884); Eduard Meyer, *Geschichte des Altertums*, 2nd ed., 5 vols. (Stuttgart: Cotta, 1907–1913); Anthony Pagden, *The Burdens of Empire: 1539 to the Present* (Cambridge: Cambridge University Press, 2015).

empire as a network of shifting relationships in which core and periphery are themselves value-laden ideas for both participants in a system and, differently, those studying those systems centuries or millennia later, allows for thicker historical description. The variegated nature of human agency itself comes into view. Since different empires face similar problems of integrating subjects into coherent social and economic networks, limiting damage from external enemies, forming alliances with potential friends, and sustaining ideological justifications for their own existence, one may speak of empire as a phenomenon distinct from nation-states, city-states, and other polities. They managed people without the benefit of a unified group identity, even while attempting to demonstrate to their subjects the advantages of compliance with centralized authority.

Nor are modern historians the first to recognize the complexity of the political phenomenon of empire. The major Europe-centered realms that arose after 1500 gave rise to both attempts at universalism and to strong reactions against such totalizing impulses.[6] Even if we do not accept fully the neo-Marxist claims of Michael Hardt and Antonio Negri that imperialism has recently been supplanted by new forms of sovereignty no longer vested in the nation-state but in transnational elites, we still should take seriously their notion of a dialectical relationship between "empire," however conceived in relationship with the state, and the "mass," the "real productive force of our social world."[7] Empire is neither an epiphenomenal structure atop "real" society nor a stage in human development (now outgrown). Empire has its own history as a type of polity.

In truth, the productive forces have always been plural, as thick descriptions of individual empires as well as comparisons of them show. Recent studies of empire and environment, for example, note the impact on ecosystems of hunting, the privileging of certain cash crops, and the creation and maintenance of large-scale waterworks, among other socially and technologically complex activities.[8] Likewise, the movement

---

6. Anthony Pagden, *Lords of All the Worlds: Ideologies of Empire in Spain, Britain and France c. 1500–c. 1800* (New Haven: Yale University Press, 1995), esp. 178–200.

7. Michael Hardt and Antonio Negri, *Empire* (Cambridge: Harvard University Press, 2000), 62.

8. For a broad-gauged approach to climatic crises in the ancient Near East, see Walter Sommerfeld, "Umweltzerstörung und ökologische Krisen im Alten Orient," in *State Formation and State Decline in the Near and Middle East*, ed. Rainer Kessler, Walter Sommerfeld, and Leslie Tramontini (Wiesbaden: Harrassowitz, 2016), 15–49.

of languages (hence speakers and their cultures) both derives from and reinforces the new networks created by or perhaps constituting the formation of empires.[9]

A half century ago, in his introduction to a collection of brief essays with the revealing title *The Decline of Empires*, Samuel Eisenstadt surmised that entities from the Roman Empire onward shared "the combination of traditional and relatively nontraditional elements and orientations within the political framework." He continues to say that successive political entities arose from "new rulers" who "came to power in periods of unrest, or during the decline of the existing political system."[10] Such generalizations do not take us much beyond the obvious, and in any case do not reveal whether imperial decline derives from the decline of material or spiritual factors or causes them. Yet Eisenstadt had already recognized that commonalities existed among otherwise unconnected polities and that studying their demise revealed their nature (a point to which I will return).

It is possible to be more precise, however. For example, in their recent volume on empires since Rome and Han dynasty China, Jane Burbank and Frederick Cooper deny that imperial repertoires of rule were either "a bag of tricks dipped into at random or a preset formula for rule."[11] Analysis of such political structures should neither assume top-down decision making nor drift into nominalism. Empires shared, Burbank and Cooper argue, several common elements: (1) They differ from nation-states in

---

Sommerfeld does not concentrate on empires per se but does offer a sophisticated attention to texts and other sources of information about ancient perceptions of ecological conditions and their relationships to human life. On ecosystems of hunting for European empires see John MacKenzie, "A Meditation on Environmental History," in *The Nature of Empires and the Empires of Nature: Indigenous Peoples and the Great Lakes Environment*, ed. Karl S. Hele (Waterloo, ON: Wilfred Laurier University Press, 2016), 1–21.

9. E.g., Josef Wiesehöfer, "The Role of Lingua Francas and Communication Networks in the Process of Empire-Building: The Persian Empire," in Kessler, Sommerfeld, and Tramontini, *State Formation and State Decline*, 121–34. More broadly, Hans Heinrich Hock and Brian D. Joseph, *Language History, Language Change, and Language Relationship: An Introduction to Historical and Comparative Linguistics* (Berlin: de Gruyter, 1996); Sarah G. Thomason, *Language Contact: An Introduction* (Washington, DC: Georgetown University Press, 2001.

10. Samuel N. Eisenstadt, ed., *The Decline of Empires* (Englewood Cliffs, NJ: Bobbs-Merrill, 1967), 3.

11. Jane Burbank and Frederick Cooper, *Empires in World History: Power and the Politics of Difference* (Princeton: Princeton University Press, 2010), 3.

their acceptance of difference and the hierarchies that inevitably (?) flow from difference. (2) The complexity of empires forces their rulers to rely on intermediaries rather than direct rule from the capital. (3) Empires interact with each other, rarely achieving complete domination of their sphere of action. (4) Rulers operate with imaginaries, often limited, that offer them options for action. Finally, (5) flexible approaches to ruling, with fluctuating concentrations of power at the center, allowed empires to survive through adaptation.[12] Burbank and Cooper explore these themes in their many manifestations rather than seeking a typology of empire. Their approach would be helpful for students of the ancient Near East in general and the Bible in particular because they avoid both nominalism ("empire" simply names big states) and essentialism (all empires are the same and all interactions with them by subjects are the same).

Their allowance for variety is useful in a discussion of the long sixth century BCE as well, for during that period previously small-scale territorial or city-states throughout the Near East suddenly found themselves part of larger, polycultural entities (just as much in Phoenicia, central Syria, or southern Mesopotamia as in Palestine). The last empire in the series, the Achaemenid Persian realm, adopted the language of the subject peoples (Aramaic) as the primary language of administration, a situation difficult to find parallels for in later empires (though the Yuan Empire and its subordinate Ilkhanate show similar practices), while nevertheless maintaining firm control over most of its territory for two centuries. Therefore, any comparative analysis of empires must show proper respect for individual cases.

In any case, each of the loci that Burbank and Cooper identify involve patterns of human behavior, hence choices by actors based on value-laden judgments. Therefore, they both rest on, and open up space for, moral reflection on the part of both the ancient subjects of empires and modern scholars studying them, not indeed the moralizing transformation of old theological terms such as *sin* and *redemption* into secular nonequivalents such as *imperial* and *liberation*, but at a deeper level.

Israelite Literature on Empire

Such reflection on the nature of life under empire does shape a number of biblical texts, some more overtly than others. In addition to the late

---

12. Burbank and Cooper, *Empires in World History*, 11–17.

examples of Daniel and Esther and the enigmatic Qoh 5:7–8, "one higher-up watches another higher-up and an even higher-up is over them; yet it is better overall for a land if a king is served for a field" (גבה מעל גבה שמר) (וגבהים עליהם: ויתרון ארץ בכל היא מלך לשדה נעבד),[13] as well as much earlier ones addressing the Assyrian invasions, a few texts do speak about the end of the Assyrian Empire (Nahum, Zephaniah), transition through Babylonian rule (Ezekiel), and the consolidation of power under the Persians (2 Chr 36:22–23; Ezra-Nehemiah).

While these texts almost invariably look at the world from the perspective of the Israelite/Judahite homeland, they also reveal a curious set of omissions. Memories of the forced migrations, resettlements in foreign lands, and even life for those who remained behind are all suppressed or sublimated in some way.

In part, as is often assumed, this suppression may reflect the absence of infrastructure for textual production during the period of Babylonian rule. Yet the absence of opportunity probably does not explain everything, even if it were possible to show that the various biblical texts usually dated to the so-called exile actually originated later. Rather, the various authors preserved in the Hebrew Bible seem to work with a theological construct that shapes how they understand the political changes during the long sixth century. Or put differently, in opposition to repertoires of rule, they use a repertoire of resistance that can exploit difference from the imperial ideal to build solidarity of a self-identifying group and can employ various elite literary forms (historiography, satire, prayer, among others) to help

---

13. The literal translation offered here masks a series of problems, no doubt. For example, what does it mean to serve the king for a field? The use of a prebendary system for officeholders seems in view, a practice that would undoubtedly involve misappropriation of land, at least from the point of view of subject peoples. Thomas Krüger, takes the verse to be an ironic quotation of Ptolemaic propaganda. See Krüger, *Qoheleth*, Hermeneia (Minneapolis: Fortress, 2004), 115; cf. Antoon Schoors, *Ecclesiastes*, HCOT (Leuven: Peeters, 2013), 410–16; Schoors, *The Preacher Sought to Find Pleasing Words: A Study of the Language of Qoheleth*, part 2, *Vocabulary*, OLA 143 (Leuven: Peeters, 2004), 298–99, 310–11 (including his understanding of the text as describing officials watching their subordinates for the sake of receiving kickbacks, 298–99). But see Aron Pinker, "The Advantage of a Country in Ecclesiastes 5:8," *JBQ* 37 (2009): 211–22. On the connection of this line, especially in LXX to 2 Samuel (2 Reigns) 8:15, see Françoise Vinel, "La texte grec de l'Ecclésiaste et ses caractéristiques: une relecture critique de l'histoire de la royauté," in *Qoheleth in the Context of Wisdom*, ed. Antoon Schoors, BETL 136 (Leuven: Peeters, 1998), 298–99.

audiences imagine, and begin to practice, an alternative to the empire, or at any rate find a way to flourish within it.

Unlike the fifth-century Greek author Ktesias of Knidos, who centuries before Eisenstadt understood the collapse of the Assyrian empire as a failure at the top, in this case of royal masculinity, the biblical writers do have access to authentic information about the names of rulers,[14] their major achievements (at least in the Levant), and the circumstances of their end. Yet the biblical writers also understand the succession of empires during the long sixth century in explicitly theological terms.[15]

The book of Ezekiel, for example, espouses the idea that the imperial conquests of Israel and Judah resulted from YHWH's disgust with the impurities that the people brought on the land and the restoration of the people as a fulfillment of the divine will that "Israel's house will never again

---

14. Mentions of emperors include Tiglath-pileser III (2 Kgs 15:19; 1 Chr 5:26), Sargon II (Isa 20:1), Sennacherib (2 Kgs 18:13; 19:16, 20, 36; Isa 36:1; 37:17, 21, 37; 2 Chr 32:1, 2, 9, 10, 22), and Esarhaddon (2 Kgs 19:37; Isa 37:38; Ezra 4:2). See n. 32 below. Ktesias organized his extraordinarily fanciful history into the three kingdoms of Assyria, Media, and Persia, attributing the end of the Assyrian empire to Sardanapalus's debauchery. For the text, see Jan P. Stronk, ed., *Ctesias' Persian History*, part 1, *Introduction, Text, and Translation*, RG 2 (Düsseldorf: Wellem, 2010), 239. According to Ktesias, the empire began through the conquests of Ninus and Semiramis, occupying most of the later Persian Empire, thus indicating both the gender bending of "empire" as a category of polity and the sense that "universal empire" coincided with the boundaries of Persia. The Greek view of Assyria closer to the life of that empire is obscure, since Herodotus's treatment of the empire has apparently gone missing. See J. G. MacQueen, "The Ἀσσύριοι Λόγοι of Herodotus and Their Position in the Histories," *ClQ* 28 (1978): 284–91. Notably, in Israelite texts the idea of a succession of empires takes on new form in Daniel, which merges the Israelite prophetic ideas with those of Hellenistic thinkers. In particular, Daniel combines the older Greek idea of four ages of human beings (seen in Hesiod, *Op.* 109–169) and the notion of emperors as irresponsible rulers (seen in Ktesias) with the prophetic ideas that the succession of empires came about because of YHWH's attempts to bring justice into the world.

15. Or they could recast the chain of empires as a single phenomenon repositioned as a primeval event revealing something of the deep structure of humanity, as in Gen 11:1–9. On the Tower of Babel story as a theological rather than "historical" text, see Angelika Berlejung, "Living in the Land of Shinar: Reflections on Exile in Genesis 11:1–9?," in *The Fall of Jerusalem and the Rise of the Torah*, ed. Peter Dubovský, Dominik Markl, and Jean-Pierre Sonnet, FAT 107 (Tübingen: Mohr Siebeck, 2016), 90–111.

defile my holy name" via corpse pollution (Ezek 43:7).¹⁶ By constructing an elaborate imaginary world centered on a rebuilt temple, the prophetic book implicitly offers an alternative to the urban visions of the great empires. Yet it does not simply substitute Jerusalem for Babylon or Susa/Persepolis, or Israel's restored and enhanced government for the real-world eastern empires. Rather, it simultaneously demotes human kingship in Israel to the role of the נשיא ("leader") and has that ruler dining in the gatehouse of the rebuilt temple otherwise closed to human access and open only to YHWH when entering the sanctuary (Ezek 44:1–3). That is, in Ezekiel's imaginarium the long sixth century ends with empires becoming irrelevant to Israelite life. This utopian fantasy critiques the imperial vision by denying all its basic assumptions. At the same time, it does not envision a return to the *status quo ante*, since the old Judahite society had caused its own demise. Ezekiel has it both ways, as utopian thinkers usually do.

In a different deployment of the repertoire of resistance, and perhaps as a complement to its interest in the destruction of Jerusalem as laid out in chapter 52,¹⁷ the long and probably composite oracles in Jer 50–51 against Babylon predict (incorrectly) the city's total destruction, reflecting less access to details of the end of the Babylonian Empire than a desire to match its end to that of Jerusalem (as, e.g., נקמת יהוה היא נקמת היכלו in Jer 51:11 ["for YHWH's vengeance it is, vengeance for his temple"]), and probably also the sense, based on the Neo-Assyrian case, that Mesopotamian empires end with the total destruction of their core.¹⁸ Indeed, Jeremiah's oracle draws a direct historiographic comparison between the end of the Neo-Babylonian and Neo-Assyrian states:

---

16. Note also several texts that, in the words of John Strong, understand the deportations as "one more step in the process of filtering out the impurities within the people." See Strong, "The Conquest of the Land and Yahweh's Honor before the Nations in Exile," in *Ezekiel: Current Debates and Future Directions*, ed. William A. Tooman and Penelope Barter, FAT 112 (Tübingen: Mohr Siebeck, 2017), 316.

17. On which note the comments of Georg Fischer, "Don't Forget Jerusalem's Destruction: The Perspective of the Book of Jeremiah," in Dubovský, Markl, and Sonnet, *Fall of Jerusalem*, 291–311, esp. 293–95. And differently, see the attempt to reclaim a Babylonian connection to Israel's future, as argued for by Adam K. Harger, "Reading Jeremiah 52 in Exile: Purpose in the Composition of Jeremiah," *JTS* 70 (2019): 511–22. See also Ian Wilson's chapter in this volume.

18. See the probably older Isa 21:9, which seems to refer to Sennacherib's sack of Babylon. See also n. 32 below.

לכן כה אמר יהוה צבאות אלהי ישראל הנני פקד אל מלך בבל ואת ארצו כאשר פקדתי אל מלך אשור:

Therefore says YHWH of Hosts, Israel's God, "I am punishing Babylon's king and his land just as I punished Assyria's king." (Jer 50:18)[19]

That is, one empire succeeds another at YHWH's chosen moment, usually with calamitous results. And yet the sovereign divine will also interacts with events in the human sphere, which in turn respond to human sinfulness. In other words, the succession of empires does not result from mere divine whim or the inevitable turning of the wheels of time,[20] but from a complex moral and political calculus to which the prophets must bear witness. Any response to the empire demands similar complexity.[21]

The difficulty of that calculus becomes obvious in later texts such as Ezra-Nehemiah, which largely accepts the legitimacy of Persian rule as a relief from prior empires but also voices criticisms of the divine plan. At least some evidence (e.g., Ezra 4:8–11)[22] exists that reflection on that history could serve rhetorical or political purposes after its expiry. Ezra-Nehemiah expresses views that are not strictly pro-Persian. In particular, the prayer in Neh 9:5–37 interweaves acceptance of responsibility, appeal to divine empathy, and protest against divine indifference to current suffering, both accepting the legitimacy of foreign occupation and protesting against. Imagined as a public address given almost in the shadow of the Persian government based at the imperial center at nearby Ramat Raḥel,[23]

---

19. Unless otherwise indicated, biblical translations are mine.

20. For those thinkers who do understand the succession of empires as a matter of divine will, see the crucial article by Peter Machinist, "The Transfer of Kingship: A Divine Turning," in *Fortunate the Eyes That See: Essays in Honor of David Noel Freedman in Celebration of His Seventieth Birthday*, ed. Astrid Beck et al. (Grand Rapids: Eerdmans, 1995), 105–20.

21. As discussed, for Jeremiah, by John Hill, *Friend or Foe? The Figure of Babylon in the Book of Jeremiah MT*, BibInt 40 (Leiden: Brill, 1999), 160–80; John Goldingay, "Jeremiah and the Superpower," in *Uprooting and Planting: Essays on Jeremiah for Leslie Allen*, ed. John Goldingay, LHBOTS 459 (New York: T&T Clark, 2007), 59–77.

22. Ezra 4:10 MT (OG) names an emperor "Osnapper" (אסנפר), arguably Assurbanipal, while at least some Greek manuscripts read Σαλμανασσαρης (LXX^L). For the idea that Osnapper was a Persian official (and the issues with the identification with Assurbanipal), see Bob Becking, *Ezra-Nehemiah*, HCOT (Leuven: Peeters, 2018), 70.

23. On the issues of the site, see Oded Lipschits, Yuval Gadot, and Dafna Langgut, "The Riddle of Ramat Raḥel: The Archaeology of a Royal Persian Period Edifice," *Transeu* 41 (2012): 57–79; Oren Tal, "Pottery from the Persian and Hellenistic

the text refers to suffering beginning "from the days of the kings of Assyria until this day" (מימי מלכי אשור עד היום הזה; v. 32), thus conceiving of the period from the eighth century to the fifth as a single period. The prayer further laments the fact that

הנה אנחנו היום עבדים והארץ אשר נתתה לאבתינו לאכל את פריה ואת טובה
הנה אנחנו עבדים עליני: ותבואתה מרבה למלכים אשר נתתה עלינו בחטאותינו

we are slaves today, and as for the land that you gave our ancestors so they could eat its fruit and its goodness, we are slaves upon it. Moreover, its vast produce is for kings whom you set over us for our sins.

Perhaps the prayer represents a perspective different from that of the Nehemiah memoir and other sources of Ezra-Nehemiah, but perhaps not, since subaltern responses to outside sovereignty can often take forms of nostalgia for an independent past, manipulation of political structures and actors, as well as more overt protest.[24] The citation of past failures—an act of antinostalgia, though not of straightforward acceptance of foreign rule—underwrites the claim that the present subordination is somehow gratuitous. The prayer can telescope time periods in order to highlight an overall assessment of them that may not seem to fit one given moment as well as another. An excess of divine justice produces injustice, which can be remedied only if YHWH frees Israel from the Persian yoke, though the text does not make that hope explicit or suggest human cooperation with such a divine action. Ezra-Nehemiah's approach to empire assumes, in short, that while some empires are better than others, independence in a context of harmonious relationships with YHWH remains preferable.[25]

Periods," in *Ramat Raḥel III: Final Publication of Yohanan Aharoni's Excavations (1954, 1959–1962)*, ed. Oded Lipschits, Yuval Gadot, and Liora Freud (Winona Lake, IN: Eisenbrauns, 2016), 1:266–71.

24. See the modern examples of such ways of interacting with states in Michael Herzfeld, "What Is a Polity? Subversive Archaism and the Bureaucratic Nation-State (2018 Lewis H. Morgan Lecture)," *Hau* 9 (2019): 23–35; Silverman, *Persian Royal-Judaean Elite*, 247–65.

25. Somewhat differently than the view worked out by David Janzen, "Yahwistic Appropriation of Achaemenid Ideology and the Function of Nehemiah 9 in Ezra-Nehemiah," *JBL* 136 (2017): 839–56. See also the discussion in Lisbeth S. Fried's chapter in this volume. The prayer relies at every turn on older traditional material, connecting the current oppression to the situation in Egypt after Joseph, as helpfully noted by Mark J. Boda, *Praying the Tradition: The Origin and Use of Tradition in Nehemiah 9*, BZAW 277 (Berlin: de Gruyter, 1999), 180–86. However, the debates about

The response to Persia in Ezra-Nehemiah thus seems at once complex and instructive. The work gives evidence of close interaction with the imperial government and its ideological discourses,[26] a complex mix that must reflect the equally mixed feelings subordinate peoples often feel even toward relatively benign overlords.

While the Persian Empire, like its predecessors (and indeed borrowing from its predecessors), employed imaginaries of rule that percolated down to the subject peoples,[27] those same subjects, at least in Israel, could also employ counterimaginaries ranging from reconstructing their own preimperial history to deploying theological concepts that relativized the allegedly universal empire as simply a small part of a divinely ruled cosmos to whose sovereign the subject people have unique access. Still other texts from the Achaemenid period assume empire as a reality to which it must respond in some way, and they operate on a similar assumption about the connection among empires as they transitioned through the long sixth century. In particular, the last chapters of the book of Isaiah draw on older

---

both the theological reasons for, and the results of, the deportations continued far into the Second Temple period. Note, for example, the recognition in 4Q372 (Apocryphon of Joseph[b]) of both the deportations as divine punishment and the tragedy of foreign occupation (with the foreigners "eating his strength," אכלים את כחו; l. 15). The discussion of Eileen Schuller and Moshe Bernstein helpfully points to a Samaritan connection for such a discussion. See Douglas M. Gropp, James VanderKam, and Monica Brady, eds., *Wadi Daliyeh II and Qumran Miscellanea, Part 2*, DJD 28 (Oxford: Oxford University Press, 2002), 171–72.

26. See notably Lisbeth S. Fried, "150 Men at Nehemiah's Table? The Role of the Governor's Meals in the Achaemenid Provincial Economy," *JBL* 137 (2018): 821–23. The fact that the imperial administration circulated key inscriptions in multiple languages for educational purposes is clear from the presence of the Aramaic translation of the Bisitun inscription (plus lines from Darius's tomb inscription) at the garrison town of Elephantine. For the text, see Bezalel Porten and Ada Yardeni, eds., *Textbook of Aramaic Documents from Ancient Egypt*, vol. 3, *Literature, Accounts, Lists* (Winona Lake, IN: Eisenbrauns, 1993), 59–70; on the combination of texts from Bisitun and Darius's burial inscriptions in the Elephantine text, see the study of Jan Tavernier, "An Achaemenid Royal Inscriptions: The Text of Paragraph 13 of the Aramaic Version of the Bisitun Inscription," *JNES* 60 (2001): 161–76. Note also the observations of Pamela Barmash in her chapter in this volume.

27. A good example appears in the seal impressions from Wadi Daliyeh portraying the Persian version of the old master-of-animals theme. See the definitive study of Mary Joan Winn Leith, *Wadi Daliyeh I: The Wadi Daliyeh Seal Impressions*, DJD 24 (Oxford: Clarendon, 1997), 209–28 and pls. xvii–xx; and, more broadly, the discussion by Matt Waters in this volume.

traditions embedded in the book in order to deal with challenges that the Persian Empire posed to its creators and their audiences.

The View from Third Isaiah

The book of Isaiah, among its many other commendable attributes, is a sort of literary tell, its strata meditating on encounters with imperial rule in the eighth–sixth centuries BCE and probably slightly later. After sketching the treatment of empire and the long sixth century in earlier strata of the book, I will attend to aspects of the final stages in chapters 56–66. In part, the incomplete merging of the encounters into a tight mental image derives from deliberate editorial activity in several stages, though with a fairly consistent mental picture in play.[28] In part the book's understanding of imperial histories affecting Judah/Israel demonstrates the perseverance of repertoires of rule across the succession of empires. The continuity within the book also shows that at least some Israelite/Judahite thinkers saw their predecessors' work as a fundamental tool for working out new ways of living under foreign control.

The Assyrian encounter is arguably the best understood, though a large scholarly literature also addresses the texts responding to Babylonian and early Persian rule, especially in Isa 40–55.[29] The later stages of the book of Isaiah offer, however, another important cluster of ideas

---

28. Note the discussion of Matthijs J. de Jong, *Isaiah among the Near Eastern Prophets: A Comparative Study of the Earliest Stages of the Isaiah Tradition and the Neo-Assyrian Prophecies*, VTSup 117 (Leiden: Brill, 2007). But against his view of a late seventh-century BCE redaction of the eighth-century material, and the extent of the latter, see the commentary of Jimmy J. M. Roberts, *First Isaiah: A Commentary*, ed. Peter Machinist, Hermeneia (Minneapolis: Fortress, 2015).

29. An extensive bibliography appears in my earlier essay: Mark W. Hamilton, "After Politics: Reflections on 2 Isaiah," in *Enemies and Friends of the State: Ancient Prophecy in Context*, ed. Christopher Rollston (University Park, PA: Eisenbrauns, 2018), 411–30; also notably Hanspeter Schaudig, "'Bel Bows, Nabu Stoops!': The Prophecy of Isaiah xlvi 1–2 as a Reflection of Babylonian 'Processional Omens'," *VT* 58 (2008): 557–72. On the Assyrian encounter, see, e.g., Peter Machinist, "Assyria and Its Image in the First Isaiah," *JAOS* 103 (1983): 719–37; Machinist, "Royal Inscriptions in the Hebrew Bible and Mesopotamia: Reflections on Presence, Function, and Self-Critique," in *"When the Morning Stars Sang": Essays in Honor of Choon Leong Seow on the Occasion of His Sixty-Fifth Birthday*, ed. Scott C. Jones and Christine Roy Yoder, BZAW 500 (Berlin: de Gruyter, 2018), 331–63; Shawn Zelig Aster, *Reflections of Empire in Isaiah 1–39*, ANEM 19 (Atlanta: SBL Press, 2017); Martin Leuenberger,

responding both to the stimuli of Persian rule and to the weight of the literature preceding it in the Isaiah corpus. Chapters 56–66, so-called Third Isaiah, offer an oft-neglected cluster of meditations on the long sixth century, drawing simultaneously on the literary traditions that the creators of these poems received and on their own experiences and reflections.

In its final form, again, Isaiah layers references to the Neo-Assyrian, Neo-Babylonian, and Persian empires, while preserving a proper sense of their order as a series of successor states. Oracles about the incursions of Tiglath-pileser III (Isa 7), defeat of Sennacherib (Isa 14:24–27), and the rise of Cyrus (Isa 44:24–45:13) peg a timeline on which the book can hang its memories of the encounters with the Mesopotamian empires, though the omission of most overt references to the seventh century BCE and the near silence on the early sixth century together create a strangely ahistorical sense of the whole. If, as Shawn Zelig Aster argues, Judahite intellectuals (including the prophet Isaiah) knew firsthand the Assyrian propaganda through written, oral, and visual media,[30] perhaps this gap derives from the lack of such interaction during the later Assyrian period, during which the empire focused its energies elsewhere and when Judah experienced straitened circumstances.

Perhaps most significant are those texts that reflect directly on the succession of empires. Again, the texts do not use special terminology for empires as opposed to other states, and indeed the structure of the oracles against the nations in chapters 13–23 presupposes the system of notionally equal states predating Assyrian expansion in the mid-eighth century BCE.[31] At the same time, the legacy idea coexisted with a realistic awareness of the asymmetry of the international system.

This awareness of the dynamics of power exercised over time appears in several texts in the book. The First Isaiah strata propose the alteration of the eighth-century BCE political structure, either by the destruction of Assyrian might (14:24–27; cf. 27:12–13) or the creation of a tripartite regional power structure (17:19–24). Some texts appear to understand the

---

"Kyros-Orakel und Kyros-Zylinder: Ein religionsgeschichtlicher Vergleich ihrer Gottes-Konzeptionen," *VT* 59 (2004): 244–56.

30. Aster, *Reflections of Empire*, 316–17 (and infra).

31. This seems true whatever the redactional history of these chapters and their relationship to the Babylonian Empire. See Bernard Gosse, *Isaïe 13,1–14,23: dans la tradition littéraire du livre d' Isaïe et dans la tradition des oracles contre les nations*, OBO 78 (Göttingen: Vandenhoeck & Ruprecht, 1988), esp. 16–30; Roberts, *First Isaiah*, 194–200.

collapse of the Neo-Babylonian Empire as parallel to the similar fate of Assyria (23:13–18), with the fall of the empires involving their extended peripheries of trading routes.³² Isaiah 25:6–7 envisions Jerusalem as the scene of a banquet for the now obedient nations, thus depicting the end of empire, or perhaps an Israelite center for it.³³

Building on this older tradition of reflection on empire and imperial transition from a religious perspective, the core of the so-called Third Isaiah, chapters 60–62, draws extensively on earlier Isaianic texts while also creating new texts reflecting on the political realities of the stabilizing Persian Empire.³⁴ The oracles structured around that core expand on the ideas. Strikingly, these chapters do not mention the (Persian or other) empire overtly, its political or economic structure, or its officials or intermediaries by name. Yet empire as a political structure remains the presupposition for the poems' description of the world. While much of the poetry focuses on the internal Israelite theological discourse and therefore says little about everyday life in the empire, either for its leaders or its subjects, at several points the political world shines though. This is true in chapters 60, 59, and 66 in particular. We should consider each in turn.

Isaiah 60

Whatever its precise date and place of origin, Isa 60:1–22 dilates on a drama of empire centered on Jerusalem. As the text opens, the dawn illuminates

---

32. And leaving aside the difficult case of Isa 21:9's נפלה נפלה בבל ("fallen, fallen is Babylon"), which may refer either to Sennacherib's destruction of that city or (less likely, to my mind) to the later Persian absorption of it. See the discussion in Michael H. Floyd, "The Meaning of Maśśā' as a Prophetic Term in Isaiah," *JHebS* 18.9 (2018): 21–23.

33. On the banquet as an inversion of the social order, see Andrew T. Abernethy, "Feasts and Taboo Eating in Isaiah: Anthropology as a Stimulant for the Exegete's Imagination," *CBQ* 80 (2018): 393–408; Abernethy, "Eating, Assyrian Imperialism, and God's Kingdom in Isaiah," in *Isaiah and Imperial Context: Isaiah in the Times of Empire*, ed. Andrew T. Abernethy et al. (Eugene, OR: Wipf & Stock, 2013), 35–50.

34. On Isa 60–62 as the core around which chs. 56–59 and 63–66 grew, see John Goldingay, *Isaiah 56–66*, ICC (London: T&T Clark, 2014), 6–9 (who is very skeptical of our ability to know); Jan L. Koole, *Isaiah III*, vol. 1, *Isaiah 40–48*, HCOT (Kampen: Kok, 1997), 28–33; Paul A. Smith, *Rhetoric and Redaction in Trito-Isaiah: The Structure, Growth and Authorship of Isaiah 56–66*, VTSup 62 (Leiden: Brill, 1995); with reservations based on a redaction-critical model, Odil Hannes Steck, "Der Grundtext in Jesaja 60 und sein Aufbau," *ZTK* 83 (1986): 261–96.

a scene of foreign rulers and merchants bringing valuable goods to the rebuilt temple in Zion. It thus creates the verbal equivalent of the Assyrian, Babylonian, and Persian (at Persepolis at any rate) presentation scenes in which an enthroned king receives tribute and obeisance from appreciative, obedient subjects.[35]

The poem is structured chiastically:

A The bringing of light (60:1–5)
  B Tribute (60:6–9)
    C City building (60:10–11)
      D A summary (60:12)
    C′ City building (60:13–16)
  B′ Tribute (60:17–18)
A′ The bringing of light (60:19–20)

The structure points inward to the summary statement in verse 12:

כי הגוי והממלכה אשר לא יעבדוך יאבדו והגוים הרב יחרבו
For the people and kingdom that doesn't serve you will perish,
Yes, the peoples will surely be devastated.

Far from being a gloss added to an earlier version of the poem,[36] this blunt threat of divine violence against political entities resisting Israel sums up the poem's overall development. Verses 21–22 close off the poem with a theme stated earlier, the reassessment of the surviving Israelites as "vindicated" (צדיקים) and a promise of their renewed vitality. The combination of verse 12 with verses 21–22 sets up a contrast between the renewed Israel as a vital center and its unpliant neighbors, now played out.

These framing lines reinforce an expectation of a new political reality that the structure and successive images of the overall poem set forth. The opening and closing scenes play on images of light and darkness, images that appear either singly or coupled at several points in the evolving book of Isaiah.[37] The closest connections to chapter 60 occurs in Isa 30:26,

---

35. The technique appears earlier in the Isaiah corpus, as well, as shown by Aster, *Reflections of Empire*, 41–80.

36. Contra Steck, "Grundtext," 261–62; cf. Jan L. Koole, *Isaiah III*, vol. 3, *Isaiah 56–66*, HCOT (Leuven: Peeters, 2001), 220–21, with bibliography.

37. For אור: Isa 2:5; 5:20, 30; 9:1; 10:17; 13:10; 18:4; 30:26; 42:6, 16; 43:3; 45:7; 49:6; 51:4, 9; 58:8; and חשך: 5:20, 30; 9:1; 29:18; 42:7; 45:3, 19; 47:5; 49:9; 58:10; 59:9.

which expects a supernova to illuminate the return of Israel from its forced migrations: the sevenfold brightness of the sun (ואור החמה יהיה שבעתים) anticipates 60:20's expectation that the sun will disappear altogether in favor of the refulgence of YHWH itself.

The solar imagery of Isa 60:1–5, 19–20 primarily serves as backlighting to the movement of peoples and rulers, however. The dawn of the new era reveals such movement as the poem conceives of the Near East as a space for movement, first of Israelite refugees (see Hos 11:10–11), then of goods and their bearers (vv. 6–9, 17–18). Two aspects of the B/B′ section take the idea of movement in space further.

First, verses 6–9 play with a cluster of pairs (camels, sheep; Midian, Qedar/Nebaioth; islands, ships of Tarshish) to underscore the movement of goods toward the sanctuary in Jerusalem, which now takes its place as the focal point of that movement. Granting that the list of place names constitutes a merism, the conception of space here is nevertheless instructive. Unlike Esther's conception of an empire of contiguous provinces (Esth 1:1) in which the state staged power in various media,[38] or Second Isaiah's view of Persia as a connected realm of urban centers whose ruler (based in Babylon? [Isa 44:1–13, esp. vv. 11–13]) could capture or rebuild a city in his territory, Isa 60 pictures Jerusalem as a node in a network of sites connected by caravan or ship, not centrally ruled by a state. In a sense, the view hearkens back to the preimperial period. Or, rather, it shifts the imperial center from the east toward Jerusalem itself.

Second, the movement of goods includes items usable in the temple in Jerusalem and materials used in building or fabricating implements, perhaps for the temple but also more generally useful. The assemblage bronze-iron-wood-stone gives way to gold-silver-bronze-iron. The contrasts rely partly on color similarities (bronze resembles gold, silver resembles iron), but clearly simple substitution cannot be intended since ironworking did not extend to construction technique and so could not simply fill in for stone. Nor could the trade networks that moved about one material simply pick up another. So verse 17a–b's expectation of an enriched flow of materials to Jerusalem must attend less to the practicalities of ancient economics and more to the more generalized idea of the

---

38. On the state as a display of royal in Esther and Aeschylus, see Peter Machinist, "Achaemenid Persia as Spectacle. Reactions from Two Peripheral Voices: Aeschylus, *The Persians* and the Biblical Book of Esther," *ErIsr* 33 (2018): 109*–23*.

city as an important center attracting wealth, as implied in verse 17c's vague but exciting promise of שלום and צדקה.

This concept of refocused, enhanced movement of goods leading to peace appears also in the C and C′ sections of the poem (vv. 10–11, 13–16). Verses 10–11 expect both the rebuilding of Jerusalem's walls and the perpetual opening of its gates. Since open gates render a city all but defenseless, the text must envision both the ends of external threats (since foreign kings now serve Jerusalem) and the reimagination of ramparts not as defensive structures but as both a demarcation between urban and rural space (or sanctuary and nonsanctuary) and an expression of the city's monumentality. The walls' symbolic nature crowds out their practical uses.

This symbolic freighting comes to the surface in verses 13–16, which step back in time to the rebuilding of the temple (employing the figure of speech hysteron proteron) to describe the splendor of the building, which is constructed from Lebanese trees (foreign space surrendering its glory to Jerusalem) in order properly to represent the "place of my feet" (מקום רגלי). Foreign space exists to serve Jerusalem less as human space than as divine space, with the temple and its host city iconizing the heavenly throne itself.

The text's conception of inhabited space points, then, to our discussion of empire, for Isa 60 presupposes the interconnectedness of many far-flung societies centered on a single point. In other words, the text envisions an empire without a human emperor, a bureaucracy, or any human means of coercion.[39] Yet, as the pivotal line of the poem indicates, revolt against Israelite hegemony leads to the destruction of the insurgents, surely an imperial response even if executed only by the deity. That is, the poem does not envision a lack of resistance to Jerusalem's newfound rule, only the illegitimacy and futility of such resistance.

To return to Burbank and Cooper's pentad of empire (difference, use of intermediaries, interempire interaction, imaginaria, and flexible ruling strategies), the poem describes the sort of polity that its subjects should embrace. That empire centers on Jerusalem, picking up the sym-

---

39. See Isa 62:8, which expects a future that reverses the prerestoration era's experience of imperial appropriation of Israelite/Judahite resources. YHWH promises, "I will never again give your grain as food to your enemies, nor will foreigners drink your new wine that you struggled for" (אם אתן את דגנך עוד מאכל לאיביך ואם ישתו בני נכר תירושך אשר יגעת בו). The understanding of empire as an instrument of collecting tribute and imprisoning people runs throughout the text.

bolic freighting of that city, though now purged of those sins of its past that brought it into other empires in the first place. Periphery has become the center of an archipelago of sites giving up humans and capital to support the new center's religiously layered activities. The kings of the various lands no longer owe allegiance to Persia or another empire but to Jerusalem. The poem envisions not a return to the polycephalous system of notionally equal states (or of smaller clusters of patron and client states as in the Sefire texts), but a new empire that is not one.[40]

However, unlike Ps 72, which it otherwise closely resembles, Isa 60 does not expect a human king to sit at the focal point of this new empire.[41] The deity will rule in a more immediate sense.

Isaiah 61 and 59

The so-called Third Isaiah develops this idea of a new empire or anti-empire or transmogrified empire (depending on one's lights) in several ways, of which I note two that directly bear on the work's understanding of the imperial dimensions of the events of the long sixth century BCE.

First, Isa 61:1–3 describes a new world in which the prophet, possessed by the divine spirit, must proclaim a new state of affairs:

לבשר ענוים שלחני
לחבש לנשברי לב
לקרא לשבוים דרור
ולאסורים פקחקוח[42]
לקרא שנת רצון ליהוה
היום נקם לאלהינו
לנחם כל אבלים

---

40. This view differs somewhat from that of Jones, who sees here an attempt to "sear an image of Jerusalem's restoration into its audience's retina." See Christopher M. Jones, "'The Wealth of Nations Shall Come to You': Light, Tribute, and Implacement in Isaiah 60," VT 64 (2014): 611–22, esp. 622.

41. As often noted (see, e.g., Goldingay, Isaiah 56–66, 277–79, 285). Note also the observations of Martin Arneth, "Sonne der Gerechtigkeit": Studien zur Solarisierung der Jahwe-Religion im Lichte von Psalm 72, BZABR 1 (Wiesbaden: Harrassowitz, 2000), 187–95. He argues that Ps 72 postdates Isa 60. That thesis seems impossible to sustain, however, given the presence of a human king in Ps 72 and his absence in Isa 60.

42. Following the reading of 4QIsa^a (4Q55) rather than L. However, see the discussion in Joseph Blenkinsopp, Isaiah 56–66, AB 19B (New York: Doubleday, 2003), 219.

לשום לאבלי ציון
<לתת> להם פאר תחת אפר
שמן ששון תחת אבל
מעטה תהלה תחת רוח כהה[43]
וקרא להם אילי הצדק
מטע יהוה להתפאר

> To announce release for the poor,
> To mend the broken-hearted,
> To proclaim manumission to the captives,
>   Openings up to the imprisoned,
> To proclaim YHWH's year of grace,
>   Our God's day of repayment,
> To comfort all the mourning,
> <To give> them a scarf not soil,
>   oil of happiness not mourning,
>   a prayer wrap not a colorless spirit,
> To call them straight oaks,
> That YHWH planted to his own credit.

While this text has exerted enormous influence on Christian theology, thanks to its quotation in the Third Gospel's programmatic story of Jesus at Nazareth (Luke 4:18–19), the Persian-period creator of the text simply speaks to a more immediate reality, the end of the deportations that culminated in the Babylonian incursions from 604–586 BCE but whose influence persisted far later. The virtuosic word play contrasting present suffering with future happiness, and the overall rhetorical brilliance of the poem, serves a religious and political purpose of deconstructing the imperial imaginaries according to which subject peoples existed to serve the center (Nineveh or Babylon). Israelites no longer live to serve their imperial masters. Their very bodies no longer bear signs of subordination.

Moreover, the liberation of Israel (and other subject peoples) allows the rebuilding of Jerusalem (61:4: ובנו ירבות עולם ["and they will rebuild the ancient ruins"]), thus completing the reversal of the sixth century's catastrophes. The collocation of (sun-)light in chapter 60 with the freeing of YHWH's subjects and their rebuilding of the deity's city echoes another

---

43. L as it stands seems to contain a conflate reading of infinitive constructs in this clause (contrast to the LXX's single verb, δοθῆναι); see Blenkinsopp, *Isaiah 56–66*, 219.

text that both Neo-Assyrian and Neo-Babylonian rulers trumpeted, and which the book of Isaiah seems otherwise to know: Enuma Elish.[44] Tablet 6 of that text reports that, following the defeat of Tiamat, Marduk cemented his reign by destroying Qingu and creating humanity from his blood, liberating the gods (*ilāni umtaššir* [6.34]), arranging the gods into heavenly and netherworld cohorts, and appointing appropriate sacrifices for them. In gratitude for his saving acts, the Annunaki offer to build for him a city and a temple, Babylon and Esagila. He responds, as the text puts it

Marduk annitu ina šemêšu
kīma ūmu immeru zīmušu māʾdiš
Marduk upon hearing this
Had his glint shining greatly like the day. (6.55–56)[45]

The collocation of city building, divine delight, and the ordering of the chief deity's subjects reflects a mythic viewpoint in which Babylon exists as a response to chaos and an earthly representation of the divine order atop which Marduk sits. Likewise (or perhaps contrariwise), the laying out of these ideas in Isa 60–61 places the mythic idea in service of an anti-imperial idea.

Second, the echoes of Enuma Elish seem to be heard in chapter 59 as well, for again a divine warrior appears. Isaiah 59:17 describes YHWH accoutered for war:

וילבש צדקה כשריון
ויכבע ישועה בראשו
וילבש בגדי נקם תלבשת
ויעט כמעיל קנאה

He wears loyalty like scale armor,
A helmet of deliverance on his head,
Yes, he wears a retribution garb as a vestment,
And dons relentless commitment like a mantle.

---

44. As argued by, among others, Joseph Blenkinsopp, "The Cosmological and Protological Language of Deutero-Isaiah," *CBQ* 73 (2011): 493–510; Mark W. Hamilton, "What Are *ʾElilim*?," *Journal of Hebrew Scriptures* 19 (2019): article 9, 1–9 (esp. 7–8).

45. For the text, see Wilfred G. Lambert, *Babylonian Creation Myths*, MC 16 (Winona Lake, IN: Eisenbrauns, 2016).

The third clause is difficult, since תלבשת seems redundant.⁴⁶ The LXX of verse 17bα (καὶ τὸ περιβόλαιον ὡς ἀνταποδώσων ἀνταπόδοσιν ὄνειδος τοῖς ὑπεναντίοις) does not seem to lack an equivalent of the Hebrew *hapax legomenon* תלבוש, as is sometimes argued, but does reflect a different understanding of the line's scansion, taking the noun with what follows rather than what precedes. The choice of an Akkadian loanword (*talbuštu*) seems to reinforce the exotic character of the depiction of the intervening god.

Isaiah 66

The intervening deity appears most dramatically at the end of the book, with a promise of war against "all the nations" (כל הגוים). The faraway lands reached by ship (66:19) will experience YHWH's sovereignty. The language of sense impression describes the deprivation of these lands: "they have not heard my report [see Isa 53:1], seen my glory," but they will "report my glory among the nations" (והגידו את כבודי בגוים). And then the now-enlightened foreign peoples will return the deportees to their homeland (see Isa 49:8–12). In short, the prosaic ending of the book in 66:18–20 reclaims themes of the Second Isaiah and expects their fulfillment in the near future. Curiously, the spaces named (Tarshish, Pul,⁴⁷ Lud, Meshech, Tubal, Yavan) lie at the edge of the Persian Empire or in its extended periphery.

This geographical array seems to mean several things. (1) It carefully avoids naming any part of the Achaemenid Empire. Yet it also frames the empire as a sort of negative space in the mental picture of the region's geography, not unlike the way in which the anaphora of Amos 1–2 brings the audience at last to Israel. As in other texts in Third Isaiah, this poem focuses on the empire while simultaneously diverting attention from it. (2) At another level, the geographical imaginarium reclaims distant foreign lands, erstwhile refuges for YHWH's people, as lands that will simultaneously respect the deity's glory and be free of his people.

This paradoxical state concludes, however, in the catastrophic defeat of any foreign power that would challenge YHWH's hegemony. On the one hand, "all flesh will come to worship before" YHWH (יבוא כל בשר)

---

46. Goldingay, *Isaiah 56–66*, 228; Koole, *Isaiah 56–66*, 202; Blenkinsopp, *Isaiah 56–66*, 195.

47. LXX adds Φουδ (Punt). See Jer 46:9.

להשתחות לפני), and on the other "they will come and see the corpses of the humans who sinned against" the deity (ויצאו וראו בפגרי האנשים הפשעים בי). These lines in Isa 66:23–24 close the book with the same understanding of YHWH's exercise of divine kingship that has informed earlier texts. The era of deportations and imperial displays of power compelling a public audience will end at last.

Conclusions

The so-called Third Isaiah presents a paradox, then: without naming an empire or analyzing its economic, military, or political practices and structures, these poems take the political form that arose and evolved from the eighth–sixth centuries BCE as a given against which it must react. As a foil for Israelite thinkers envisioning a new postimperial future, the interplay of royal display, movement of peoples and goods toward a center, the existence of transnational networks of power and submission, empire becomes the reality without which the texts can make no sense. Their visions of the future are, therefore, self-erasing. Heaven needs hell for contrast.

Yet despite its problems with the Greeks, Egyptians, and Bactrians at its edges, Achaemenid Persia was not the netherworld, in part because, as such Israelite thinkers as the creators of Isa 40–55, Chronicles, and Ezra-Nehemiah knew, that empire had abandoned the most Plutonic elements, various forms of mass deportations, while retaining many of the artistic and literary conventions worked out by the Neo-Assyrian rulers. So Third Isaiah's reticence may derive less from fear of political repercussions or even distaste of foreign occupation than from a more theologically oriented sensibility. According to that view, the politics of YHWH transcended human politics even while adopting its outward forms.

If this is so, repertoires of resistance may also erase themselves because the texts do not assume that imagining a counterempire, or even its realization in the human sphere, marks the end of the journey. Something unnamable lies beyond even that: YHWH's reign, elusive yet inescapable.

The Far Side of the Long Sixth Century: Mesopotamian Political Influences on Early Achaemenid Persia

Matt Waters

The Achaemenid Persians adopted and adapted previous structures as they forged an empire that lasted more than two hundred years and at its height included territory on three continents stretching across southeastern Europe, northeastern Africa, and central Asia. In its political structure and organization the Achaemenid Empire far surpassed its predecessors in Iran (Elam and the Medes), Mesopotamia (Assyria and Babylonia), and Egypt. It was something new in its scale and its effective staying power, but, without any rival of comparable size or power, for imperial models the Achaemenids had no choice but to look to the past.[1] Within this volume's emphasis on the long sixth century, the topic at hand involves the influence of Mesopotamian political thought on the Achaemenid system. Only a few examples may be discussed in an article-length treatment, focusing on those illustrative of a deep and lasting imprint, most evident in various forms of ideological expression.

Tracing continuity of imperial signatures, as they are sometimes called, ranges from the straightforward—for example, images and descriptions of

---

1. The observation of Amélie Kuhrt on the exceptional historical circumstances of the Achaemenid Empire is well applied here: "During that time, no power of remotely comparable size, capable of challenging it effectively, existed.... The Achaemenid rulers were not in competition (or dialogue) with contemporary rulers. Rather their dialogue was with imperial powers of the past, on whose structures and imagery they drew, while simultaneously formulating and promoting a distinctive Persian identity of their kingship." See Kuhrt, "Achaemenid Images of Royalty and Empire," in *Concepts of Kingship in Antiquity*, ed. Giovanni Lanfranchi and Robert Rollinger (Padova: S.A.R.G.O.N., 2010), 87.

the royal hero—to the (relatively) more subtle but still readily identifiable phrase or epithet in a royal inscription; an accoutrement of the royal costume, regalia, or court; or an image on a seal. Apprehending the full significance of such adaptations, as they were formulated into an Achaemenid code, is another matter, continued grist for the scholarly mill applied to a variety of recipes (i.e., interpretations). Even if the main messages are obvious, many of the symbols or words in which they were coded are often multivalent—involving several levels of interpretation.

Much depends on where one stands in the literal sense of the phrase. One would not expect to find prominent within Egypt, for example, explicitly "Mesopotamianized" expressions of Persian ideology, but Egyptianized ones. Continuity was at times an extension of expediency: appropriating local conventions to facilitate acceptance of new political realities. It was not a static phenomenon, however. For example, reliance on Babylonian traditions and local elites was a higher priority during the reigns of Cyrus and Cambyses, but some of these links ruptured during the reigns of Darius and (especially) Xerxes. This shift has been undergoing increased scrutiny, a critical phenomenon in understanding Achaemenid rule in Babylonia during the fifth and fourth centuries, but the particulars of which run far afield from the focus of this paper.[2] In considering the continuation of Mesopotamian political thought, however such a phrase is to be precisely defined, herein the focus is on manifestations of previous concepts that were adopted for the projection of political authority via the crafting of a systematic royal ideology.

Assyriologists typically define the long sixth century as beginning with the reign of Nabopolassar through the Babylonian revolts early in the reign of Xerxes (see below). As set within Mesopotamia itself, these parameters are fairly straightforward. They become more nebulous when considering the empire as a whole. The term generally encompasses the last decade or two (at least) of the Assyrian Empire through its fall in 609

---

2. Some examples of focused cultural studies include Kristin Kleber with Johannes Hackl, "*Dātu ša šarri*: Gesetzgebung in Babylonien unter den Achämeniden," *JANEBL* 16 (2010): 49–75; Caroline Waerzeggers, "The Babylonian Priesthood in the Long Sixth Century BC," *BICS* 54 (2011): 59–70; Michael Jursa, "Families, Officialdom, and Families of Royal Officials in Chaldean and Achaemenid Babylonia," in *Tradition and Innovation in the Ancient Near East*, ed. Alfonso Archi (Winona Lake, IN: Eisenbrauns, 2015), 597–606. Note also the chapters by Bonfiglio, Cooke, and Hamilton in this volume.

BCE; the span of the Neo-Babylonian Empire (ca. 626–539 BCE) and its contemporary powers the Medes, Lydians, and Egyptians; and the early Achaemenid period. Where one draws the end line of the early Achaemenid period also may vary. Historiographic periodization deserves a treatment in itself, especially for pedagogical purposes.

The Achaemenid Empire, as a historical period, has always been an outlier. In the classroom, it bursts onto the scene overwhelming the wider ancient Near East after centuries of Mesopotamian and Egyptian kingdoms stretching back to the third millennium; or shares time with—but, paradoxically, is entirely overshadowed by—late archaic and classical Greece; or sets the stage, as a foil, for the arrival of Alexander of Macedon and his singular but ephemeral achievement. The long sixth century by any definition does not run through most of the fifth. Whether one draws an end line for a variable, historiographic construct with Cyrus's conquest of Babylon in 539 BCE, his death in 530 BCE, the usurpation of Darius I in 522 BCE, or the reign of Xerxes (486–465 BCE) depends mainly on locus and is, in the end, somewhat arbitrary. For Mesopotamia, as noted above, the failed Babylonian revolts against Xerxes in 484 and their aftermath are a logical endpoint of the long sixth century, though the ramifications for Persian rule there—and a concomitant loss of status for Babylonian temples—continued to play out for some years thereafter.

The long sixth century—inevitably gravitating toward its beginning (the fall of Assyria) or its end (the rise of Persia)—runs some risk of overlooking the dominant power within that time frame, that is, Babylonia. Among the reasons why this happens, a main one is that Neo-Babylonian royal sources (mainly inscriptions) tend to focus much more on building works than on military campaigns or other deeds, around which a colorful narrative may be written.[3] Neo-Babylonian royal ideology shared

---

3. The apropos cliché still applies that Neo-Babylonian royal inscriptions are fewer in quantity and quality (with regard to the types of imperialistic and ideological information they convey) than their Neo-Assyrian counterparts. That cliché, though, overlooks the usefulness of some of the Babylonian material for these same questions; inter alia see Rocio Da Riva, *The Neo-Babylonian Royal Inscriptions: An Introduction* (Münster: Ugarit-Verlag, 2008), and Hanspeter Schaudig, "The Magnanimous Heart of Cyrus: The Cyrus Cylinder and Its Literary Models," in *Cyrus the Great: Life and Lore*, ed. M. Rahim Shayegan (Boston: Ilex/Center for Hellenic Studies, 2018), 67–91, especially for the reign of Nabonidus. For a historical review, see Michael Jursa, "The Neo-Babylonian Empire," in *Imperien und Reiche in der Weltgeschichte: Epochenübergreifende und globalhistorische Vergleiche*, ed. Sabine Fick (Wiesbaden: Harrassowitz,

some similarities with Neo-Assyrian, though it is testimony from the latter that is most often invoked, again, as much a quantitative feature of the extant evidence as anything else. Barring the important exception of Darius I's Bisitun inscription (inscribed ca. 520 BCE; see below), the typical content of Achaemenid royal inscriptions may be viewed as closer to the Babylonian model, in that they generally eschew accounts of military campaigns.

But such a generalization oversimplifies the issue. Assyrian influence was hardly lacking. Parallels between Assyrian and Achaemenid ideologies of kingship and imperialistic expression are pervasive; the main component of such was the centrality of the king in a universal empire.[4] By that is meant not merely the truism that the king is the focal point of the empire but that concepts of king and kingship are incorporated into an elaborate and systematically developed package of ideological expression, which included multiple mechanisms of application. The phenomenon goes beyond typological similarities. One may begin with an overarching comparison. Assyrian kings were Assur's representative on earth, while Achaemenid kings were Auramazda's representative on earth, and both positions were predicated on profound religiosity that encompassed the ultimate in prestige, power, and responsibility as the deity's chosen one.[5] Both kings were tasked with a mandate to uphold stability. This was a big job, parts of which involved providing for the people (e.g., through agricultural productivity), directing appropriate building works (e.g., the building or restoration of temples), ensuring justice, and maintaining—where necessary, imposing—order on the surrounding lands.

Assyrian annals are replete with narratives of conquest, as an extension of the imposition of order, supplying—if in embellished form—the official record of the king's exploits. These were often narrated in the first person. A direct echo of the Assyrian annals is manifest in Darius I's Bisitun inscription, which relays in stylized form his triumph

---

2014), 121–48, especially 121–22. Jursa includes a brief excursus on these very problems. Note Hamilton in this volume for further discussion on the problem of empire.

4. A phenomenon that goes back far earlier than the Neo-Assyrian period, all the way back to Sargon of Akkad; see below.

5. There are multiple variations and spellings of this deity's name in the modern literature, the most typical being "Ahuramazda." The spelling "Auramazda" is becoming more commonplace in the scholarly literature on the Achaemenid period, as a normalized rendering of the deity's name as spelled in Old Persian inscriptions as Auramazdā.

over multiple enemies (i.e., liars and rebels,[6] as described by Darius), such as the following:

> Darius the king proclaims: Then I left Babylon; I went to Media. When I arrived in Media, a town called Kunduru, in Media, there this Fravartish, who called himself king in Media, came with his army against me to join battle. Then we joined battle. Auramazda helped me; by the favour of Auramazda, I utterly defeated the army of Fravartish. Twenty-five days of the month Adukanaisha had gone—then we fought that battle.... Then this Fravartish fled with a few horsemen. A place called Raga, in Media, he went there. Then I sent an army in pursuit. Fravartish was seized; he was brought before me. I cut off his nose, ears and tongue, and tore out one eye. He was held in fetters at my palace entrance; all the people saw him. After that, I impaled him at Ecbatana; and the men who were his foremost followers, those I hanged at Ecbatana in the fortress. (DB §§31–32)[7]

With few exceptions, even such terse military narratives disappear after Darius I's reign. The humiliation of the defeated rebels prominent on the Bisitun relief becomes an anomaly; in Achaemenid monumental sculpture there are no further portrayals of humiliated enemies. The graphic punishments afflicted on enemies that find copious forerunners in the Assyrian annals and in the reliefs, for example, of Assurbanipal,[8] were eschewed by Darius after Bisitun. This was a conscious decision to place a different sort of emphasis on public display, both in sculpture and in inscriptions (and by extension, proclamations). Specific battles with specific enemies at specific times and places are replaced by generalized statements of royal dominion such as "king of this wide earth unto the far"[9] or

---

6. Punishment of rebels is a standard theme in Assyrian royal inscriptions, but liars were also implicated; see, e.g., Erle Leichty, *The Royal Inscriptions of Esarhaddon, King of Assyria (680–669 BC)*, RINAP 4 (Winona Lake, IN: Eisenbrauns, 2011), 203, ll. 20–25 (an inscription of Esarhaddon).

7. Translation from Amélie Kuhrt, *The Persian Empire: A Corpus of Sources from the Achaemenid Period* (London: Routledge, 2007), 145–46; note DB §52 for the full list of liars and rebels.

8. Two examples appear in John Malcolm Russell, *Writing on the Wall: Studies in the Architectural Context of Late Assyrian Palace Inscriptions* (Winona Lake, IN: Eisenbrauns, 1999), 177. For more on this aspect of Achaemenid messaging, see Bonfiglio in this volume.

9. The so-called *dahyu*-lists (of which seven survive from the reigns of Darius and Xerxes) enumerate specific places ruled, or that the kings claimed to rule. These

vague, stylized expressions of the king's imposition of order. Consider one of Xerxes's inscriptions from Persepolis:

> Xerxes the king proclaims: When I became king, there was among those countries one which was in turmoil. Afterwards Auramazda brought me aid; by the favour of Auramazda I defeated that country and put it in its proper place.... And there was something else, that had been done wrong, that too I put right. That which I have done, all that I have done by the favor of Auramazda. Auramazda brought me aid, until I had done the work. (XPh §4)[10]

The Persians followed, with some adaptation, Mesopotamian conventions of royal title. Epithets of the sort "great king" and "mighty king" (or as sometimes translated: "strong king") are ubiquitous in Assyrian inscriptions, though they are used by Neo-Babylonian kings as well.[11] The titles

---

lists also serve ideological purposes, and many elements of their interpretation are still debated. See Bruno Jacobs, "Achaemenid Satrapies," *Encyclopaedia Iranica*, online ed., 2011, https://tinyurl.com/SBL1735b; Pierre Briant, *From Cyrus to Alexander: A History of the Persian Empire*, trans. Peter T. Daniels (Winona Lake, IN: Eisenbrauns, 2002), 172–75; and Matt Waters, *Ancient Persia: A Concise History of the Achaemenid Empire, 550–330 BCE* (Cambridge: Cambridge University Press, 2014), 96–98.

10. Translation slightly modified from Kuhrt, *Persian Empire*, 305. The phrase "among those countries" alludes to the lengthy list of subject territories included earlier in the inscription; no specificity is given as to which country(ies) are meant, i.e., it is an intentionally timeless statement.

11. For the inscriptions of Cyrus at Pasargadae, most likely installed by Darius, see David Stronach, "On the Genesis of the Old Persian Cuneiform Script," in *Contribution à l'histoire de l'Iran: melanges offerts a Jean Perrot*, ed François Vallat (Paris: ERC, 1990), 195–203; Matthew Waters, "Darius and the Achaemenid Line," *AHB* 10 (1996): 13–15; Philip Huyse, "Some Further Thoughts on the Bisitun Monument and the Genesis of the Old Persian Script," *BAI* 13 (1999): 51–52; Briant, *From Cyrus to Alexander*, 63. For the Cyrus Cylinder, many translations are available; see Irving Finkel, ed., *The Cyrus Cylinder: The King of Persia's Ancient Proclamation from Babylon* (London: I. B. Tauris, 2013). For Nabopolassar, see Rocio Da Riva, *The Inscriptions of Nabopolassar, Amel-Marduk, and Neriglissar* (Berlin: de Gruyter, 2013), 71–72 (inscription C22) and commentary on ll. 2–4; Hayim Tadmor, "Nabopalassar and Sin-shum-lishir in a Literary Perspective," in *Festschrift für Rykle Borger zu seinem 65. Geburtstag am 24. Mai 1994*, ed. Stefan Maul (Groningen: Sytx, 1998), 355–56, on the titles of Neo-Assyrian kings, echoed by Cyrus in the Cyrus Cylinder. Note also Paul-Alain Beaulieu, *The Reign of Nabonidus, King of Babylon 556–539 B.C.* (New Haven: Yale University Press, 1989), 137–43 on Nabonidus and his attitude toward Assyrian kings.

have a long history, going back to the third millennium and the first pan-Mesopotamian dynasty, that of Sargon of Akkad.[12] Sargon and his grandson Naram-Sin left an indelible mark on Mesopotamian traditions; they became prototypes for the establishment of political and ideological matrices that persisted for centuries. These matrices were consciously adopted and adapted by the Persians at the end of the long sixth century, nearly two millennia later.

Surviving royal inscriptions securely attributable to Cyrus the Great are all from Babylonia—Babylon, Uruk, and Ur—and unsurprisingly follow Babylonian paradigms. Line 20 of the Cyrus Cylinder contains the formal presentation of Cyrus's Babylonian titles: "I am Cyrus king of the world, great king, strong king, king of Babylon, king of Sumer and Akkad, king of the four quarters."[13] Cyrus's royal inscription from Ur also contains the title "king of the world" (*šar kiššati*) and, as a display inscription, adds the further touch of having been inscribed with archaizing signs. The use of archaizing signs was a device adopted from Neo-Babylonian royal inscriptions that was meant to highlight a link to earlier times, another prestige marker linking these kings to a centuries-old stream of tradition. The discovery of Cyrus's inscriptions near the Esagila temple complex, though intended for the Imgur-Enlil wall, of Babylon, in the temple of Nanna-Suen at Ur, and in the Eanna temple complex at Uruk also followed age-old precedent. Many previous rulers, dating all the way back to Naram-Sin for the Eanna temple complex,[14] left dedications in these same spots. There was certainly advantage in continuing these political traditions in Babylonia, and for that matter it met an expectation.

The Cyrus Cylinder's longer excursus adheres to typically Mesopotamian patterns of rightful kingship. It describes Cyrus's selection by Marduk because of his righteousness; his concern for the welfare of Babylon; proper observance of cult and ritual; and his restoration of sanctuaries.[15] That Cyrus did all these things was no doubt true; they were neces-

---

12. The classic reference for attestations of Akkadian royal titles is Marie-Joseph Seux, *Epithetes royales akkadiennes et sumeriennes* (Paris: Letouzey et Ane, 1967).

13. Unless otherwise indicated, all translations herein are mine.

14. Andrew R. George has a list of kings who left inscriptions at the Eanna temple complex. See George, *House Most High: The Temples of Ancient Mesopotamia* (Winona Lake, IN: Eisenbrauns, 1993), 67–68.

15. Finkel, *Cyrus Cylinder*, 4–7 for translation, 130–33 for transliteration. Note Schaudig, "Magnanimous Heart of Cyrus," for the strong links to Babylonian tradition

sary components for any Babylonian ruler, let alone a foreign one who lacked any link to the previous dynasty, to legitimize his position. Lineage was also a key legitimizing factor, and Cyrus rehearsed his lineage back to Teispes, who, if in a direct line, was Cyrus's great-grandfather. The term that Cyrus used to describe Teispes, Akkadian *liblibbu*, may be translated as "great-grandfather" or as "descendant"; the translation chosen affects assessment of Cyrus's genealogy.[16] By listing his ancestors Cyrus reinforced the standard proclamation that he was of an "eternal lineage" (literally "eternal seed"—NUMUN *darû*) that had always exercised kingship: a long-standing Mesopotamian motif.[17]

Darius I began his first royal inscription, at Bisitun, with the titles great king, king of kings, king in Persia, and king of lands (DB §1).[18] Only

---

and, specifically, the inscriptions of Nabonidus. Nabonidus's inscriptions show greater affinity with Assyrian royal convention than his Neo-Babylonian predecessors, so it is a matter of interpretation whether Cyrus patterned his inscriptions on one or the other, or both. Nabonidus's were closer in time (and presumably more accessible), but this is a complex issue; see also below. See Jason M. Silverman, *Persian Royal-Judaean Elite Engagements in the Early Teispid and Achaemenid Empire: The King's Acolytes*, LHBOTS 690 (London: T&T Clark, 2020), and Caralie Cooke in this volume on Persian-period Yehud and the transmission of the biblical text via the (returned) Babylonian exiles.

16. *CAD* 9:179–81; Wouter F. Henkelman, "Cyrus the Persian and Darius the Elamite: A Case of Mistaken Identity," in *Herodot und das Persische Weltreich/Herodotus and the Persian Empire*, ed. Robert Rollinger, Brigitte Truschnegg, and Josef Wiesehöfer (Wiesbaden: Harrassowitz, 2011), 602–3 n. 71; Matt Waters, "Cyrus Rising: Reflections on Word Choice, Ancient and Modern," in Shayegan, *Cyrus the Great*, 26–45. Darius I mentions the same Teispes, labeled in literal, genealogical terms as his great-great-grandfather in DB §2. That iteration supports the translation of "great-grandson" for *liblibbu* in the Cyrus Cylinder with regard to Cyrus's genealogical relationship with Teispes.

17. *CAD* 21:89–97; Robert Rollinger, "Der Stammbaum des achaimenidischen Königshauses oder die Frage des Legitimität der Herrschaft de Dareios," *AMIT* 30 (1998): 193; Paul-Alain Beaulieu, "Nabopolassar and the Antiquity of Babylon," *ErIsr* 27 (2003): 2*; Matthew Stolper, "The Form, Language, and Contents of the Cyrus Cylinder," in *Cyrus the Great: An Ancient Iranian King*, ed. Touraj Daryaee (Santa Monica, CA: Afshar, 2013), 44–45. Darius uses the same expression in DB §4.

18. This is the order in the Old Persian and Elamite versions, but not in the Babylonian, which has his parentage (son of Hystaspes) first, then the epithets Achaemenid, king of kings, a Persian, king of Persia. Chul-Hyun Bae relays all the versions in transliteration and translation. See Bae, "Comparative Studies of King Darius's Bisitun Inscription" (PhD diss., Harvard University, 2001), 76–79.

"king in Persia" was not in the traditional lexicon of Mesopotamian royal titles, for obvious reasons.[19] These various superlative titles—Assyrian, Babylonian, or Persian—of course served to highlight the king's unique position: any other kings were subject to him, just as other lands even far beyond the core were subject to him. The centrality of the king radiated a universality of rule. A fundamental feature in Darius I's royal inscriptions, from Bisitun onward, is the threat posed by the Lie (Old Persian *drauga*), that is, falsehood. The implied opposition highlights the king's special status as a guardian of truth and guarantor of order, again, main components of his centrality to a stable and prosperous kingdom, and for that matter, cosmos. As described in the Bisitun inscription, when "the Lie became great" (as often translated, DB §10) it threatened to splinter the entire empire—all those who engaged in falsehood were by definition enemies of the king, rebels who must be destroyed. Untruths, disloyalty, and rebellion were affronts not just to the king but to the gods. This sentiment, if cast differently, also finds a home in earlier traditions. Neo-Assyrian kings applied the motif to treacherous underlings fomenting rebellion or to claims of pretenders, especially in instances of irregular succession to the throne, a practice that finds a direct echo in Darius's emphasis on those rebels he defeated as liars.[20] Darius's emphasis on the antithesis between right and wrong finds simple but compelling expression in his tomb relief, "I am not a friend of the man who is a follower of the Lie" (DNb §2), a sentiment echoed by Xerxes (XPl §2).

These aspects, centrality and universality, are manifest in other ways as well. The king's command of vast resources from far-flung territories meant that they could be marshaled for the construction of palaces and lush gardens. Sennacherib and other Assyrian kings tamed rivers and sur-

---

19. The title "king of lands" also frequently occurs after Persian kings' names in Babylonian administrative documents.

20. Kuhrt, *Persian Empire*, 143 and 504 for translations of the passages DB §10 and DNb/XPl §2. See Bruce Lincoln, *"Happiness for Mankind": Achaemenian Religion and the Imperial Project* (Leuven: Peeters, 2012), 213–17, with references on the nuances of translation of *drauga*. On the lie as a rhetorical strategy in Neo-Assyrian (and earlier) inscriptions and treaties, see Beate Pongratz-Leisten, "'Lying King' and 'False Prophet': The Intercultural Transfer of a Rhetorical Device within Ancient Near Eastern Ideologies," in *Ideologies as Intercultural Phenomena: Proceedings of the Third Annual Symposium of the Assyrian and Babylonian Intellectual Heritage Project*, ed. A. Panaino and G. Pettinato (Milan: Università di Bologna, 2002), 215–43.

mounted great distances to move this material, all of the finest quality and craftsmanship.²¹ The Achaemenids did likewise, just on a larger scale of dominion. The so-called foundation charter from Darius's palace at Susa is the exemplary testimonial:

> The cedarwood was brought from a mountain called Lebanon; the Assyrian people brought it as far as Babylon; from Babylon, the Carians and Ionians brought it as far as Susa; the *yaka*-wood was brought from Gandara and Carmania. The gold which was worked here was brought from Lydia [Sardis] and Bactria; the lapis lazuli and the carnelian which was worked here was brought from Sogdiana; the turquoise which was worked here was brought from Chorasmia. The silver and the ebony were brought from Egypt; the decoration, with which the walls were ornamented, was brought from Ionia; the ivory which was worked here was brought from Nubia, India and Arachosia. The stone columns which were worked here were brought from a village called Abiradu in Elam; the masons who crafted the stone were Ionians and Sardians. The goldsmiths who worked the gold were Medes and Egyptians; the men who worked the wood were Sardians and Egyptians; the men who crafted the bricks were the Babylonians; the men who decorated the wall were Medes and Egyptians. (DSf §9–13)²²

Similarly, as Sennacherib dedicated a lot of clay to record his creation of gardens and orchards for his palace—likewise manifestations of the extent of Assyrian rule—the Persians placed great priority on *paradeisoi* (a Greek word, presumably from Old Persian *paradayadā-* and Elamite *partetaš*).²³ The word is often translated as "paradises," from the Greek, and in the figurative sense the English connotation likely applied. These were, in fact, gardens or even parks or preserves of sometimes many acres, in which exotic plants and animals were cultivated for the enjoyment of the king

---

21. On Sennacherib's "palace without rival," see, e.g., A. Kirk Grayson and Jamie Novotny, eds., *The Royal Inscriptions of Sennacherib, King of Assyria (704–681 BC), Part 2*, RINAP 3/2 (Winona Lake, IN: Eisenbrauns, 2014), inscription 42 (51); John Malcolm Russell, *Sennacherib's Palace without Rival at Nineveh* (Chicago: University of Chicago Press, 1991).
22. Translation from Kuhrt, *Persian Empire*, 492.
23. As normalized after Roland G. Kent, *Old Persian: Grammar, Texts, Lexicon* (New Haven: Yale University Press, 1953), 195, translated "perhaps 'pleasant retreat'"; Rüdiger Schmitt. *Wörterbuch der altpersischen Königsinschriften* (Wiesbaden: Reichert, 2014), 225 (*paradai̯dā-*).

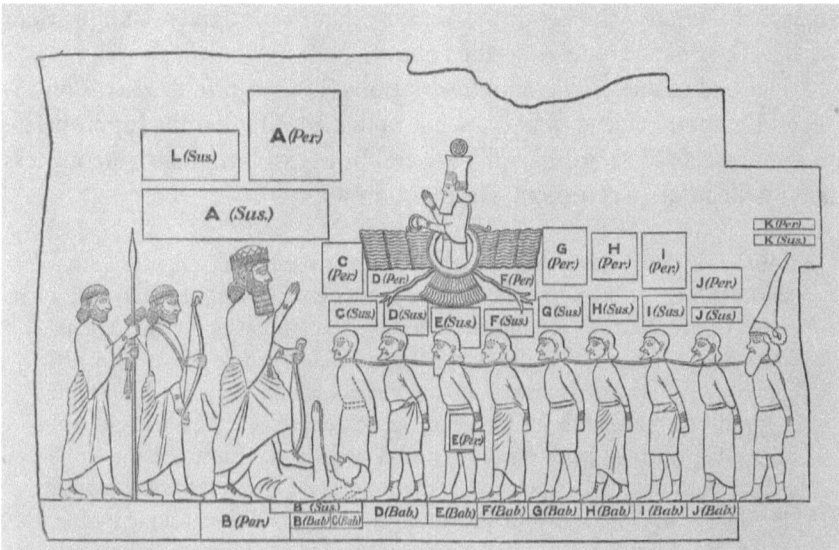

Fig. 8.1. Drawing of Bisitun Relief. Source: L. W. King and R. Campbell Thompson, *The Sculptures and Inscription of Darius the Great, on the Rock of Behistûn in Persia* (London: British Museum, 1907), pl. XIII. The capital letters indicate separate inscriptions, and the abbreviations Per., Sus., and Bab. stand for Old Persian, Susian (rather: Elamite), and Babylonian (Akkadian), respectively.

and elite, a spectacle of Achaemenid power. Archaeological evidence for such exists at Cyrus's Pasargadae, and there are numerous allusions in the literary record.[24]

The Persian portrayal—in both text and image—of the glorified king also finds numerous parallels from earlier Mesopotamian traditions. In

---

24. For Pasargadae, see inter alia Rémy Boucharlat, "Gardens and Parks at Pasargadae: Two 'Paradises'?," in *Herodot und das Persisiche Weltreich*, ed. Robert Rollinger, Brigitte Truschnegg, and Josef Wiesehöfer (Wiesbaden: Harrassowitz, 2011), 557–74; Boucharlat, "The 'Paradise' of Cyrus at Pasargadae, the Core of the Royal Ostentation," in *Bau- und Gartenkultur zwischen "Orient" und "Okzident": Fragen zu Herkunft, Identität und Legitimation*, ed. Joachim Ganzert und Joachim Wolschke-Bulmahn (Munich: Meidenbauer, 2009), 47–64; Boucharlat, "À propos de *paradayadām* et paradis perse: perpléxité de l'archéologue et perspectives," in *Des contrées avestiques à Mahabad, via Bisoton: études offertes en homage à Pierre Lecoq*, ed. Celine Redard (Paris: Recherches et Publications, 2016), 61–80. Kuhrt provides several excerpts from Greek and Roman texts, and one notable Elamite example from the Persepolis fortification archive (*Persian Empire*, 510–14).

image, the king is the central, or largest, figure in a given composition, such as the Bisitun relief described above.

Darius I in one of his tomb inscriptions (DNb) summarizes his physical and mental qualities and his sense of justice, all the things appropriate to the exercise of kingship. After several lines extolling his righteousness and intellectual discernment, Darius continues:

> Moreover this (is) my ability, that my body is strong. As a fighter I am a good fighter. At once my intelligence stands in its place. whether I see a rebel or not. Both by intelligence and by command at that time I regard myself as superior to panic, when I see a rebel just as when I do not see (one).... As a horseman I am a good horseman. As a bowman I am a good bowman, both on foot and on horseback. As a spearman I am a good spearman, both on foot and on horseback. These are the skills which Auramazda has bestowed upon me and I have had the strength to bear them. By the favour of Auramazda, what has been done by me, I have done with these skills which Auramazda has bestowed upon me. (DNb/XPl §2)[25]

This is about as strident as it gets beyond the recitation of standard titles, and in tenor closer to Neo-Babylonian kings' assertions of personal attributes.[26] Darius's and Xerxes's claims seem downright modest when compared to the megalomania manifest in some of the Neo-Assyrian inscriptions. Here is one of the shorter examples from Assurnasirpal II (884–858 BCE):

> Ashurnasirpal, great king, strong king, king of the world, king of Assyria ... valiant man who acts with the support of Ashur, his lord, and has no rival among the princes of the four quarters, marvelous shepherd, fearless in battle, mighty flood-tide which has no opponent, the king who subdued ... [a list of several regions follows].[27]

---

25. Translation from Kuhrt, *Persian Empire*, 504–5, also discussed above with *drauga*.

26. Parts of Nabopolassar's inscriptions are striking in their humility (somewhat ironically), with an implied humble origin—and that relative only to one born of a sitting king; see Jursa on Nabopolassar's origins ("Neo-Babylonian Empire," 124). Even the standard superlative epithets are not as much emphasized as piety and justice; see, e.g., Da Riva, *Inscriptions of Nabopolassar*, 62, 71.

27. Examples are legion, this one from A. Kirk Grayson, *Assyrian Rulers of the Early First Millennium BC I*, RIMA 2 (Toronto: University of Toronto Press, 1991), 301–2; cf. inscription 1 (p. 194) for an even more verbose version.

In all cases, Assyrian, Babylonian, and Persian, kingly qualities are conjoined with divine favor, selection, or blessing. In Achaemenid contexts, as per the norm, these recitations are prefaced (and sometimes suffixed) by an invocation and the standard Old Persian attribution, *vašnā Auramazdāhā* ("By the support [or will][28] of Auramazda ...").

In some instances in Neo-Assyrian texts, there is a not-so-subtle intonation of the kings' divine essence: having been created of divine material, the literal offspring of Ishtar, elevated to rank just below the warrior god Ninurta, or the very image of Enlil or Marduk. The interpretation of these unambiguously translated but seemingly contradictory assertions of the king's divine essence, if not outright divinity, is undergoing renewed scrutiny. Similar ambiguity with regard to the god-king relationship has been ascribed to some of Darius I's portrayals (in image, not text). However one interprets the phenomenon from the time of Darius, any manifestation of it, even if just experimental, may be traced to Assyrian precedents.[29]

---

28. Translation varies; see, e.g., Schmitt, *Wörterbuch*, 277 (with references); Waters "By All Means, Auramazda: Help, Support, and Protect the King," for *Contextualizing Iranian Religions in the Ancient World*, ed. M. Rahim Shayegan (Vienna: Verlag der Österreichischen Akademie der Wissenschaften, forthcoming).

29. For the Assyrians see Peter Machinist, "Kingship and Divinity in Imperial Assyria," in *Text, Artifact, and Image: Revealing Ancient Israelite Religion*, ed. Gary Beckman and Theodore Lewis (Providence: Brown University Press, 2006), 151–88; Irene Winter, "Touched by the Gods: Visual Evidence for the Divine Status of Rulers in the Ancient Near East," in *Religion and Power: Divine Kingship in the Ancient World and Beyond*, ed. Nicole Brisch (Chicago: University of Chicago Press, 2008), 75–102; Eckhart Frahm, "Rising Suns and Falling Stars: Assyrian Kings and the Cosmos," in *Experiencing Power, Generating Authority: Cosmos, Politics, and the Ideology of Kingship in Ancient Egypt and Mesopotamia*, ed. Jane A. Hill, Philip Jones, and Antonio J. Morales (Philadelphia: University of Pennsylvania Museum, 2013), 97–120. For Darius, see especially Margaret Cool Root, "Defining the Divine in Achaemenid Persian Kingship: The View from Bisitun," in *Every Inch a King: Comparative Studies on Kings and Kingship in the Ancient and Medieval Worlds*, ed. Lynette Mitchell and Charles Melville (Leiden: Brill, 2013), 23–65; and note Mark B. Garrison, "Beyond Auramazdā and the Winged Symbol: Imagery of the Divine and Numinous at Persepolis," in *Persian Religion in the Achaemenid Period*, ed. Wouter F. Henkelman and Celine Redard (Wiesbaden: Harrassowitz, 2017), 185–246; Matt Waters, "Darius I and the Greater Glory: Ambiguity in Representation and Relationship with the Divine," in *Art/ifacts and ArtWorks: Image, Object, and Aesthetics in the Ancient Near East*, ed. Karen Sonik (Philadelphia: University of Pennsylvania Press, forthcoming).

Mesopotamian and Persian kings typically shaped their image, projecting legitimacy, through the typical means: divine selection and favor as well as their royal lineage (embellished or fabricated, if necessary), but other conventions could be tapped. For example, the Neo-Assyrian king Sargon (r. 722–705 BCE) and his successors consciously modeled their rule on the kingship of Sargon of Akkad and his successors in the late twenty-fourth and twenty-third centuries. (This was hardly a new approach but one taken to an enhanced level by the Sargonid kings.) Likewise, Neo-Babylonian kings tied themselves to the heritage of the dynasty of Akkad; this was especially the case with Nabonidus, who took pains to find and restore inscriptions and artifacts from that time. One component of the Sargonic renaissance in the Sargonid period, and thereafter in the Neo-Babylonian and Achaemenid, was the compelling power of the motif of the infant exposed at birth (e.g., Moses), or of having a humble upbringing. Because one of its earliest attributions was to Sargon of Akkad, the motif has become labeled the "Sargon Legend" in modern literature.[30] We are confident that Sargon II of Assyria, Nabopolassar of Babylon, or Cyrus the Great of Persia were not commoners (quite the reverse), but the motif had great utility nonetheless and not just for those kings. For Cyrus, we must rely on the Greek tradition, mainly Herodotus and Ctesias for the legendary details of Cyrus's youth and upbringing. These Greek authors provide different takes on the subject: Herodotus (*Hist.* 1.107–123) has the infant Cyrus exposed, rescued, and initially raised by shepherds before discovery of his true identity, while Ktesias has Cyrus a completely self-made man, born in penury to ignoble parents: a bandit and a goatherd.[31] Both versions are beholden to the "Sargon Legend" of Mesopotamian tradition.

---

30. Note the seminal treatment of Brian Lewis, *The Sargon Legend: A Study of the Akkadian Text and the Hero Who Was Exposed at Birth* (Cambridge: ASOR, 1980). The adjective *Sargonic* is used in Assyriological literature to refer to Sargon of Akkad and his dynasty, while *Sargonid* is used to refer to the Neo-Assyrian king Sargon (II) and his successors Sennacherib, Esarhaddon, and Assurbanipal. See Amélie Kuhrt, "Making History: Sargon of Agade and Cyrus the Great of Persia," in *A Persian Perspective: Essays in Memory of Heleen Sancisi-Weerdenburg*, ed. Wouter F. Henkelman and Amélie Kuhrt, AH 13 (Leiden: Nederlands Instituut voor het Nabije Oosten, 2003), 354–55 on Nabonidus's (and Cyrus's) interest in the kings of Akkad. Despite Cyrus's intensive vilification of Nabonidus, their similarities often outweigh their differences.

31. Matt Waters, *Ctesias' Persica and Its Near Eastern Context* (Madison: University of Wisconsin Press, 2017), ch. 3 (especially for the Ctesian version).

There was also great store set by the continued reapplication of visual tropes, expressions of political thought via image. Darius I also harked back to late third-millennium models, including a motif adapted from Naram-Sin: defeating nine kings in one year.[32] Darius and his planners found direct inspiration for the Bisitun relief from the nearby relief of Anubanini dating almost two millennia earlier.[33] The Achaemenid king is portrayed in some sculptures as battling monsters, a standard image in the Mesopotamian visual lexicon, a vivid image of the king's import in defending order against the forces of chaos cast at a metaphorical, cosmic level.[34] Such portrayals are extensions of similar images such as the elaborate relief sequences of lion hunts adorning Assyrian palace walls.[35] The famous, but enigmatic, winged figure from Pasargadae provides a paradigmatic distillation of Mesopotamian—as well as Elamite and Egyptian—artistic influences coalesced into a highly symbolic, Persian conceptualization. Its full ramifications, however, are yet to be understood; in other words, it is unclear what the combined symbolism was meant to convey.[36]

---

32. On the wider connections manifest in the Bisitun relief, see Marian H. Feldman, "Darius I and the Heroes of Akkad: Affect and Agency in the Bisitun Relief," in *Ancient Near Eastern Art in Context: Studies in Honor of Irene Winter by Her Students*, ed. Jack Chang and Marian H. Feldman (Leiden: Brill, 2007), 265–93. On the one-year motif, see Waters with references to earlier literature (*Ancient Persia*, 73–74).

33. Note the important discussion in Margaret Cool Root, *The King and Kingship in Achaemenid Art: Essays on the Creation of an Iconography of Empire*, Acta Iranica 19, TM 9 (Leiden: Brill, 1979), 196–201.

34. Root, *King and Kingship*, 303–8 (including discussion on the identity and regalia of the hero and Neo-Assyrian influences). For sealings, see Mark B. Garrison and Margaret Cool Root, *Seals on the Persepolis Fortification Tablets, Images of Heroic Encounter*, OIP 117 (Chicago: Oriental Institute of the University of Chicago, 2001).

35. The bibliography here is enormous as well. Note Richard D. Barnett, *Sculptures from the North Palace of Assurbanipal at Nineveh (668–627 B.C.)* (London: British Museum Press, 1976); Barnett, Erika Bleibtreu, and Geoffrey Turner, *Sculptures from the Southwest Palace of Sennacherib at Nineveh* (London: British Museum Press, 1998); Russell, *Sennacherib's Palace* (valuable with its conjoined study of epigraphic material); Irene Winter, *On Art in the Ancient Near East*, vol. 1, *Of the First Millennium BCE*, CHANE 34/1 (Leiden: Brill, 2010), 1–184.

36. David Stronach, *Pasargadae: A Report on the Excavations Conducted by the British Institute of Persian Studies from 1961 to 1963* (Oxford: Oxford University Press, 1978), 47–50; Root, *King and Kingship*, 300–303, for seminal discussion of this figure, "whether it represents a syncretic deity, some metaphorical vision of an abstract idea of imperial domain, or a vision of Cyrus himself in a mythical aspect of ideal kingship" (303). The image has not been found in monumental form elsewhere, but note the

Fig. 8.2. Winged figure, Pasargadae. Courtesy of David Stronach.

The guardian figure is of Assyrian inspiration (e.g., the figure's wings), with Elamite robe and hairstyle, and an Egyptian crown. It is an internationalizing figure that, while clearly inspired by these other traditions, seems a uniquely Persian creation and has not been found outside this context at Pasargadae.

We have already encountered several instances previously where the king's special relationship with the gods has been noted. Divine favor, support, and, at times, active involvement in the king's engenderment, upbringing, elevation to the throne, and military success are ubiquitous in Mesopotamian royal inscriptions. The same applies, if in more abstract formulae, in the much smaller corpus of Achaemenid inscriptions as well. Auramazda was continuously invoked as the creator, the source of all that is good and right in the world, and the Achaemenid king's place as the guarantor of such on Auramazda's behalf is the ineluctable inference.[37] The invocations were reiterated by Darius I so many times that, for the modern reader, they can distract from the fundamental message of the royal inscriptions. The Assyrian and Babylonian traditions were distilled further into a purely Achaemenid form: abstract

---

parallel image on an Achaemenid seal impression. See Mark B. Garrison, Charles E. Jones, and Matthew W. Stolper, "Achaemenid Elamite Administrative Tablets, 4: BM 108963," *JNES* 77 (2018): 1–14.

37. See Lincoln, "Happiness for Mankind," for a comprehensive treatment, emphasizing a Mazdean interpretive milieu. Most scholars now avoid labeling the Achaemenids as Zoroastrians per se, as the discussion moves toward considering their import in the early stages of that religious tradition, preferring the term *Mazdean* or something similar. Note that the emphasis herein is on the royal inscriptions. Persian religion—however that is to be defined—was a much larger phenomenon. Several royal inscriptions refer to other gods (even if not identified) beyond Auramazda; see inter alia the contributions to Wouter F. Henkelman and Celine Redard, eds., *Persian Religion in the Achaemenid Period* (Wiesbaden: Harrassowitz, 2017).

to the point where, if an individual king did not name himself, we would often have no idea to whom to assign many inscriptions. This is not an accident, as these timeless features served to codify Achaemenid kingship as an institution.

To take an example, a prayer of Darius inscribed at Persepolis encapsulates many elements of these timeless formulae; leaving out the name, this inscription and its elements could apply to any Achaemenid king:

> Great is Auramazda, greatest of the gods—he made Darius king, he bestowed kingship upon him; by the favour of Auramazda Darius is king. Darius the king proclaims: This country, Persia, which Auramazda bestowed upon me, which is good, containing good horses, good men, by the favour of Auramazda and of me, Darius the king, it fears no one else. King Darius proclaims: May Auramazda bring me aid, together with all the gods; and may Auramazda protect this country from the army (of the enemy), from famine, from the lie! May there not come upon this country the army (of the enemy), famine, the lie! This I pray as a favour from Auramazda together with all the gods; this favour may Auramazda grant me together with all the gods. (DPd)[38]

The special relationship between king and god is also manifest in images, and the foremost example of such is the figure in winged disk offering support for and protection of the king. The winged disk (with or without figure) is another symbol with a long history; in Assyrian sculpture it is often identified as Assur or Shamash, and the winged disk itself finds its origins even earlier in Egyptian and Hittite iconography. For the Achaemenids, we again start with Darius and Bisitun, the relief sequence (see fig. 8.1) showing the prominent Darius triumphant over the prostrate Gaumata, flanked (behind) by two unlabeled attendants, and standing before a chain of other defeated rebels. The other key figure in the relief is the winged disk, clearly in special association with the king, and the figure within showing remarkable (and not coincidental) similarity to the portrayal of the king and mirroring the same hand gesture: barring the crowns, the figures are the same. While the winged disk appears in many forms in various contexts,[39] the

---

38. After Kuhrt, *Persian Empire*, 487.

39. Note the observations in Mark B. Garrison, "Visual Representation of the Divine and the Numinous in Achaemenid Iran: Old Problems, New Directions," in *Iconography of Deities and Demons*, electronic prepublication, 2009, https://tinyurl.com/SBL1735c, 38–40; Root, "Defining the Divine," 37–44. For a more recent over-

manifestation including the figure resembling the king is most prominent in Darius's relief at Bisitun and his tomb at Naqsh-i Rustam.

The connection between Darius and Auramazda does not end at the physical similarity in sculpture. Recent research has postulated an identification between god and king, especially in a Neo-Assyrian milieu. It is an ongoing question, and a controversial topic, how this idea—apparently not a consistent phenomenon through time in any case—may have carried over into the Achaemenid period. One important element from the Mesopotamian context is the *melammu*, a divine power exclusive to gods and kings, often associated with radiance.[40] At the risk of oversimplifying a complex phenomenon, this power, the *melammu*, finds a corollary in Elamite *kitin*, also a gods-given protection (or put differently, a shared divine essence and power) but one that also carries implications of active agency. While there is still much to unpack from this phenomenon and its Mesopotamian corollary, the idea was still viable in the Achaemenid period. It makes an appearance in an Elamite version of one of Xerxes's inscriptions from Persepolis, the so-called *daiva* inscription (XPh).[41] In line 31 of the Elamite version *kitin* is invoked by Xerxes as an instrument whereby the offending place of *daiva*-worship was destroyed and placed under an interdiction.

The Elamite legacy has proven no less significant than the Mesopotamian, perhaps more so. Simply based on geographical proximity, that is,

---

view with references to previous literature, see Garrison, "Beyond Auramazdā," 193–200. See also Bonfiglio in this volume.

40. *CAD* 10.2:9–12; Mehmet-Ali Ataç, "The *Melammu* as Divine Epiphany and Usurped Entity," in Chang and Feldman, *Ancient Near Eastern Art*, 295–313; Shawn Zelig Aster, *The Unbeatable Light: Melammu and Its Biblical Parallels* (Münster: Ugarit-Verlag, 2012).

41. See Wouter F. Henkelman, *The Other Gods Who Are: Studies in Elamite-Iranian Acculturation Based on the Persepolis Fortification Texts* (Leiden: Nederlands Instituut voor het Nabije Oosten, 2008), 364–71, for seminal treatment of this passage. Note Garrison for potential associations with the winged disk; and Christopher Tuplin's comments on Elamite *kitin*. See Garrison, "Visual Representation," 36–39; Tuplin, "The Justice of Darius: Reflections on the Achaemenid Empire as a Rule-Bound Environment," in *Assessing Biblical and Classical Sources for the Reconstruction of Persian Influence, History and Culture*, ed. Anne Fitzpatrick-McKinley (Wiesbaden: Harrassowitz, 2015), 89–90. Salvatore Gaspa postulates the *melammu* connection. See Gaspa, "State Theology and Royal Ideology of the Neo-Assyrian Empire as a Structuring Model for the Achaemenid Imperial Religion," in Henkelman and Redard, *Persian Religion*, 161; cf. Waters, "Darius I and the Greater Glory."

that the Elamites and Persians lived on the same ground, acculturation is hardly a surprise but, because of a variety of factors (e.g., the paucity of and difficulty with the extant evidence), the Elamite imprint is not always as evident. Thus, we do not yet fully appreciate on how many levels these intentional borrowings and reworkings of political thought—Assyrian, Babylonian, and Elamite—operated; understanding their full significance in the formulation of Achaemenid ideology and political thought, as well as their application, remains a work in progress. Several other political and institutional influences not discussed here have been treated in the literature: the provincial system and its governance; the land tenure system, especially as it relates to military organization and corvée obligations; the royal roads and messenger relays; deportations; *inter multa alia*.[42] And much remains to be done.

Beyond an accounting of continuities and influences lies the question as to how they were transmitted. With their defeat by the Medes and Babylonians, the Assyrians as a political power were swept away. How much, and to what extent, did any of the Assyrian palatial centers survive? How realistic is it to think that these no-longer-imperial centers—and the ideological messages they broadcast—could have served as viable models for Achaemenid successors roughly a century later during the final decades of the long sixth century? (This is not to imply that viewing the palatial centers was the only means of absorbing the ideological messages.) The Neo-Babylonian Empire—and its still-flourishing urban centers, temples, libraries, and scribal schools, which persisted even after Cyrus's conquest—of course would have served as a main conduit for Mesopotamian ideological traditions of all sorts: bureaucratic, literary, architectural, and sculptural. But how do we account for more distinctively Assyrian elements that carried through?

---

42. See Muhammad Dandamayev, "Assyrian Traditions during Achaemenid Times," in *Assyria 1995: Proceedings of the Tenth Anniversary of the Neo-Assyrian Text Corpus Project*, ed. Simo Parpola and Robert Whiting (Helsinki: Neo-Assyrian Text Corpus Project, 1997), 41–48. Examples abound and include Assyrian (and other) antecedents for the throne- and platform-bearers at Persepolis and Naqsh-i Rustam as well as the Persians kings' participation in an investiture ceremony at the temple of Nabû in Babylon, at least through the time of Cyrus and Cambyses (one of whom wore Elamite attire; Root, *King and Kingship*, 147–53). For discussion of the broken passage, see Andrew R. George, "Studies in Cultic Topography and Ideology," *BO* 53 (1996): 379–84.

Even if many questions about the earliest Persians in western and southwestern Iran remain unanswered at present, Assyrian influences on the Achaemenid system did not come out of a vacuum. The Persians were a known commodity to their neighbors for a few centuries before Cyrus, increasingly so in the documentation from the reign of Assurbanipal onward.[43] Another means of transmission, in my opinion a main one, would have resulted from the compelled presence—and implied eventual return—of royal hostages (or "guests," if one prefers a more neutral term) and their entourages at the Assyrian court. The case of Arukku, son of Cyrus of Parsumash (often identified with Cyrus the Great's grandfather, though this is disputed), offers one possibility.[44] Assurbanipal's annals are silent beyond Cyrus's submission and the delivery of his son Arukku to the Assyrian court, so we do not know Arukku's fate. But if he and his entourage had, potentially, years of experience with the Assyrian court, and then returned to Parsumash (i.e., Parsa, i.e., Persia in the strict sense of Fars in this period), one may imagine the formative impact this may have had on a nascent Persian kingdom in the late seventh and early sixth centuries, from which the Achaemenids eventually descended.

Nor need we rely on one hypothetical, if grounded, interchange. The phenomenon was not unique and played out consistently over time and among many peoples in the Assyrian Empire's orbit.[45] Beyond this, com-

---

43. Matthew Waters, "The Earliest Persians in Southwestern Iran: The Textual Evidence," *IrSt* 32 (1999): 99–107; Waters, "Cyrus Rising"; Robert Rollinger, "Zur Lokalisation von Parsu(m)a(š) in der Fārs und zu einigen Fragen der frühen persischen Geschichte," *ZA* 89 (1999): 115–39; Henkelman, "Cyrus the Persian," 597–606. This discussion leaves aside for the present context the complicated but formative process labeled ethnogenesis or acculturation of the Persians as the within the crucible of an originally Elamite region. See especially Pierre de Miroschedji, "La fin du royaume d'Anšan et de Suse et la naissance de l'Empire perse," *ZA* 75 (1985): 295–96.

44. The Cyrus, king of Parsumash, episode is recorded in two extant inscriptions, Prism H2 ii′ 7′–25′ and the so-called Ishtar temple inscription. See Rykle Borger, *Beiträge zum Inscriftenwerk Assurbanipals* (Wiesbaden: Harrassowitz, 1996), 191–92 and 280–81, respectively. Arukku is mentioned only in the prism inscription; see Matt Waters, "Parsumaš, Anšan, and Cyrus," in *Elam and Persia*, ed. Javier Álvarez-Mon and Mark Garrison (Winona Lake, IN: Eisenbrauns, 2011), 292–93.

45. A prime example is the exchange of Assyrian and Elamite royal children is referenced in ABL 918, published in Mikko Luukko and Greta Van Buylaere, *The Political Correspondence of Esarhaddon*, SAA 16 (Helsinki: Helsinki University Press, 2002), text 1 (p. xxi); cf. Matthew Waters, *A Survey of Neo-Elamite History*, SAAS 12 (Helsinki: State Archives of Assyria, 2000), 43–44. Note also Karen Radner, "After Eltekeh:

mercial interchange is another mechanism of transmission. As evident by recent analyses of the transition from Neo-Babylonian to Persian rule, many Babylonian institutions and enterprises continued as before—the most logical course, and a necessary one, for the new conquerors to attain and then maintain stability in that region. Far more difficult to track than to conceptualize, these mechanisms of interchange certainly would have played a role in transmission of ideas.

Only over time do we see a shift in Persian reliance on, or tolerance of, indigenous Babylonian elites and institutions continuing to wield great influence. The shift is most marked after the failed Babylonian revolts against Xerxes in 484 BCE. The ramifications of this watershed are still being analyzed, but for periodization purposes in Babylonia itself, Xerxes's reprisals and the changes implemented thereafter (e.g., increased Persian intrusiveness in Babylonian affairs) seem a more appropriate endpoint for the long sixth century.[46] What is just as intriguing, and even more elusive, are the means and mechanisms—the conscious choices and real-time situations—by which and why decisions were made for the placement, phrasing, and imaging of inscriptions, sculpture, and architectural works.

To consider one example, let us briefly return to the Cyrus Cylinder discussed above. This text, recall, is a document found in Babylon,[47] written by Babylonian scribes well-versed in centuries of tradition, and thus indebted to Babylonian norms and expectations. In line 43 of the cylinder, Cyrus—who must have given some level of approval for the cylinder's contents—explicitly noted that he saw an inscription of the Assyrian king Assurbanipal. Why Assurbanipal? There were undoubtedly several other

---

Royal Hostages from Egypt at the Assyrian Court," in *Stories of Long Ago: Festschrift für Michael D. Roaf*, ed. Heather D. Baker, Kai Kaniuth, and Adelheid Otto (Münster: Ugarit Verlag, 2012), 471–79.

46. Caroline Waerzeggers, "The Babylonian Revolts against Xerxes and the End of Archives," *AfO* 50 (2003/2004): 150–73; Michael Jursa, "The Transition of Babylonia from the Neo-Babylonian Empire to Achaemenid Rule," in *Regime Change in the Ancient Near East and Egypt: From Sargon of Agade to Saddam Hussein*, ed. Harriet Crawford (Oxford: Oxford University Press, 2007), 73–94; Jursa, "Factor Markets in Babylonia from the Late Seventh to the Third Century BCE," *JESHO* 57 (2014): 173–202.

47. Even if, as is evident, its message was propagated beyond the barrel cylinder foundation deposit, see John Curtis, *The Cyrus Cylinder and Ancient Persia: A New Beginning for the Middle East* (London: British Museum Press, 2013); and contributions to Finkel, *Cyrus Cylinder*.

deposits from other kings that would have been known or uncovered in the process of the wall's restoration.

The legacy of the Assyrian kings in Babylon is another topic. Assurbanipal, whatever virtues he may have displayed toward Babylonia, in 648 BCE was responsible for the sack and burning of the city at the end of a protracted siege and bitter war with his brother Shamash-shum-ukin—an event just over a century previous. It does not seem a stretch to assume that Assurbanipal left a controversial legacy there.[48] Despite the Persians' evident debt to their Assyrian predecessors, given the cylinder's Babylonian context, Assurbanipal seems an unusual choice for Cyrus's attention. There was, at some point in the composition and redaction process, a conscious choice made to include this reference to Assurbanipal, as opposed to any of the other kings, a multitude, who had left dedications there. We may speculate, but in the end we do not know why this choice was made. Such conscious choices reflect a significant outlay of resources—time, money, and effort—for the project in question. It is worth asking why a specific person or place, or a specific phrase, or a particular symbol was chosen for attention for reuse or for reconfiguration. The answers to such questions will reveal much about the continuity of political thought.

---

48. I discuss this issue further in "Ashurbanipal's Legacy," in *The Persian-Achaemenid Empire as a "World-System": New Approaches and Contexts*, ed. Touraj Daryaee and Robert Rollinger, PSPCAIH (Wiesbaden: Harrassowitz, forthcoming).

Remembering the Future: Prophetic Literature's Archives of Exile and Judah's Social Memory in the Persian Era

Ian D. Wilson

The ultimate focus of this essay is exile and its representations in prophetic literature. But in the course of thinking about exile, I would also like to make some programmatic observations about the prophetic books themselves and their social function in ancient Judah (i.e., Yehud). Remembering the prophets—that is, reading the books that archived prophetic messages of old—would complicate understandings of exile and its outcomes in contemporary Judean life. But such complications would effectively balance the complex representations of exile as an experience of the Judean *past*. Understandings of past exile and understandings of its present and future outcomes would thus work in concert in the construction of Judean social identity and historical consciousness, in the Persian period (the so-called postexilic era). This would be the case for exile, as it would be for other major complexes of thought that spanned the ancient discourse now contained in the Hebrew Bible.

I dedicate this essay to my friend and colleague Diana Edelman, who, at the time of this writing (July 2019), has just retired from a long and fruitful career in the academy. Her work has had a significant influence on my thinking about these issues. Many thanks to Diana for her scholarship and friendship. I would also like to thank those who provided feedback on the essay as I worked on it. I presented a draft at the 2018 Annual Meeting of the Society of Biblical Literature in Denver, in the Exile in Biblical Literature program unit. There I received helpful questions and comments from many in attendance, including Pamela Barmash and Mark Hamilton. Thanks to Pamela, Mark, and the audience in Denver for their thoughtful contributions to the work.

"Exile," Robert Carroll once wrote, "is a biblical trope.... It should be treated as a fundamental element in the cultural poetics of biblical discourses."[1] Exile is everywhere in the Bible, from beginning to end. In that same essay, in the midst of demonstrating how truly ubiquitous exile is in biblical texts, Carroll jokes, "Read Genesis in order to save yourself reading the rest of the Hebrew Bible."[2] It is true. All the major themes are there, right at the beginning: exile and exodus, being cast out of a homeland, journeying from one place to another at YHWH's command, dispersion of family and people and resources, and YHWH's acting as eventual gatherer and provider, the deity behind the scenes of it all.

Of course, Carroll's tongue-in-cheek comment about reading Genesis betrays the fact that exile means many things in the Bible's texts, and it betrays his own nuanced approach to the issue, which is to consider the trope in its many discursive settings and to see what these poetics might reveal to us about the cultural history, and historical culture, of the texts.[3] Genesis only introduces readers to the complex of exile. It is only by taking in the diverse perspectives of, say, Deuteronomy, Ezekiel, Ezra-Nehemiah, and Chronicles, among many other texts, that one can realize the conceptual complexity involved in the narrative of leaving one land and entering into another, of leaving one life behind in order to forge a new one. And it is only by keeping Genesis in mind, as a statement of human and Israelite

---

1. Robert P. Carroll, "Exile! What Exile? Deportation and the Discourses of Diaspora," in *Leading Captivity Captive: "The Exile" as History and Ideology*, ed. Lester L. Grabbe, JSOTSup 278, ESHM 2 (Sheffield: Sheffield Academic, 1998), 64.

2. Carroll, "Exile! What Exile?," 63.

3. For an overview of Carroll's extensive work on the topic, see Robert P. Carroll, "Exile, Restoration, and Colony: Judah in the Persian Empire," in *The Blackwell Companion to the Hebrew Bible*, ed. Leo G. Perdue (Malden, MA: Blackwell, 2001), 102–16. See also Adele Berlin, "The Exile: Biblical Ideology and Its Postmodern Ideological Interpretation," in *Literary Construction of Identity in the Ancient World*, ed. Hanna Liss and Manfred Oeming (Winona Lake, IN: Eisenbrauns, 2010), 341–56. Berlin takes aim at "postmodernists" and "minimalists" who would deny the Babylonian exile any historicity, as that exile is described in biblical texts. She also critiques the work of Carroll, which does not deny the historicity of a Babylonian exile per se but which argues that "a small exclusivist minority" imposed an "ideology of return" on those who had not gone into exile (Berlin, "Exile," 347). Berlin thus takes issue with how Carroll interprets exile as hegemonic ideology among Judeans in Jerusalem in the Persian period. But her general approach to the texts—that is, her basic understanding of exile and its ideological complexities in the literature—is actually complementary to Carroll's.

beginnings, that one can fully appreciate the challenge of understanding what exile would mean for the ancient Judean writers and readers of this literature. In other words, in order to understand how the concept of exile would function in ancient Judean literary culture and social memory, how it would produce meanings in its original social contexts, we should follow the work of Carroll and others who take holistic approaches to the discourse, examining the variety of possible meanings that were available to ancient readers and how those meanings might have worked together to inform social life.[4]

Given that exile is such a central concept in Judean literature, it is remarkable (at least from our modern perspective) that the literature's understandings of the concept are so diverse, that it contains so many different voices concerning exile. The multivocality of many ancient Judean texts, on the one hand, speaks to their long compositional history. On the other hand, the fact that various voices were preserved in individual texts, and that these voices were collated with certain and sometimes diverse narrative aims, also says something about the mindset of those who received the texts in antiquity.[5] Here I focus on the latter. I approach prophetic literature from the perspective of its primary reading community, emphasizing the fact of its diversity as initially received within Persian-era Judah, and asking what this diversity might tell us about Judean society and its literary interests in exile past and present.[6]

To think about exile (and other major complexes) in prophetic literature is also to think about empire and its effects. Empire was the political context in which Judah's exile occurred and in which it was remembered. The books that now reside in the Hebrew Bible took shape in the wake of Assyrian, Babylonian, and Persian imperialism in the ancient Near East. Judean society was just a small part of a much larger, multinational, and politically interconnected world.

---

4. For another example of a holistic approach to exile in biblical discourse, see David M. Carr, *Holy Resilience: The Bible's Traumatic Origins* (New Haven: Yale University Press, 2014), 91–140.

5. David Jobling, *1 Samuel*, Berit Olam (Collegeville, MN: Liturgical Press, 1998), 19.

6. For a more detailed discussion of this kind of approach, see Ian D. Wilson, *Kingship and Memory in Ancient Judah* (New York: Oxford University Press, 2017), 5–17. See also Pamela Barmash's essay in this volume, which addresses the book of Ezra in this regard.

In the days of Babylonian and then Persian rule especially, when Jerusalem and its environs were slowly recovering from the devastations of Babylonian campaigning, the province of Yehud was something of a backwater in a sea of empire. The province's entire population was thirty thousand at best, perhaps much lower, and within that population only a very small percentage were responsible for fostering and maintaining literary culture.[7] This tightly knit group of literati, as it were, fostered discourse about the Israelite and Judean past within this larger landscape of empire. And, even though the imperial center was hundreds upon hundreds of miles away, empire was ever present. Jerusalemites, for example, did not have to travel to Persepolis to take in the glories of Persia; they could walk just a short distance to Ramat Raḥel, which was likely the local seat of Persian rule and which contained luxuries (e.g., its garden) unmatched elsewhere in the province.[8] Moreover, the Achaemenid rulers of the empire propagated the idea of a "common destiny" between themselves and the ruled, between center and periphery, thus creating a sense of sociocultural and political interrelatedness and stability throughout the empire; so it was possible that those in Judah would look on the great kings of Persia and their empire with some admiration.[9]

---

7. On Yehud's population, see, e.g., the different perspectives in Charles E. Carter, *The Emergence of Yehud in the Persian Period: A Social and Demographic Study*, JSOTSup 294 (Sheffield: Sheffield Academic, 1999); Oded Lipschits, *The Fall and Rise of Jerusalem* (Winona Lake, IN: Eisenbrauns, 2005); Oded Lipschits and Oren Tal, "The Settlement Archaeology of the Province of Judah," in *Judah and the Judeans in the Fourth Century B.C.E.*, ed. Oded Lipschits, Gary N. Knoppers, and Rainer Albertz (Winona Lake, IN: Eisenbrauns, 2007), 33–52; Oded Lipschits, "Persian Period Finds from Jerusalem: Facts and Interpretations," *JHebS* 9 (2009): article 20, https://doi.org/10.5508/jhs.2009.v9.a20; and Israel Finkelstein, "Persian Period Jerusalem and Yehud Rejoinders," in *Focusing Biblical Studies: The Crucial Nature of the Persian and Hellenistic Periods; Essays in Honor of Douglas A. Knight*, ed. Jon L. Berquist and Alice Hunt, LHBOTS 544 (New York: T&T Clark, 2012), 49–62. See also Lisbeth S. Fried in this volume.

8. See, e.g., Oded Lipschits et al., "Palace and Village, Paradise and Oblivion: Unravelling the Riddles of Ramat Raḥel," *NEA* 74 (2011): 2–49; Oded Lipschits, Yuval Gadot, and Dafna Langgut, "The Riddle of Ramat Raḥel: The Archaeology of a Royal Persian Period Edifice," *Transeu* 41 (2012): 57–79; and Diana V. Edelman, "City Gardens and Parks in Biblical Social Memory," in *Memory and the City in Ancient Israel*, ed. Diana V. Edelman and Ehud Ben Zvi (Winona Lake, IN: Eisenbrauns, 2014), 115–55.

9. See Josef Wiesehöfer, "Achaemenid Rule and Its Impact on Yehud," in *Texts, Contexts and Readings in Postexilic Literature: Explorations into Historiography and Identity Negotiation in Hebrew Bible and Related Texts*, ed. Louis Jonker, FAT 2/53 (Tübingen: Mohr Siebeck, 2011), 171–85; Jason M. Silverman, *Persian Royal-Judean*

Yet the realities of imperial domination and its potential to destroy loomed large in Judean life. The area's political and economic capital had shrunk dramatically since the days when Judah and its neighbors had their own indigenous monarchies. Urban life in Judah had essentially collapsed since then, and much of the area remained in ruins after Babylon's conquests. The experience of empire, and of exile and forced migration within it, was foundational to Judeans' understandings of their place in the world, of how they got there, and of where they might go from there.[10]

Prophetic literature, I argue in this essay, was key to Judah's social remembering in that historical context. The prophetic book, as a genre that came into its own in the Persian period,[11] appears to have been

---

Elite Entanglements in the Early Teispid and Achaemenid Empire: The King's Acolytes, LHBOTS 690 (London: T&T Clark, 2020), 5–15. Silverman, in particular, emphasizes the variety of experiences Judeans would have had throughout the Near East, under Persian rule. In Judah and in Jerusalem itself, however, as both Wiesehöfer and Silverman argue, Judeans would have benefited both politically and socially from aligning with the Persian elite, thus seeking to maintain universal "peace" via the great king's divinely sanctioned rule and authority.

10. For further discussion of the social and economic experience of Judean exile and return under Persian rule, see Fried in this volume.

11. On the emergence and production of prophetic books in this era, see, e.g., Michael H. Floyd, "The Production of Prophetic Books in the Early Second Temple Period," in *Prophets, Prophecy, and Prophetic Texts in Second Temple Judaism*, ed. Michael H. Floyd and Robert D. Haak, LHBOTS 427 (New York: T&T Clark, 2006), 276–97; Diana V. Edelman, "From Prophets to Prophetic Books: The Fixing of the Divine Word," in *The Production of Prophecy: Constructing Prophecy and Prophets in Yehud*, ed. Diana V. Edelman and Ehud Ben Zvi (London: Equinox, 2009), 29–54; Martti Nissinen, *Ancient Prophecy: Near Eastern, Biblical, and Greek Perspectives* (Oxford: Oxford University Press, 2017), 150–62. To be clear, by saying that the prophetic book "came into its own" during the Persian period, I am not suggesting that prophetic texts were nonexistent before that time. Biblical scholarship has long demonstrated that some material in the Bible's prophetic literature comes from an era prior to the rise of the Neo-Babylonian and Persian empires (e.g., much of Hosea, and the so-called First Isaiah, inter alia). From the Iron Age Levant, too, there are the eighth-century BCE plaster texts from Tell Deir ʿAlla, on the eastern side of the Jordan valley, for example, which perhaps mentioned the "scroll"/"book" (ספר) of Balaam the seer. For the texts and bibliography, see Martti Nissinen with Choon-Leong Seow and Robert K. Ritner, *Prophets and Prophecy in the Ancient Near East*, ed. Peter Machinist, WAW 12 (Atlanta: Society of Biblical Literature, 2003), 207–12. The reading of ספר is usually taken for granted in scholarship, but see Jo Ann Hackett, *The Balaam Text from Deir ʿAllā*, HSM 31 (Chico, CA: Scholars Press, 1984), 31. Hackett comments

something like a literary archive, an organized collection of speeches and visions associated with a particular personage from the past. And these literary archives served to remember the future. In other words, prophetic books provided means to access past imaginings of possible futures. As such, this literature would play a key role in Judean readers' negotiation of dissonance in their remembering of exile (and exoduses from lands of exile) under imperial rule. By complicating the imagining of exile and its outcomes in a community's past, the reading of prophetic texts would enable ongoing debate about the significance of the concept for the community going forward. This thesis, I argue, makes a contribution to our understandings of how central concepts such as exile would function specifically in Judean literary culture in the Persian period, and it also makes a contribution to our general knowledge of the processes of social remembering in Near Eastern antiquity.

Prophetic Literature's Metageneric and Archival Functions

Elsewhere I have argued at length that we should reconsider the generic interrelationship between the historiographic and the prophetic in ancient Judah.[12] Prophetic literature is composed of ancient written texts, texts that were meant to be read and consulted on an ongoing basis in their context. These texts have a keen sense of possible futures, of course, but they

---

that the reading is not entirely certain. Such a "scroll" or collection, if that is indeed what is referenced in the Deir ʿAlla texts, might have been a generic precursor to the kind of prophetic literature we know from the Bible. However, it was only in the Persian period that the prophetic book emerged as a fully fledged generic category in its own right, with its own particular literary features—both structural and thematic. On this issue, I agree with Nissinen, who writes, "The perspective of the advanced (but not 'final') literary form of *all prophetic books* includes the destruction of Jerusalem, the subsequent diaspora or 'exile,' and the socio-religious developments of the Second Temple period" (*Ancient Prophecy*, 151, emphasis added).

12. See Wilson, *Kingship and Memory*, esp. chs. 5–6. To be clear, when I draw parallels between historiography and prophetic writings, my goal is not to make claims about the historicity of the texts' contents. To me, questions of historicity (e.g., Was Jeremiah a real person in the kingdom of Judah at the turn of the sixth century BCE?) and questions of genre and its import in a given sociocultural context (e.g., What does the book of Jeremiah tell us about how Persian-period Judean society imagined its past?) are two different kinds of issues. One can research the latter without necessarily addressing the former. See also Ian D. Wilson, *History and the Hebrew Bible: Culture, Narrative, and Memory*, BRPBI 3.2 (Leiden: Brill, 2018), esp. 34–42.

are primarily writings about the past, as ancient Judeans understood it, and about the work of social actors in that past. Their contents are largely concerned with group identity formation and maintenance vis-à-vis the group's relationship with its deity in past time, and so—as texts that were read and consulted repeatedly—they most certainly contributed to social remembering within the communities that read them. Thus, the texts share features with historiography, which gives them a kind of metageneric character, but they are not histories per se.[13] The texts would have been formative for a kind of historical consciousness and thought even though they did not present formal historical narratives. They were something in between, recording messages of old and contributing to a sense of history without formalizing the story. We should think of the prophetic book, therefore, as a kind of archive of speech and vision, as something that would contribute to historical thought in an intentionally organized fashion, but without fully forming such thought.[14]

---

13. See Megan Bishop Moore, "Writing Israel's History Using the Prophetic Books," in *Israel's Prophets and Israel's Past: Essays on the Relationship of Prophetic Texts and Israelite History in Honor of John H. Hayes*, ed. Megan Bishop Moore and Brad E. Kelle, LHBOTS 446 (New York: T&T Clark, 2006), 23–36. On the metageneric characteristics of prophetic literature, see, e.g., Carol Meyers and Eric Meyers, "The Future Fortunes of the House of David: The Evidence of Second Zechariah," in *Fortunate the Eyes That See: Essays in Honor of David Noel Freedman*, ed. Astrid B. Beck et al. (Grand Rapids: Eerdmans, 1995), 207–22, esp. 210; Ehud Ben Zvi, *Signs of Jonah: Reading and Rereading in Ancient Yehud*, JSOTSup 367 (London: Sheffield Academic, 2003), 80–98; James R. Linville, "Mythoprophetics: Some Thoughts," in *History, Memory, Hebrew Scriptures: A Festschrift for Ehud Ben Zvi*, ed. Ian D. Wilson and Diana V. Edelman (Winona Lake, IN: Eisenbrauns, 2015), 403–15; Wilson, *Kingship and Memory*, 223–34.

14. See Michael H. Floyd, "New Form Criticism and Beyond: The Historicity of Prophetic Literature Revisited," in *The Book of the Twelve and the New Form Criticism*, ed. Mark J. Boda, Michael H. Floyd, and Colin M. Toffelmire, ANEM 10 (Atlanta: SBL Press, 2015), 17–36. Floyd argues that the compilers of prophetic books were, in some sense, historiographers. His argument is based on the idea that prophetic literature had its generic roots in oracle lists, that is, in organized collections of prophecies that Judean scribes associated with a particular personage. In making such lists, scribes "imaginatively elaborated on the records of a prophet from the past" (Floyd, "New Form Criticism," 34). See also Walther Eichrodt, *Ezekiel: A Commentary*, trans. Cosslett Quin, OTL (Philadelphia: Westminster, 1970), 18–22; Nissinen, *Ancient Prophecy*, 150–62. I agree with Floyd but would like to utilize different terminology. On the whole I find the concept of *archive* to be more productive than that of *list*, for thinking about prophetic literature's generic functions in antiquity. List making

That said, not all archives are created equal, and this reality is apparent in the variety of organization one finds in prophetic literature. Ezekiel, for example, is rather meticulously organized and structured with a chronological framework and relatively precise dating of material.[15] Jeremiah seems haphazard and thrown together with less attention to detail, at least in comparison to Ezekiel.[16] Also, our modern concept of an archive is of course anachronistic in relation to the ancient Levant. The Judeans did not have archives such as those that national museums, state governments, or local interest groups have today.[17] To be sure, Judeans had libraries or collections of texts—ranging from mundane economic records to arcane literary works—held in individual locales, what we might call "textual deposits."[18] But it is debatable whether these were anything like the Greek ἀρχεῖον, the home and record of official legal power, or like any of the other official record houses in the ancient world. In any case, the concept of archive, as it has been theorized in recent years, can be productive for thinking about prophets as written texts in their ancient Judean context, as loci of power and sources of recorded and ordered information, sources that would inform possible futures by accounting for the past.

---

and archiving, generally speaking, have much in common. How one organizes a list affects how readers interact with the list, as Floyd demonstrates in his study. Likewise, an archive's organization affects how one interacts with it. The term *archive*, however, at least in our contemporary usage, specifically relates to the issue of understanding the past and to the preservation and organization of certain records for the study of history. Thus I find it to be more helpful for discussions of how ancient Judean readers (and writers) would interact with the prophetic books. For additional discussion, see Ian D. Wilson, "Ezekiel as Written Text: Archiving Visions, Remembering Futures," in *Oxford Handbook of the Book of Ezekiel*, ed. Corrine Carvalho (Oxford: Oxford University Press, forthcoming).

15. See, e.g., Tyler D. Mayfield, *Literary Structure and Setting in Ezekiel*, FAT 2/43 (Tübingen: Mohr Siebeck, 2010).

16. On the organization and structure of Jeremiah, see, e.g., Carly L. Crouch, *An Introduction to the Study of Jeremiah* (London: T&T Clark, 2017), 11–37.

17. On archives and their usages in the modern era, see, e.g., Terry Cook, "What Is Past Is Prologue: A History of Archival Ideas since 1898, and the Future Paradigm Shift," *Archivaria* 43 (1997): 17–63; Cook, "Evidence, Memory, Identity, and Community: Four Shifting Archival Paradigms," *ArchS* 13 (2013): 95–120.

18. Reinhard G. Kratz, *Historical and Biblical Israel: The History, Tradition, and Archives of Israel and Judah*, trans. Paul Michael Kurtz (Oxford: Oxford University Press, 2015), 135. See also Jacqueline S. Du Toit, *Textual Memory: Archives, Libraries and the Hebrew Bible* (Sheffield: Sheffield Phoenix, 2011).

Jacques Derrida, via his deconstructive readings of Sigmund Freud, argues that the archive is at once a place where authority is held and from whence it comes; the archive recalls order and imposes it, conserves power and institutes it.[19] In other words, archives organize and preserve what has come before, but they do so with the result of fostering possibility. One of Freud's most famous texts, notices Derrida, hints at this archival function, when, in *Civilization and Its Discontents*, the psychoanalyst observes that, while it seems he is saying nothing new, he is in fact reassessing what has come before in order to rechart the course of analytic theory and its doctrine of the drives.[20] Freud has gone to his own archive, so to speak, for a fresh perspective.

Similarly, Laura Carlson Hasler argues that archives both preserve and represent a community's collective remembering; they contain the materials that foster ongoing recollection and, at the same time, they stand for the fact of social memory in that context.[21] She argues, too, that the work of archiving can be a productive analogy for thinking about the formation of Judean literary texts.[22] She writes, "When we interpret scribal practice in terms of archiving, the acts and aesthetics of collection may become vital literary strategies in their own right."[23] Examining Ezra 4, for example, Carlson Hasler suggests that what appears to be literary fragmentation (sometimes attributed to poor or sloppy composition and editing) may actually represent acts of intentional and structured literary collection. "If read as an archival structure as well as a narrative," comments Carlson

---

19. See Jacques Derrida, *Archive Fever: A Freudian Impression*, trans. Eric Prenowitz (Chicago: University of Chicago Press, 1996), esp. 1–3, 7–8.

20. See Sigmund Freud, *Civilization and Its Discontents*, trans. David McLintock, GI 19 (New York: Penguin Books, 2004), 68.

21. See Laura Carlson Hasler, "Writing in Three Dimensions: Scribal Activity and Spaces in Jewish Antiquity," in *Scribes and Scribalism in Social Context*, ed. Mark Leuchter (London: T&T Clark, forthcoming); Carlson Hasler, *Archival Historiography in Jewish Antiquity* (New York: Oxford University Press, 2020). Many thanks to Dr. Carlson Hasler for sharing her work with me in advance of its publication. See also Pernille Carstens, "The Torah as Canon of Masterpieces: Remembering in Archives," in *Cultural Memory in Biblical Exegesis*, ed. Pernille Carstens, Trine Bjørnung Hasselbalch, and Niels Peter Lemche, PHSC 17 (Piscataway, NJ: Gorgias, 2012), 309–23, esp. 312.

22. See also Eva Mroczek, *The Literary Imagination in Jewish Antiquity* (New York: Oxford University Press, 2016), 15 and passim.

23. Carlson Hasler, "Writing in Three Dimensions."

Hasler, "the optics of textual accumulation become integral to the literary achievements of these texts."[24] There are several issues here that can inform our understanding of prophets as written texts in ancient Judah.

Like an archive, the prophetic book provided for its Judean readers a catalogued or intentionally organized record of literary artifacts (and again, some of them are catalogued better than others). Like archives, these texts played a role in a kind of historiographical process, but they were not the end products of any such process. The texts were meant to be read, reread, continuously consulted—researched, so to speak—for fresh insights concerning the past's role in shaping things to come (e.g., Hos 14:10; Sir 38:34b–39:3). As the archive contributes to historical thought and historiographical pursuits in our day, so prophetic literature would contribute to knowledge of the past, and the continual reshaping and application of such knowledge, in its day.

Prophetic literature's job, however, was not to offer a critical assessment of the past's various conflicting narrative possibilities, a task that historians today frequently call their own. Its purpose was simply to represent and make apparent those possibilities inherent in Judah's past time, as they were revealed through the deity's messages to his people, and as they might have ongoing import for those people. Within prophetic literature, the deity's ultimate rule and authority over Israel (and the world) are never questioned, of course, but problematic aspects of the people's past existence in relation to the deity—exodus, monarchy, exile, temple, priesthood, and so on—are repeatedly laid bare, with a variety of possible future outcomes in view. In this way, Judeans would perceive themselves holding a source of divine information and power in an imperial world that afforded them little real political and economic power. Like archives, which contain various records and literary artifacts in order to maintain and even promote their collective significance, prophetic literature would preserve Israel's past and its variety—as Judean society understood it—thus remembering and promoting Israel's future possibilities.

Social Remembering in Ancient Judah

All that said, how would the reading of prophetic literature inform the processes of Judean social remembering? To situate my argument concerning

---

24. Carlson Hasler, "Writing in Three Dimensions."

prophetic archives and representations of exile within the broader landscape of Judean culture, here I offer a few comments on social memory as it would relate to the literature. Take Davidic kingship as a prime example.[25] It has long been observed that there are different ideas about the Davidic dynasty, its victories and failures, its hopes and disappointments, preserved in the books of the Hebrew Bible. Again, these texts are clearly multivocal. The book of Samuel, for instance, promises that the dynasty will be established "forever" (עַד עוֹלָם; 2 Sam 7:13, 16) and the book of Kings presents David as the royal benchmark, Israel's prototypical ruler.[26] Still, the dynasty comes to an end that one might call embarrassing, with the last Judahite monarch ironically elevated to a position of status in Babylon, not in Jerusalem, and under the aegis of a less than noteworthy Babylonian king (2 Kgs 25:27–30).[27]

Typically, tightly knit societies tend not to allow such multivocality to stand. It is remarkable that a community like the one in Persian Judah, in the early years of the Second Temple, would maintain such ambiguous accounts of a central figure and institution such as David and his dynasty. The processes of social remembering tend to minimize options, tend to focus on a single great hero or a single villain responsible for a given course of events.[28] It is therefore striking that Davidic kingship carries a thoroughgoing ambiguity in Judean narratives about the past. This fact becomes less surprising, however, if we take into account Judean prophetic imagination. For Judean readers, prophetic books would stand with feet in both the monarchic past and the postmonarchic present, but they were nevertheless oriented toward an imminent future. In these texts we find a myriad of images concerning Davidic kingship, its effects and outcomes.

Taking only the book of Isaiah, for example, we find future images in which a kind of superhuman Davidide reigns as YHWH's regent (e.g., Isa 11:1–5), in which Davidic kingship is democratized, as it were (e.g., Isa

---

25. See also Wilson, *Kingship and Memory*, 131–81.

26. See Alison L. Joseph, *Portrait of the Kings: The Davidic Prototype in Deuteronomistic Poetics* (Minneapolis: Fortress, 2015); and Joseph, "Who Is like David? Was David like David? Good Kings in the Book of Kings," *CBQ* 77 (2015): 20–41.

27. See Ian D. Wilson, "Joseph, Jehoiachin, and Cyrus: On Book Endings, Exoduses and Exiles, and Yehudite/Judean Social Remembering," *ZAW* 126 (2014): 521–34.

28. See Barry Schwartz, "Collective Forgetting and the Symbolic Power of Oneness: The Strange Apotheosis of Rosa Parks," *SPQ* 72 (2009): 123–42.

55:3–5), and in which Davidic kingship plays no apparent role whatsoever (e.g., Isa 2:2–4).[29] We also find an image of the Persian ruler Cyrus acting in a David-like role, as YHWH's anointed shepherd-king, restoring Jerusalem and its temple (Isa 44:24–45:8)—an image that seems to contradict Deuteronomy's legal precedent for kingship in Israel (Deut 17:14–20).[30] Similar discursive contributions are found in the books of Jeremiah, Ezekiel, Hosea, and Micah.[31] As Ehud Ben Zvi has put it, prophetic books often delineate "a horizon of an ideal future by suggesting a kind of dialogue among different and yet related images of that future."[32] In accomplishing this horizon of related images, prophetic literature would provide a balancing effect in Judean social remembering. The multivocality of the prophetic future would enable and maintain multivocality in the historiographic past, and vice versa. Just as Judean discourse does not know what to do with kingship in the past, it cannot decide on kingship's future, whether that kingship is Davidic, foreign, or otherwise. Thus, as counterintuitive as it may seem, incertitude is the ballast that would have achieved some sense of unity in Judean social remembering. It is the one feature that would stand on both sides of the temporal divide, in readings of Judah's past and of its future.

Kingship discourse is one example of these mnemonic processes. Exodus is another, as Pamela Barmash has convincingly shown. She writes, "Part of the potential of the Exodus lies in its multidimensionality."[33] It is

---

29. The bibliography relating to kingship (Davidic or otherwise) in Isaiah is, of course, extensive. For an overview of the texts and issues, see, e.g., Hugh G. M. Williamson, *Variations on a Theme: King, Messiah and Servant in the Book of Isaiah* (Carlisle: Paternoster, 1998).

30. Blurring the identities of Cyrus and David is one way that Judean readers could have understood Cyrus as a kind of Israelite, thus qualifying him for Israelite kingship in accord with Deuteronomy's expectations and ultimately promoting Persian rule over Judah. See Ian D. Wilson, "Yahweh's Anointed: Cyrus, Deuteronomy's Law of the King, and Yehudite Identity," in *Political Memory in and after the Persian Empire*, ed. Jason M. Silverman and Caroline Waerzeggers, ANEM 13 (Atlanta: SBL Press, 2015), 325–61. For a broader discussion of Second Isaiah's discourse within the Persian context, see Silverman, *Persian Royal-Judean Elite Entanglements*, 108–17.

31. See Wilson, *Kingship and Memory*, 182–222.

32. Ehud Ben Zvi, *Micah*, FOTL 21B (Grand Rapids: Eerdmans, 2000), 103; see also 88–94.

33. Pamela Barmash, "The Exodus—Central, Enduring, and Generative," in *Exodus in the Jewish Experience: Echoes and Reverberations*, ed. Pamela Barmash and W. David Nelson (Lanham, MD: Lexington Books, 2015), x.

represented as an event in the distant past, but one that will always have ongoing significance. The narrativity of the exodus, a story that is foundational and heroic but also open-ended (after all, the future success of the people in the promised land is never secured or certain), would lend itself to many different readings and interpretive applications, in different contexts.

Psalm 78, for example, proposes to "gush forth with riddles from antiquity" (v. 2). אביעה חידות מני־קדם, the psalmist states, in order to ensure that future generations of Israel will know the wonders of YHWH. The text then begins its account with the divine marvels of the exodus: the splitting of the sea, the guidance of cloud by day and fire by night, and the flowing of water from rock. In the course of its story, it compares God's sinful people to the bowmen of Ephraim (v. 9), and it ends, tellingly, with David the shepherd tending his people with care and skill. The psalm thus uses exodus as history "to amplify the ideology of the Davidic monarchy in the southern kingdom and to heighten the excoriation of the northern kingdom," as Barmash puts it.[34] Isaiah 40–55 does something similar: it contains numerous allusions to the exodus and draws on the narrative of exodus to describe the eventual restoration of YHWH's people. But, unlike Ps 78, this Isaiah passage replaces David with a foreign ruler, the Persian Cyrus, as mentioned above.

Other prophetic texts have different takes. Hosea, for example, presents the exodus as the crucial link between YHWH and his people (Hos 9:10; 11:1). It utilizes the exodus as a point of reference for understanding the current status of YHWH and Israel's relationship. The people are special, because YHWH brought them out of Egypt; but the book emphasizes that the deity can also send them back there if they fail him (Hos 8:13; 9:3; 11:5). Amos, too, highlights the special relationship between YHWH and Israel, making reference to the exodus (Amos 3:1–2). But later the book challenges the uniqueness of Israel's exodus experience, calling into question whether the Israelites are really any different from the Ethiopians, Philistines, or Arameans, whom the deity also brought from one place to another (Amos 9:7). Barmash's study clearly demonstrates how psalms and prophetic texts present an array of exodus images, how they "use the Exodus as a means of promoting alternate events and ideologies."[35] In this

---

34. Pamela Barmash, "Out of the Mists of History: The Exaltation of the Exodus in the Bible," in Barmash and Nelson, *Exodus in the Jewish Experience*, 7.

35. Barmash, "Out of the Mists," 7. See also Barmash's discussion of Ezra and the return in this volume.

way, the images both draw on and reinforce the exodus story's open-endedness and multidimensionality.

A close look at some of the major tropes of ancient Judean literature—kingship and exodus, for example—reveals a number of positions that stand in tension with one another. These tensions would exist on both sides of the temporal divide between past and future, from the perspective of readers in the Persian era. Accounts of the past offer no clear outcomes. Was kingship a good thing or a bad thing? Where exactly did the exodus lead the people, both literally and figuratively? And so on. Visions of the future, too, present a horizon of possibilities for how those past events and issues might affect the community as it forges ahead. From a sociological perspective this is perhaps curious. But it makes sense if we consider understandings of the past and understandings of the future as two sides of a scale, so to speak, balancing each other in Judean discourse. And it is the genre of prophetic literature that enabled this balancing act. The prophetic book was archival in function. Reading it would provide the opportunity and resources for drawing on the past in order to understand future possibilities, and to understand the deity's role in the people's ongoing story. But reading such literature, in and of itself, would provide no straightforward paths to understanding. In the same way, archives today do not simply tell one how it was; they preserve artifacts in order to foster the possibility of history.

Remembering Exile with Prophetic Imagination

Within Judean literature, we find many examples of how representations of the past and of the future have a mutually reinforcing effect on each other. This is true for texts concerning kingship, as it is for those concerning the exodus. It is also true for texts concerning exile, which, of course, is the other side of exodus. To quote Carroll again, "Any journey out of the land or out of a country is equally a journey into a different land or country (it is a zero sum game). So *exodus equals exile or deportation* and vice versa."[36] Much like kingship and exodus, exile and its meanings and purposes are manifold in Judean literary discourse. Exile is both necessary punishment, as in Deut 28, and an opportunity for cleansing land and people, as in Lev 26. It is a kind of new beginning, as in Haggai and parts

---

36. Carroll, "Exile! What Exile?," 63, emphasis original.

of Zechariah, Ezra-Nehemiah, and Chronicles (with each of those texts offering different perspectives, of course). Yet it is a never-ending state of existence, as the "night visions" of Zech 1–8 suggest and as Genesis implies from the get-go—part of being human is to be exiled from the garden.[37]

Martien Halvorson-Taylor writes, "At each juncture, the redactors who shaped the canon highlighted exile not only to reinforce its historical importance, but further to sharpen and reshape the memory of it as a formative and definitive experience. This is one of the ways that exile endures, as a context that makes scripture make sense."[38] With this statement in mind, my concluding comments here are meant to reinforce the thesis outlined above, about social remembering and prophetic literature in ancient Judah, and thus to inform our knowledge of Judean literary culture and thought in general.

Exile, as already stated, is there at the very beginning of the human story in the Hebrew Bible, and for ancient Judean readers, in the wake of multiple forced migrations and in the context of Persian imperial rule, it would be understood as a fundamental aspect of human identity. To be human is to be forced out of the garden, with everything that that migration would entail. More specifically, exile was thought to be written into the people of Israel's foundational texts, into the divine instruction given to and communicated by Moses. Both Lev 26 and Deut 28, for example, divinely dictate exile to come, sparing the reader none of the atrocities that go along with human conquest and capture. So, in the end, the narrative of first Assyrian and then Babylonian subjugation, which plays out in Judah's historiographical literature, is a fait accompli.

The question here is, finally, what would all this mean for Judean readers who were reflecting on exile past and exile present? One way to specify the question would be to ask: Who is "in" and who is "out"? Who counts among the people of YHWH in the wake of such experiences? Leviticus 26 sets a *torah*-precedent for the question, when in verses 39–45

---

37. On Zech 1–8 see, e.g., Martien Halvorson-Taylor, *Enduring Exile: The Metaphorization of Exile in the Hebrew Bible*, VTSup 141 (Leiden: Brill, 2011), 165–98. On exile as essential to human identity and experience in Judean discourse, see, e.g., James R. Linville, "Myth of the Exilic Return: Myth Theory and the Exile as an Eternal Reality in the Prophets," in *The Concept of Exile in Ancient Israel and Its Historical Contexts*, ed. Ehud Ben Zvi and Christoph Levin, BZAW 404 (Berlin: de Gruyter, 2010), 295–308.

38. Halvorson-Taylor, *Enduring Exile*, 199.

it is said that a certain number of survivors will "atone for their iniquity" (ירצו את־עונם; vv. 41, 43) and the deity will remember the covenant with their ancestors.[39]

If we look to the prophetic books, the Judean archives of remembered futures—as I have presented them above—we find an array of possible answers as to who constitutes this group.[40] In general, prophetic literature, like other genres of text in the Bible, tends to link Israelite identity with the experience of exile; that is, to be Israel is to be or to have been in exile, especially exile in Babylon.[41] Prophetic texts, again like other biblical texts, also tend to draw on the narrative and themes of the exodus in order to define the exilic experience. The book of Isaiah, for example, repeatedly refers to and appropriates tropes found in the Song of the Sea (Exod 15:1–21; cf. Isa 10:5–12:6; 43:1–44:5; 51:9–11; 63:7–14), thus evoking for its Persian-era readers a sense of liminality with respect to geography, time, and the processes of atonement and redemption.[42] Similarly, Hosea—with its references to the exodus (e.g., Hos 8:13; 9:3, 10; 11:1, 5; also discussed above) and its onomastic metaphors of rejection and restoration (e.g., Hos 2:25)—fuses the interrelated ideas of going into exile

---

39. Julius Wellhausen famously argued that Lev 26 is a kind of prophetic text composed after the Babylonian exile. See Wellhausen, *Prolegomena to the History of Ancient Israel* (New York: Meridian, 1957), 380–84. The text shares language with Ezek 34, though Ezek 34:23–30 ties the people's restoration to a Davidic shepherd to come. For a recent discussion of the Leviticus text, see, e.g., Reinhard Müller, "A Prophetic View of the Exile in the Holiness Code: Literary Growth and Tradition History in Leviticus 26," in Ben Zvi and Levin, *Concept of Exile*, 207–28. It is worth noting, too, that Deut 28—the other Torah text that deals with exile—does not mention any possibility of atonement and restoration. That text has well known and much-discussed parallels with Assyrian treaties, and so does not imagine any hope for those who would break their covenant with the deity (see Halvorson-Taylor, *Enduring Exile*, 25–31).

40. See, e.g., Ehud Ben Zvi, "Inclusion in and Exclusion from Israel as Conveyed by the Use of the Term 'Israel' in Post-monarchic Biblical Texts," in *The Pitcher Is Broken: Memorial Essays for Gösta W. Ahlström*, ed. Steven W. Holloway and Lowell K. Handy, JSOTSup 190 (Sheffield: Sheffield Academic, 1995), 95–149; also John Kessler, "Images of Exile: Representations of the 'Exile' and 'Empty Land' in Sixth to Fourth Century BCE Yehudite Literature," in Ben Zvi and Levin, *Concept of Exile*, 309–51.

41. Ben Zvi, "Inclusion in and Exclusion from Israel," 95–100.

42. See Ian D. Wilson, "The Song of the Sea and Isaiah: Exodus 15 in Post-monarchic Prophetic Discourse," in *Thinking of Water in the Early Second Temple Period*, ed. Ehud Ben Zvi and Christoph Levin, BZAW 461 (Berlin: de Gruyter, 2014), 123–47.

and overcoming exile.[43] Again, the two—exile and exodus, going out and coming in—work in tandem in a kind of zero-sum game. Indeed, one so-called distinctive feature of Israelite identity, as represented in a variety of biblical statements, is the people's ongoing status as outsiders, despite any specific geographic locale in which they might reside or to which they might be headed.[44] This thoroughgoing identification with outsider status makes sense, of course, given that Genesis presents a fundamental aspect of human existence as being cast out from one's place of origin. Within this larger conceptual framework for Israelite (and human) identity, prophetic literature makes statements about the status of YHWH's people that range from the very general to the more particular, from the global to the local, and from the *golah* to those who would remain in the land of Judah.

Parts of Isaiah and Zechariah (e.g., Isa 41:8–10; Zech 8:7–8), for example, imagine a gathering of groups from a variety of lands from here to there, without always specifying where those lands might be.[45] These texts, on account of their generality, represent a more inclusive vision of who constitutes God's people in the wake of exile. But other texts have very specific ideas about who is "in" and who is not. The classic example is Jer 24, with its metaphor of good figs and bad figs, which distinguishes between the exiles of 597 BCE and those who would remain in Jerusalem with King

---

43. See Ehud Ben Zvi, *Social Memory among the Literati of Yehud*, BZAW 509 (Berlin: de Gruyter, 2019), 294–303.

44. See Peter Machinist, "The Question of Distinctiveness in Ancient Israel," in *Essential Papers on Israel and the Ancient Near East*, ed. Frederick E. Greenspahn (New York: NYU Press, 1991), 420–42, esp. 432.

45. Hence the real confusion over whether Isa 40–55 was penned in Babylonia or in Judah. There is a general consensus in scholarship that this portion of Isaiah contains texts composed in Babylonia. However, the many references to "coastlands" (איים), for example (40:15; 41:1, 5; 42:4, 12, 15; 49:1; 51:5), seem out of place for a Babylonian context, as do texts such as 41:9 and 44:23, which imply a completed return from exile. See Joseph Blenkinsopp, *Isaiah 40–55*, AB 19A (New Haven: Yale University Press, 2002), 197. See also Hans M. Barstad and Lena-Sofia Tiemeyer, both of whom situate the composition of these texts in Judah. See Barstad, *The Babylonian Captivity of the Book of Isaiah: "Exilic" Judah and the Provenance of Isaiah 40–55* (Oslo: Novus, 1997); Tiemeyer, *For the Comfort of Zion: The Geographical and Theological Location of Isaiah 40–55*, VTSup 139 (Leiden: Brill, 2011). For a recent discussion that ultimately situates the composition in Babylonia, see Hugh G. M. Williamson, "The Setting of Deutero-Isaiah: Some Linguistic Considerations," in *Exile and Return: The Babylonian Context*, ed. Jonathan Stökl and Caroline Waerzeggers, BZAW 478 (Berlin: de Gruyter, 2015), 253–67.

Zedekiah (see Jer 21:8–10; 29:16–17). It sees no hope for those who would remain, including, it seems to imply, those who would eventually go into Babylonian exile in 586 BCE.⁴⁶ So, in Jer 24 at least, not all who will go to Babylon share equal status, thus complicating any general idea that the experience of exile in Mesopotamia is essential to Israelite identity. Ezekiel 11 has a similar message, favoring the exiles of 597, although it is not so categorical in its condemnation of others—it focuses on the deity's eventual restoration of the *golah* without necessarily damning those who remained at any given time. But elsewhere in that same book, in Ezek 33, remainees are given no quarter. There YHWH states,

> As I live, surely those who are in the waste places shall fall by the sword; and those who are in the open field I will give to the wild animals to be devoured; and those who are in strongholds and in caves shall die by pestilence. I will make the land a desolation and a waste, and its proud might shall come to an end; and the mountains of Israel shall be so desolate that no one will pass through. Then they shall know that I am YHWH, when I have made the land a desolation and a waste because of all their abominations that they have committed. (Ezek 33:27–29, after NRSV)

Ezekiel 33 thus clearly condemns those who would remain in the land. Yet, in other texts, certain groups among the *golah* are shown no mercy. Jeremiah, perhaps ironically, rails against those who would go to Egypt to escape the Babylonians (Jer 42:1–22), before being taken to Egypt himself (Jer 43:6)—a position that supports the general preference for exile in Babylon as opposed to Egypt, and one that stands in tension with more inclusive texts that imagine a gathering of YHWH's people from all lands. Prophetic literature thus paints a multidimensional picture of diaspora and exile and the status of YHWH's people in the wake of these experiences. To quote John Kessler, who provides a good survey of these issues and the related texts, the concept of exile is "a composite image, a cord made of many distinct strands."⁴⁷

One way to think about this diversity of views is to situate the different texts diachronically, with each representing different understandings

---

46. See Robert P. Carroll, who discusses the "puzzling features" of Jeremiah's understandings of the attacks and deportations of both 597 and 586 BCE. See Carroll, *Jeremiah: A Commentary*, OTL (London: SCM, 1986), 483–84.

47. Kessler, "Images of Exile," 348.

at different times.⁴⁸ But another way to approach the issue is to focus on the question of why readers and writers in Judah, within the context of imperial domination, allowed this diversity to remain in the discourse. Why did Judeans maintain the multivocality of their traditions? Why did they hold so many ideas in tension with one another, sometimes within individual texts? Jeremiah, for example, is something of a quagmire when it comes to its thoughts on exile, and that is only one book.⁴⁹ Kessler, noted above, presents what is perhaps the majority view. He states that the literati of Judah "saw themselves as inscribers of sacred texts" and that, since the deity's knowledge was thought to surpass any human knowledge, there was no reason to question what would be perceived as inconsistency or even contradiction."⁵⁰ In other words, from the Judean perspective, these texts had come from YHWH, so it was best to leave them alone, just to wait and see how it would all work out. Christoph Levin has put it this way, that Judean literati had a "reverent attitude" and "saw themselves as in duty bound to preserve the religious tradition in all its variety, and to pass it on unchanged."⁵¹

To be sure, there is truth in these statements. Judean literati undoubtedly revered these texts, and they revered the divinity believed to be the texts' ultimate source. But there was more going on in ancient Judah. Halvorson-Taylor's work on exile, Barmash's work on exodus, and my own work on kingship—to mention again some of the examples I discuss above—each demonstrates that there are thoroughgoing ambivalences within these Judean literary artifacts. Scribes in Judah preserved and read these ambivalences not simply out of reverence, but because they were also ambivalent about these issues themselves in their particular social context. There are apparent tensions and even contradictions in the texts because there were tensions and contradictions in the mindsets that initially received and subsequently maintained them, to riff again on the phras-

---

48. See the work of Halvorson-Taylor (e.g., *Enduring Exile*), who tracks the development of the exile motif during the Second Temple period, and also that of Jill Middlemas. See, e.g., Middlemas, "Prophecy and Diaspora," in *The Oxford Handbook of the Prophets*, ed. Carolyn J. Sharp (New York: Oxford University Press, 2016), 37–54.

49. See Carroll, *Jeremiah*, 483–84; also Mark Leuchter, *The Polemics of Exile in Jeremiah 26–45* (Cambridge: Cambridge University Press, 2008); Leuchter, "Jeremiah: Structure, Themes, and Contested Issues," in Sharp, *Oxford Handbook of the Prophets*, 171–89, esp. 178–80.

50. Kessler, "Images of Exile," 350.

51. Christoph Levin, "Introduction," in Ben Zvi and Levin, *Concept of Exile*, 10.

ing of David Jobling.[52] Put very simply, social remembering draws on the shared past to make sense of a shared present, and the present simultaneously provides a framework for viewing that shared past. In the early Second Temple period, in the era of Persian (and eventually Hellenistic) imperial dominance, the jury was still out on exile, and thus Judean society required an imagination that could embrace multiple possibilities for understanding its present circumstances. Prophetic literature—received as the archives of the prophets of old—was that imagination.

---

52. Jobling, *1 Samuel*, 19.

Bibliography

Abernethy, Andrew T. "Eating, Assyrian Imperialism, and God's Kingdom in Isaiah." Pages 35–50 in *Isaiah and Imperial Context: Isaiah in the Times of Empire*. Edited by Andrew T. Abernethy, Mark G. Brett, Tim Bulkeley, and Tim Meadowcroft. Eugene, OR: Wipf & Stock, 2013.

———. "Feasts and Taboo Eating in Isaiah: Anthropology as a Stimulant for the Exegete's Imagination." *CBQ* 80 (2018): 393–408.

Ackroyd, Peter R. *Exile and Restoration: A Study of Hebrew Thought of the Sixth Century B.C.E.* Philadelphia: Westminster, 1968.

Akee, Randall, and Maggie R. Jones. "Immigrants' Earnings Growth and Return Migration from the U.S.: Examining Their Determinants Using Linked Survey and Administrative Data." NBER Working Paper Series, 2019. #25639.

Albertz, Rainer. *Israel in Exile: The History and Literature of the Sixth Century B.C.E.* Translated by David Green. SBLStBL 3. Atlanta: Society of Biblical Literature, 2003.

Alexander, Jeffrey C. *Trauma: A Social Theory*. Cambridge: Polity, 2012.

Amiran, Ruth, and Ze'ev Herzog. *Arad*. Tel Aviv: Tel Aviv University Press, 1997.

Andersen, Francis I., and David Noel Freedman. *Micah*. AB 24E. New York: Doubleday, 2006.

Andrews, D. K. "Yahweh the God of the Heavens." Pages 45–57 in *The Seed of Wisdom: Essays in Honour of Th. J. Meek*. Edited by William Stuart McCullough. Toronto: University of Toronto Press, 1964.

Arneth, Martin. *"Sonne der Gerechtigkeit": Studien zur Solarisierung der Jahwe-Religion im Lichte von Psalm 72*. BZABR 1. Wiesbaden: Harrassowitz, 2000.

Assmann, Jan. *Cultural Memory and Early Civilization: Writing, Remembrance, and Political Imagination*. New York: Cambridge University Press, 2011.

Aster, Shawn Zelig. *Reflections of Empire in Isaiah 1–39.* ANEM 19. Atlanta: SBL Press, 2017.

———. *The Unbeatable Light: Melammu and Its Biblical Parallels.* Münster: Ugarit-Verlag, 2012.

Ataç, Mehmet-Ali. "The *Melammu* as Divine Epiphany and Usurped Entity." Pages 295–313 in *Ancient Near Eastern Art in Context: Studies in Honor of Irene Winter by Her Students.* Edited by Jack Chang and Martin H. Feldman, Leiden: Brill, 2007.

Bae, Chul-Hyun. "Comparative Studies of King Darius's Bisitun Inscription." PhD diss., Harvard University, 2001.

Barkay, Gabriel. "Batei hakevurot shel yerushalayim bimei habayit harishon" [The necropoli of Jerusalem in the First Temple period]. Pages 233–70 in *Sefer yerushalayim: Tekufat hamikra* [The history of Jerusalem: the biblical period]. Edited by Shmuel Aḥituv and Amichai Mazar. Jerusalem: Yad Yitzhak ben Zvi, 2000.

———. "Hakever uvet hamegurim bihudah bitkufat habarzel hasheni: Hashlakhot hehevratiyot" [Burial caves and dwellings in Judah during the Iron Age II: sociological sspects]. Pages 96–102 in *Tarbut homerit, hevrah ve'idiologiyah: Kivunim hadashim be'arkhei'ologiyah shel eretz Yisrael* [Material culture, society and ideology: new directions in the archaeology of the land of Israel]. Edited by Aren M. Maeir and Avi Faust. Ramat-Gan: Bar-Ilan University Press, 1999.

———. "Kevarim ukevurah bihudah bitkufat hamikra" [Burial caves and burial practices in Judah in the Iron Age]. Pages 96–164 in *Kevarim venohagei kevurah be'eretz Yisrael be'et ha'atikah* [Graves and burial practices in Israel in the ancient period]. Edited by Itamar Singer. Jerusalem: Yad Yitzhak ben Zvi, 1994.

Barmash, Pamela. "At the Nexus of History and Memory: The Ten Lost Tribes." *AJSR* 29 (2005): 207–36.

———. "The Exodus—Central, Enduring, and Generative." Pages vii–xiv in *Exodus in the Jewish Experience: Echoes and Reverberations.* Edited by Pamela Barmash and W. David Nelson. Lanham, MD: Lexington Books, 2015.

———. "Out of the Mists of History: The Exaltation of the Exodus in the Bible." Pages 1–22 in *Exodus in the Jewish Experience: Echoes and Reverberations.* Edited by Pamela Barmash and W. David Nelson. Lanham, MD: Lexington Books, 2015.

Barnett, Richard D. *Sculptures from the North Palace of Assurbanipal at Nineveh (668–627 B.C.).* London: British Museum Press, 1976.

Barnett, Richard D., Erika Bleibtreu, and Geoffrey Turner. *Sculptures from the Southwest Palace of Sennacherib at Nineveh*. London: British Museum Press, 1998.

Barstad, Hans M. "After the 'Myth of the Empty Land': Major Challenges in the Study of Neo-Babylonian Judah." Pages 3–20 in *Judah and the Judeans in the Neo-Babylonian Period*. Edited by Oded Lipschits and Joseph Blenkinsopp. Winona Lake, IN: Eisenbrauns, 2003.

———. *The Babylonian Captivity of the Book of Isaiah: "Exilic" Judah and the Provenance of Isaiah 40–55*. Oslo: Novus, 1997.

———. *The Myth of the Empty Land: A Study in the History and Archaeology of Judah during the "Exilic" Period*. Oslo: Scandinavian University Press, 1996.

Battista, Giovanni, Raija Mattila, and Robert Rollinger, eds. *Writing Neo-Assyrian History: Sources, Problems, and Approaches*. SAA 29. Helsinki: Neo-Assyrian Text Corpus Project, 2019.

Beaulieu, Paul-Alain. "Nabopolassar and the Antiquity of Babylon." ErIsr 27 (2003): 1*–9*.

———. *The Reign of Nabonidus, King of Babylon 556–539 B.C.* New Haven: Yale University Press, 1989.

Becker, Eve-Marie, Jan Dochhorn, and Else Kragelund Holt, eds. *Trauma and Traumatization in Individual and Collective Dimensions: Insights from Biblical Studies and Beyond*. SAN. Göttingen: Vandenhoeck & Ruprecht, 2014.

Becking, Bob. *Ezra-Nehemiah*. HCOT. Leuven: Peeters, 2018.

Bedford, Peter Ross. *Temple Restoration in Early Achaemenid Persia*. JSJSup. Leiden: Brill, 2001.

Ben Zvi, Ehud. "Inclusion in and Exclusion from Israel as Conveyed by the Use of the Term 'Israel' in Post-monarchic Biblical Texts." Pages 95–149 in *The Pitcher Is Broken: Memorial Essays for Gösta W. Ahlström*. Edited by Steven W. Holloway and Lowell K. Handy. JSOTSup 190. Sheffield: Sheffield Academic, 1995.

———. *Micah*. FOTL 21B. Grand Rapids: Eerdmans, 2000.

———. *Signs of Jonah: Reading and Rereading in Ancient Yehud*. JSOTSup 367. London: Sheffield Academic, 2003.

———. *Social Memory among the Literati of Yehud*. BZAW 509. Berlin: de Gruyter, 2019.

Berlejung, Angelika. "Living in the Land of Shinar: Reflections on Exile in Genesis 11:1–9?" Pages 90–111 in *The Fall of Jerusalem and the Rise of the Torah*. Edited by Peter Dubovský, Dominik Markl, and Jean-Pierre Sonnet. FAT 107. Tübingen: Mohr Siebeck, 2016.

Berlin, Adele. "The Exile: Biblical Ideology and Its Postmodern Ideological Interpretation." Pages 341–56 in *Literary Construction of Identity in the Ancient World*. Edited by Hanna Liss and Manfred Oeming. Winona Lake, IN: Eisenbrauns, 2010.

Berman, Joshua. "The Narratological Purpose of Aramaic Prose in Ezra 4:4–6:18." *AS* 5.2 (2007): 1–27.

———. "The Narratorial Voice of the Scribes of Samaria: Ezra 4:8–6:18 Reconsidered." *VT* 56 (2006): 313–26.

Blenkinsopp, Joseph. "The Cosmological and Protological Language of Deutero-Isaiah." *CBQ* 73 (2011): 493–510.

———. *Isaiah 40–55*. AB 19A. New Haven: Yale University Press, 2002.

———. *Isaiah 56–66*. AB 19B. New York: Doubleday, 2003.

Bloch-Smith, Elizabeth. *Judahite Burial Practices and Beliefs about the Dead*. JSOTSup 123. Sheffield: Sheffield Academic, 1992.

Boardman, John. *Greek Gems and Finger Rings*. New York: Abrams, 1970.

Boase, Elizabeth, and Christopher G. Frechette, eds. *Bible through the Lens of Trauma*. SemeiaSt 86. Atlanta: SBL Press, 2016.

Boda, Mark J. "Babylon in the Book of the Twelve." *HBAI* 3 (2014): 225–48.

———. *Praying the Tradition: The Origin and Use of Tradition in Nehemiah 9*. BZAW 277. Berlin: de Gruyter, 1999.

Bonfiglio, Ryan P. "Divine Warrior or Persian King? The Archer Metaphor in Zechariah 9." Pages 227–42 in *Iconographic Exegesis of the Hebrew Bible/Old Testament*. Edited by Izaak J. de Hulster, Brent A. Strawn, and Ryan P. Bonfiglio. Göttingen: Vandenhoeck & Ruprecht, 2015.

———. *Reading Images, Seeing Texts: Towards a Visual Hermeneutics for Biblical Studies*. OBO 280. Fribourg: Academic Press; Göttingen: Vandenhoeck & Ruprecht, 2016.

Bonnie, Rick. *Judeans in Babylonia: A Study of Deportees in the Sixth and Fifth Centuries BCE*. Leiden: Brill, 2020.

Borger, Rykle. *Beiträge zum Inscriftenwerk Assurbanipals*. Wiesbaden: Harrassowitz, 1996.

———. *Die Inschriften Asarhaddons, Königs von Assyrien*. AfOB. Osnabrück: Biblio-Verlag, 1967.

Borkowski, Sebastian. "'Of Marshes, Kings and Rebels': On the Perception and Representation of Southern Mesopotamian Wetlands at the Neo-Assyrian Royal Court." Pages 103–15 in *Text and Image: Proceedings of the 61e Rencontre Assyriologique Internationale, Geneva and Bern,*

22–26 June 2015. Edited by Pascal Attinger, Antoine Cavigneaux, Catherine Mittermayer, and Mirko Novák. OBO.SA 40. Leuven: Peeters, 2018.

Boucharlat, Rémy. "Gardens and Parks at Pasargadae: Two 'Paradises'?" Pages 557–74 in *Herodot und das Persisiche Weltreich*. Edited by Robert Rollinger, Brigitte Truschnegg, and Josef Wiesehofer. Wiesbaden: Harrassowitz, 2011.

———. "The 'Paradise' of Cyrus at Pasargadae, the Core of the Royal Ostentation." Pages 47–64 in *Bau- und Gartenkultur zwischen "Orient" und "Okzident": Fragen zu Herkunft, Identität und Legitimation*. Edited by Joachim Ganzert und Joachim Wolschke-Bulmahn. Munich: Meidenbauer, 2009.

———. "À propos de *paradayadām* et paradis perse: perpléxité de l'archéologue et perspectives." Pages 61–80 in *Des contrées avestiques à Mahabad, via Bisoton: études offertes en homage à Pierre Lecoq*. Edited by Celine Redard. Paris: Recherches et Publications, 2016.

Bousquet, Bernard, Michel Chauveau, Peter Dils, Sylvie Marchand, and Annie Schweitzer. "Première Rapport Préliminaire des Travaux sur le Site de 'Ayn Manawir (Oasis de Kharga)." *BIFAO* 96 (1996): 385–451.

Braudel, Fernand. *The Mediterranean and the Mediterranean World in the Age of Philip II*. 2 vols. Translated by Siân Reynolds. New York: Harper & Row, 1972.

Braulik, Georg. "Deuteronomy and the Commemorative Culture of Israel: Redactio-historical Observations of the Use of למד." Pages 183–98 in *The Theology of Deuteronomy: Collected Essays of Georg Braulik, O.S.B.* Translated by Ulrika Lindblad. North Richland Hills, TX: BIBAL, 1994.

Briant, Pierre. *From Cyrus to Alexander: A History of the Persian Empire*. Translated by Peter T. Daniels. Winona Lake, IN: Eisenbrauns, 2002.

Burbank, Jane, and Frederick Cooper. *Empires in World History: Power and the Politics of Difference*. Princeton: Princeton University Press, 2010.

Burke, Peter. *The French Historical Revolution: The Annales School, 1929–2014*. Palo Alto, CA: Stanford University Press, 2015.

Cardasçia, Guillaume. *Les Archives Des Murašû, une Famille d'Hommes d'Affaires À l'Époque Perse (455–503 Av. J.-C.)*. Paris: Impr. nationale, 1951.

Carlson Hasler, Laura. *Archival Historiography in Jewish Antiquity*. New York: Oxford University Press, 2019.

———. "Writing in Three Dimensions: Scribal Activity and Spaces in Jewish Antiquity." In *Scribes and Scribalism in Social Context*. Edited by Mark Leuchter. London: T&T Clark, forthcoming.

Carr, David M. *The Formation of the Hebrew Bible*. New York: Oxford University Press, 2011.

———. *Holy Resilience: The Bible's Traumatic Origins*. New Haven: Yale University Press, 2014.

Carradice, Ian. "The 'Regal' Coinage of the Persian Empire." Pages 73–95 in *Coinage and Administration in the Athenian and Persian Empires: The Ninth Oxford Symposium on Coinage and Monetary History*. Edited by Ian Carradice. BARIS 343. Oxford: British Archaeological Reports, 1987.

Carroll, Robert P. "Exile, Restoration, and Colony: Judah in the Persian Empire." Pages 102–16 in *The Blackwell Companion to the Hebrew Bible*. Edited by Leo G. Perdue. Malden, MA: Blackwell, 2001.

———. "Exile! What Exile? Deportation and the Discourses of Diaspora." Pages 62–79 in *Leading Captivity Captive: "The Exile" as History and Ideology*. Edited by Lester L. Grabbe. JSOTSup 278. ESHM 2. Sheffield: Sheffield Academic, 1998.

———. *Jeremiah: A Commentary*. OTL. London: SCM, 1986.

Carstens, Pernille. "The Torah as Canon of Masterpieces: Remembering in Archives." Pages 309–23 in *Cultural Memory in Biblical Exegesis*. Edited by Pernille Carstens, Trine Bjørnung Hasselbalch, and Niels Peter Lemche. PHSC 17. Piscataway, NJ: Gorgias, 2012.

Carter, Charles E. *The Emergence of Yehud in the Persian Period: A Social and Demographic Study*. JSOTSup 294. Sheffield: Sheffield Academic, 1999.

Cassarino, Jean-Pierre. "Theorizing Return Migration: A Revisited Conceptual Approach to Return Migrants." Pages 1–33 in *EUI Working Papers*. San Domenico di Fiesole, Italy: European University Institute Badia Fiesolana, 2004.

Childs, Brevard. *Introduction to the Old Testament as Scripture*. Philadelphia: Fortress, 1979.

Cogan, Morton (Mordechai). *Imperialism and Religion: Assyrian, Judah, and Israel in the Eighth and Seventh Centuries B.C.E.* SBLMS 19. Missoula, MT: Scholars Press, 1974.

Colburn, Henry P. *Archaeology of Empire in Achaemenid Egypt*. Edinburgh: Edinburgh University Press, 2020.

Constant, Amélie, and Douglas S. Massey. "Return Migration by German Guest-Workers: Neoclassical versus New Economic Theories." *IM* 40 (2002): 5–38.

Cook, Terry. "Evidence, Memory, Identity, and Community: Four Shifting Archival Paradigms. *ArchS* 13 (2013): 95–120.

———. "What Is Past Is Prologue: A History of Archival Ideas since 1898, and the Future Paradigm Shift." *Archivaria* 43 (1997): 17–63.

Cooley, Robert E., and Gary D. Pratico. "Gathered to His People: An Archaeological Illustration from Tell Dothan's Western Cemetery." Pages 70–92 in *Scripture and Other Artifacts: Essays on the Bible and Archaeology in Honor of Philip J. King*. Edited by Michael D. Coogan, J. Cheryl Exum, and Lawrence E. Stager. Louisville: John Knox, 1994.

Coser, Lewis A. Introduction to *On Collective Memory*, by Maurice Halbwachs. Edited by Lewis A. Coser. Chicago: University of Chicago Press, 1992.

Cross, Frank Moore. *Canaanite Myth and Hebrew Epic: Essays in the History of the Religion of Israel*. Cambridge: Harvard University Press, 1973.

Crouch, Carly L. *An Introduction to the Study of Jeremiah*. London: T&T Clark, 2017.

Curtis, John. *The Cyrus Cylinder and Ancient Persia: A New Beginning for the Middle East*. London: British Museum Press, 2013.

Da Riva, Rocio. *The Inscriptions of Nabopolassar, Amel-Marduk, and Neriglissar*. Berlin: de Gruyter, 2013.

———. *The Neo-Babylonian Royal Inscriptions: An Introduction*. Münster: Ugarit-Verlag, 2008.

Dahood, Mitchell. *Psalms*. 3 vols. AB 16–17A. Garden City, NY: Doubleday, 1965–1970.

Dandamayev, Muhammad. "Assyrian Traditions during Achaemenid Times." Pages 41–48 in *Assyria 1995: Proceedings of the Tenth Anniversary of the Neo-Assyrian Text Corpus Project*. Edited by Simo Parpola and Robert Whiting. Helsinki: Neo-Assyrian Text Corpus Project, 1997.

———. "The Domain-Lands of Achaemenes in Babylonia." *AoF* 1 (1974): 123–27.

———. "Die Lehnsbeziehungen in Babylonien unter den ersten Achämeniden." Pages 37–42 in *Festschrift für Wilhelm Eilers: Ein Dokument der Internationalen Forschung zum 27. September 1967*. Edited by Gernot Wiessner and Wilhelm Eilers. Wiesbaden: Harrassowitz, 1967.

Derrida, Jacques. *Archive Fever: A Freudian Impression*. Translated by Eric Prenowitz. Chicago: University of Chicago Press, 1996.

Dhorme, Edouard. "Les tablettes babyloniennes de Neirab." *RA* 25 (1928): 53–82.

Dieulafoy, Marcel. *L'art antique de la Perse: Achéménides, Parthes, Sassanides*. Paris: Librairie central d'architecture, etc., 1884–1885.

Driel, Govert van. *Elusive Silver: In Search for a Market in an Agrarian Environment; Aspects of Mesopotamia's Society*. UNINO 9. Leiden: Nederlands Instituut voor het Nabije Oosten, 2002.

———. "The Murašus in Context." *JESHO* 32 (1989): 203–29.

Du Toit, Jacqueline S. *Textual Memory: Archives, Libraries and the Hebrew Bible*. Sheffield: Sheffield Phoenix, 2011.

Edelman, Diana V. "City Gardens and Parks in Biblical Social Memory." Pages 115–55 in *Memory and the City in Ancient Israel*. Edited by Diana V. Edelman and Ehud Ben Zvi. Winona Lake, IN: Eisenbrauns, 2014.

———. "From Prophets to Prophetic Books: The Fixing of the Divine Word." Pages 29–54 in *The Production of Prophecy: Constructing Prophecy and Prophets in Yehud*. Edited by Diana V. Edelman and Ehud Ben Zvi. London: Equinox, 2009.

———. "Identities within a Central and Peripheral Perspective: The Use of Aramaic in the Hebrew Bible." Pages 109–31 in *Centres and Peripheries in the Early Second Temple Period*. Edited by Ehud Ben Zvi and Christoph Levin. FAT 109. Tübingen: Mohr Siebeck, 2016.

———. *The Origins of the "Second" Temple: Persian Imperial Policy and the Rebuilding of Jerusalem*. London: Equinox, 2005.

Eichrodt, Walther. *Ezekiel: A Commentary*. Translated by Cosslett Quin. OTL. Philadelphia: Westminster, 1970.

Eisenstadt, Samuel N., ed. *The Decline of Empires*. Englewood Cliffs, NJ: Bobbs-Merrill, 1967.

Eph'al, Israel. *Archaeology of the Land of the Bible*. Vol. 2, *The Assyrian, Babylonian, and Persian Periods (732–333 BCE)*. New York: Doubleday, 2001.

———. *The City Besieged: Siege and Its Manifestations in the Ancient Near East*. Boston: Brill, 2009.

———. "The Western Minorities in Babylonia in the Sixth and Fifth Centuries BC." *Or* 47 (1978): 74–90.

Eph'al, Israel, and Joseph Naveh. *Aramaic Ostraca of the Fourth Century BC from Idumea*. Jerusalem: Israel Exploration Society, 1996.

Fales, Frederick M. "Remarks on the Neirab Texts." *OrAnt* 12 (1973): 131–42.

Faust, Avraham. "Deportation and Demography in Sixth Century B.C.E. Judah." Pages 91–103 in *Interpreting Exile: Interdisciplinary Studies of Displacement and Deportation in Biblical and Modern Contexts*. Edited by Brad E. Kelle, Frank R. Ames, and Jacob L. Wright. Atlanta: Society of Biblical Literature, 2011.

———. "Forts or Agricultural Estates? Persian Period Settlement in the Territories of the Former Kingdom of Judah." *PEQ* 150 (2018): 34–59.

———. *Israel's Ethnogenesis: Settlement, Interaction, Expansion, and Resistance*. London: Equinox, 2006.

———. *Judah in the Neo-Babylonian Period: The Archaeology of Desolation*. ABS 18. Atlanta: Society of Biblical Literature, 2012.

———. "Judah in the Sixth Century B.C.E.: A Rural Perspective." *PEQ* 135 (2003): 37–53.

———. "Social and Cultural Changes in Judah during the Sixth Century BCE and Their Implications for Our Understanding of the Nature of the Neo-Babylonian Period." *UF* 36 (2004): 157–76.

Faust, Avraham, and Shlomo Bunimovitz. "The Judahite Rock-Cut Tomb: Family Response at a Time of Change." *IEJ* 58 (2008): 150–70.

Feldman, Marian H. "Darius I and the Heroes of Akkad: Affect and Agency in the Bisitun Relief." Pages 265–93 in *Ancient Near Eastern Art in Context: Studies in Honor of Irene Winter by Her Students*. Edited by Jack Chang and Martin H. Feldman. Leiden: Brill, 2007.

Finkel, Irving, ed. *The Cyrus Cylinder: The King of Persia's Ancient Proclamation from Babylon*. London: I. B. Tauris, 2013.

Finkelstein, Israel. "Archaeology and the List of Returnees in the Books of Ezra and Nehemiah." *PEQ* 140 (2008): 7–16.

———. "Jerusalem in the Persian (and Early Hellenistic) Period and the Wall of Nehemiah." *JSOT* 32 (2008): 501–20.

———. "Persian Period Jerusalem and Yehud: A Rejoinder." *JHebS* 9 (2009): article 24.

———. "Persian Period Jerusalem and Yehud Rejoinders." Pages 49–62 in *Focusing Biblical Studies: The Crucial Nature of the Persian and Hellenistic Periods; Essays in Honor of Douglas A. Knight*. Edited by Jon L. Berquist and Alice Hunt. LHBOTS 544. New York: T&T Clark, 2012.

———. "The Territorial Extent and Demography of Yehud/Judea in the Persian and Early Hellenistic Periods." *RB* 117 (2010): 39–54.

Fischer, Georg. "Don't Forget Jerusalem's Destruction: The Perspective of the Book of Jeremiah." Pages 291–311 in *The Fall of Jerusalem and the Rise of the Torah*. Edited by Peter Dubovský, Dominik Markl, and Jean-Pierre Sonnet. FAT 107. Tübingen: Mohr Siebeck, 2016.

Floyd, Michael H. "The Meaning of *Maśśāʾ* as a Prophetic Term in Isaiah." *JHebS* 18.9 (2018): 21–23.

———. "New Form Criticism and Beyond: The Historicity of Prophetic Literature Revisited." Pages 17–36 in *The Book of the Twelve and the New Form Criticism*. Edited by Mark J. Boda, Michael H. Floyd, and Colin M. Toffelmire. ANEM 10. Atlanta: SBL Press, 2015.

———. "The Production of Prophetic Books in the Early Second Temple Period." Pages 276–97 in *Prophets, Prophecy, and Prophetic Texts in Second Temple Judaism*. Edited by Michael H. Floyd and Robert D. Haak. LHBOTS 427. New York: T&T Clark, 2006.

Frahm, Eckhart. "Rising Suns and Falling Stars: Assyrian Kings and the Cosmos." Pages 97–120 in *Experiencing Power, Generating Authority: Cosmos, Politics, and the Ideology of Kingship in Ancient Egypt and Mesopotamia*. Edited by Jane A. Hill, Philip Jones, and Antonio J. Morales. Philadelphia: University of Pennsylvania Museum, 2013.

Freud, Sigmund. *Civilization and Its Discontents*. Translated by David McLintock. GI 19. New York: Penguin Books, 2004.

Fried, Lisbeth S. "150 Men at Nehemiah's Table? The Role of the Governor's Meals in the Achaemenid Provincial Economy." *JBL* 137 (2018): 821–31.

———. "The Exploitation of Depopulated Land in Achaemenid Judah." Pages 149–62 in *The Economy of Ancient Judah in Its Historical Context*. Edited by Marvin L. Miller, Ehud Ben Zvi, and Gary N. Knoppers. Winona Lake, IN: Eisenbrauns, 2015.

———. *Ezra, a Commentary*. SPCCS. Sheffield: Sheffield Phoenix, 2015.

———. *The Priest and the Great King: Temple-Palace Relations in the Persian Empire*. Winona Lake, IN: Eisenbrauns, 2004.

———. "A Silver Coin of Yoḥanan Hakkôhen." *Transeu* 26 (2003): 65–85, pls. II–V.

Funk, Robert W. "Beth-Zur." *NEAEHL* 1 (1993): 259–61.

Gardiner, Alan H. *Egyptian Grammar*. 3rd rev. ed. London: Oxford University Press, 1957.

Garrison, Mark B. "Achaemenid Iconography as Evidenced by Glyptic Art: Subject Matter, Social Function, Audience and Diffusion." Pages 115–63 in *Images as Media: Sources for the Cultural History of the Near East and the Eastern Mediterranean (First Millennium BCE)*. Edited by Christoph Uehlinger. OBO 175. Fribourg: University Press; Göttingen: Vandenhoeck & Ruprecht, 2000.

———. "Archers at Persepolis: The Emergence of Royal Ideology at the Heart of the Empire." Pages 337–59 in *The World of Achaemenid Persia: History, Art and Society in Iran and the Ancient Near East*. Edited by John Curtis and St. John Simpson. New York: I. B. Tauris, 2010.

———. "Beyond Auramazdā and the Winged Symbol: Imagery of the Divine and Numinous at Persepolis." Pages 185–246 in *Persian Religion in the Achaemenid Period*. Edited by Wouter F. Henkleman and Celine Redard. Wiesbaden: Harrassowitz, 2017.

———. "Visual Representation of the Divine and the Numinous in Achaemenid Iran: Old Problems, New Directions." Pages 38–40 in *Iconography of Deities and Demons*. Electronic prepublication. 2009. https://tinyurl.com/SBL1735c.

Garrison, Mark B., Charles E. Jones, and Matthew W. Stolper. "Achaemenid Elamite Administrative Tablets, 4: BM 108963." *JNES* 77 (2018): 1–14.

Garrison, Mark B., and Margaret Cool Root. *Persepolis Seal Studies: An Introduction with Provisional Concordances of Seal Numbers and Associated Documents on Fortification Tablets 1–2087*. AH 9. Leiden: Nederlands Instituut voor het Nabije Oosten, 1998.

———. *Seals on the Persepolis Fortification Tablets, Images of Heroic Encounter*. OIP 117. Chicago: Oriental Institute of the University of Chicago, 2001.

Gaspa, Salvatore. "State Theology and Royal Ideology of the Neo-Assyrian Empire as a Structuring Model for the Achaemenid Imperial Religion." Pages 125–84 in *Persian Religion in the Achaemenid Period*. Edited by Wouter F. Henkleman and Celine Redard. Wiesbaden: Harrassowitz, 2017.

George, Andrew R. *House Most High: The Temples of Ancient Mesopotamia*. Winona Lake, IN: Eisenbrauns, 1993.

———. "Studies in Cultic Topography and Ideology." *BO* 53 (1996): 363–95.

Goldingay, John. *Isaiah 56–66*. ICC. London: T&T Clark, 2014.

——— . "Jeremiah and the Superpower." Pages 59–77 in *Uprooting and Planting: Essays on Jeremiah for Leslie Allen*. Edited by John Goldingay. LHBOTS 459. New York: T&T Clark, 2007.

Gosse, Bernard. *Isaïe 13,1–14,23: dans la tradition littéraire du livre d' Isaïe et dans la tradition des oracles contre les nations*. OBO 78. Göttingen: Vandenhoeck & Ruprecht, 1988.

Grabbe, Lester L. "The 'Persian Documents' in the Book of Ezra: Are They Authentic?" Pages 531–70 in *Judah and the Judeans in the Persian Period*. Edited by Oded Lipschits and Manfred Oeming. Winona Lake, IN: Eisenbrauns, 2006.

———. Review of *The Templeless Age: An Introduction to the History, Literature, and Theology of the Exile*, by Jill Middlemas. *RBL* (July 2008): https://www.sblcentral.org/home/bookDetails/6072.

Grayson, A. Kirk. *Assyrian Rulers of the Early First Millennium BC I*. RIMA 2. Toronto: University of Toronto Press, 1991.

Grayson, A. Kirk, and Jamie Novotny. *The Royal Inscriptions of Sennacherib, King of Assyria (704–681 BC), Part 2*. RINAP 3/2. Winona Lake, IN: Eisenbrauns, 2014.

Gropp, Douglas M., James VanderKam, and Monica Brady. *Wadi Daliyeh II and Qumran Miscellanea, Part 2*. DJD 28. Oxford: Oxford University Press, 2002.

Gunneweg, Antonius H. J. *Ezra*. KAT. Gütersloh: Gütersloher Verlag Mohn, 1985.

Hackett, Jo Ann. *The Balaam Text from Deir 'Allā*. HSM 31. Chico, CA: Scholars Press, 1984.

Halbwachs, Maurice. *On Collective Memory*. Translated by Lewis A. Coser. Chicago: University of Chicago Press, 1992.

Hallock, Richard T. *The Persepolis Fortification Tablets*. OIP 92. Chicago: Oriental Institute of the University of Chicago, 1969.

Halvorson-Taylor, Martien. *Enduring Exile: The Metaphorization of Exile in the Hebrew Bible*. VTSup 141. Leiden: Brill, 2011.

Hamilton, Mark W. "After Politics: Reflections on 2 Isaiah." Pages 411–30 in *Enemies and Friends of the State: Ancient Prophecy in Context*. Edited by Christopher Rollston. University Park, PA: Eisenbrauns, 2018.

———. "What Are *ʾElilim*?" *JHebS* 19 (2019): article 9, 1–9.

Hardt, Michael, and Antonio Negri. *Empire*. Cambridge: Harvard University Press, 2000.

Harger, Adam K. "Reading Jeremiah 52 in Exile: Purpose in the Composition of Jeremiah." *JTS* 70 (2019): 511–22.

Henkelman, Wouter F. "Cyrus the Persian and Darius the Elamite: A Case of Mistaken Identity." Pages 577–634 in *Herodot und das Persische Weltreich/Herodotus and the Persian Empire*. Edited by Robert Rollinger, Brigitte Truschnegg, and Josef Wiesehöfer. Wiesbaden: Harrassowitz, 2011.

———. *The Other Gods Who Are: Studies in Elamite-Iranian Acculturation Based on the Persepolis Fortification Texts*. Leiden: Nederlands Instituut voor het Nabije Oosten, 2008.

Henkelman, Wouter F., and Celine Redard, eds. *Persian Religion in the Achaemenid Period*. Wiesbaden: Harrassowitz, 2017.

Herzfeld, Michael. "What Is a Polity? Subversive Archaism and the Bureaucratic Nation-State (2018 Lewis H. Morgan Lecture)." *Hau* 9 (2019): 23–35.

Hill, John. *Friend or Foe? The Figure of Babylon in the Book of Jeremiah MT*. BibInt 40. Leiden: Brill, 1999.

Hillers, Delbert R. "The Book of Micah." *ABD* 4:807–10.

Hock, Hans Heinrich, and Brian D. Joseph. *Language History, Language Change, and Language Relationship: An Introduction to Historical and Comparative Linguistics*. Berlin: de Gruyter, 1996.

Hoftijzer, Jean, and Karel Jongeling. *Dictionary of the North-West Semitic Inscriptions*. Leiden: Brill, 1995.

Hogland, Kenneth G. "The Achaemenid Context." Pages 54–72 in *Second Temple Studies*. Vol. 1, *The Persian Period*. Edited by Philip R. Davies. JSOTSup 117. Sheffield: Sheffield Academic, 1991.

Hulster, Izaak J. de, and Brent A. Strawn. "The Power of Images: Isaiah 60, Jerusalem, and Persian Imperial Propaganda." Pages 197–216 in *Iconographic Exegesis of the Hebrew Bible/Old Testament*. Edited by Izaak J. de Hulster, Brent A. Strawn, and Ryan P. Bonfiglio. Göttingen: Vandenhoeck & Ruprecht, 2015.

Hurowitz, Victor (Avigdor). *I Have Built You an Exalted House: Temple Building in the Bible in Light of Mesopotamian and Northwest Semitic Writings*. JSOTSup 115. Sheffield: Sheffield Academic, 1992.

Huyse, Philip. "Some Further Thoughts on the Bisitun Monument and the Genesis of the Old Persian Script." *BAI* 13 (1999): 45–66.

Jacobs, Bruno. "Achaemenid Satrapies." *Encyclopaedia Iranica*. Online ed. 2011. https://tinyurl.com/SBL1735b.

Janzen, David. *The Violent Gift: Trauma's Subversion of the Deuteronomistic History's Narrative*. LHBOTS 531. New York: T&T Clark, 2012.

———. "Yahwistic Appropriation of Achaemenid Ideology and the Function of Nehemiah 9 in Ezra-Nehemiah." *JBL* 136 (2017): 839–56.

Japhet, Sara. "Sheshbazzar and Zerubbabel against the Background of the Historical and Religious Tendencies of Ezra-Nehemiah: Part 1." Pages 77–83 in *From the Rivers of Babylon to the Highlands of Judah: Collected Studies on the Restoration Period*. Winona Lake, IN; Eisenbrauns, 2006.

Joannès, Francis, and André Lemaire. "Trois Tablettes Cunéiformes à Onomastique Ouest-Sémitique (Collection Sh. Moussaïeff)." *Transeu* 17 (1999): 17–34, pls. 1–2.

Jobling, David. *1 Samuel*. Berit Olam. Collegeville, MN: Liturgical Press, 1998.

Jones, Christopher M. "'The Wealth of Nations Shall Come to You': Light, Tribute, and Implacement in Isaiah 60." *VT* 64 (2014): 611–22.

Jong, Matthijs J. de. *Isaiah among the Near Eastern Prophets: A Comparative Study of the Earliest Stages of the Isaiah Tradition and the Neo-Assyrian Prophecies*. VTSup 117. Leiden: Brill, 2007.

Joseph, Alison L. *Portrait of the Kings: The Davidic Prototype in Deuteronomistic Poetics*. Minneapolis: Fortress, 2015.

———. "Who Is like David? Was David like David? Good Kings in the Book of Kings." *CBQ* 77 (2015): 20–41.

Jursa, Michael. "Agricultural Management, Tax Farming and Banking: Aspects of Entrepreneurial Activity—Babylonia in the Late Achaemenid and Hellenistic Periods." Pages 137–222 in *La transition entre l'empire achéménide et les royaumes hellénistiques (vers 350–300 avant J.-C.)*. Edited by Pierre Briant and Francis Joannès. Persika 9. Paris: de Boccard, 2006.

———. *Aspects of the Economic History of Babylonia in the First Millennium BC*. AOAT 377. Münster: Ugarit-Verlag, 2010.

———. "Factor Markets in Babylonia from the Late Seventh to the Third Century BCE." *JESHO* 57 (2014): 173–202.

———. "Families, Officialdom, and Families of Royal Officials in Chaldean and Achaemenid Babylonia." Pages 597–606 in *Tradition and Innovation in the Ancient Near East*. Edited by Alfonso Archi. Winona Lake, IN: Eisenbrauns, 2015.

———. "The Neo-Babylonian Empire." Pages 121–48 in *Imperien und Reiche in der Weltgeschichte: Epochenübergreifende und globalhistorische Vergleiche*. Edited by Sabine Fick. Wiesbaden: Harrassowitz, 2014.

———. "The Transition of Babylonia from the Neo-Babylonian Empire to Achaemenid Rule." Pages 73–94 in *Regime Change in the Ancient Near East and Egypt: From Sargon of Agade to Saddam Hussein*. Edited by Harriet Crawford. Oxford: Oxford University Press, 2007.

Jursa, Michael, and Ran Zadok. "Judeans and Other West Semites: Another View from the Babylonia Countryside." *HBAI* 9 (2020): 20–40.

Kapelrud, Arvid S. "Temple Building: A Task for Gods and Kings." *Or* 32 (1963): 56–62.

Keel, Othmar. *The Symbolism of the Biblical World: Ancient Near Eastern Iconography and the Book of Psalms*. Repr. ed. Winona Lake, IN: Eisenbrauns, 1997.

Keel, Othmar, and Christoph Uehlinger. *Gods, Goddesses, and Images of God: In Ancient Israel*. Rev. ed. Translated by Thomas H. Trapp. Minneapolis: Fortress, 1998.

Kent, Roland G. *Old Persian: Grammar, Texts, Lexicon*. New Haven: Yale University Press, 1953.

Kessler, John. "Images of Exile: Representations of the 'Exile' and 'Empty Land' in Sixth to Fourth Century BCE Yehudite Literature." Pages 309–51 in *The Concept of Exile in Ancient Israel and Its Historical Contexts*. Edited by Ehud Ben Zvi and Christoph Levin. BZAW 404. Berlin: de Gruyter, 2010.

King, Rhyne. "Taxing Achaemenid Arachosia: Evidence from Persepolis." *JNES* 78 (2019): 185–99.

Kleber, Kristin, with Johannes Hackl. "*Dātu ša šarri*: Gesetzgebung in Babylonien unter den Achämeniden." *JANEBL* 16 (2010): 49–75.

Klingbeil, Martin G. "Syro-Palestinian Stamp Seals from the Persian Period: The Iconographic Evidence." *JNSL* 18 (1992): 95–124.

Koole, Jan L. *Isaiah III*. Vol. 1, *Isaiah 40–48*. HCOT. Kampen: Kok, 1997.

———. *Isaiah III*. Vol. 3, *Isaiah 56–66*. HCOT. Leuven: Peeters, 2001.

Kratz, Reinhard G. *Historical and Biblical Israel: The History, Tradition, and Archives of Israel and Judah*. Translated by Paul Michael Kurtz. Oxford: Oxford University Press, 2015.

Krüger, Thomas. *The Preacher Sought to Find Pleasing Words: A Study of the Language of Qoheleth. Part 2, Vocabulary*. OLA 143. Leuven: Peeters, 2004.

———. *Qoheleth*. Hermeneia. Minneapolis: Fortress, 2004.

Kuhrt, Amélie. "Achaemenid Images of Royalty and Empire." Pages 87–105 in *Concepts of Kingship in Antiquity*. Edited by Giovanni Lanfranchi and Robert Rollinger. Padova: S.A.R.G.O.N., 2010.

———. "Making History: Sargon of Agade and Cyrus the Great of Persia." Pages 347–61 in *A Persian Perspective: Essays in Memory of Heleen Sancisi-Weerdenburg*. Edited by Wouter F. Henkelman and Amélie Kuhrt. AH 13. Leiden: Nederlands Instituut voor het Nabije Oosten, 2003.

———. *The Persian Empire: A Corpus of Sources from the Achaemenid Period*. London: Routledge, 2007.

Lambert, Wilfred G. *Babylonian Creation Myths*. MC 16. Winona Lake, IN: Eisenbrauns, 2016.

Lecoq, Pierre. *Les inscriptions de la Perse achéménide*. Paris: Gallimard, 1997.

Leichty, Erle. *The Royal Inscriptions of Esarhaddon, King of Assyria (680–669 BC)*. RINAP 4. Winona Lake, IN: Eisenbrauns, 2011.

Leith, Mary Joan Winn. *Wadi Daliyeh I: The Wadi Daliyeh Seal Impressions*. DJD 24. Oxford: Clarendon, 1997.

Lemaire, André. "Administration in Fourth-Century BCE Judah in Light of Epigraphy and Numismatics." Pages 53–74 in *Judah and the Judeans in the Fourth Century B.C.E.* Edited by Oded Lipschits, Gary N. Knoppers, and Rainer Albertz. Winona Lake, IN: Eisenbrauns, 2007.

———. "Populations et Territoires de Palestine À l'Époque Perse." *Transeu* 3 (1990): 31–74.

Leuchter, Mark. "The Aramaic Transition and the Redaction of the Pentateuch." *JBL* 136 (2017): 249–68.

———. "Jeremiah: Structure, Themes, and Contested Issues." Pages 171–89 in *The Oxford Handbook of the Prophets*. Edited by Carolyn J. Sharp. New York: Oxford University Press, 2016.

———. *The Polemics of Exile in Jeremiah 26–45*. Cambridge: Cambridge University Press, 2008.

Leuenberger, Martin. "Kyros-Orakel und Kyros-Zylinder: Ein religionsgeschichtlicher Vergleich ihrer Gottes-Konzeptionen." *VT* 59 (2004): 244–56.

Levin, Christoph. "Introduction." Pages 1–10 in *The Concept of Exile in Ancient Israel and Its Historical Contexts*. Edited by Ehud Ben Zvi and Christoph Levin. BZAW 404. Berlin: de Gruyter, 2010.

Lewis, Brian. *The Sargon Legend: A Study of the Akkadian Text and the Hero Who Was Exposed at Birth*. Cambridge: ASOR, 1980.

Lichtheim, Miriam. *Ancient Egyptian Literature, a Book of Readings*. Vol. 3. Berkeley: University of California Press, 1980.

Lincoln, Bruce. *"Happiness for Mankind": Achaemenian Religion and the Imperial Project.* Leuven: Peeters, 2012.

Linville, James R. "Myth of the Exilic Return: Myth Theory and the Exile as an Eternal Reality in the Prophets." Pages 295–308 in *The Concept of Exile in Ancient Israel and Its Historical Contexts.* Edited by Ehud Ben Zvi and Christoph Levin. BZAW 404. Berlin: de Gruyter, 2010.

———. "Mythoprophetics: Some Thoughts." Pages 403–15 in *History, Memory, Hebrew Scriptures: A Festschrift for Ehud Ben Zvi.* Edited by Ian D. Wilson and Diana V. Edelman. Winona Lake, IN: Eisenbrauns, 2015.

Lipschits, Oded. "Achaemenid Imperial Policy, Settlement Processes in Palestine, and the Status of Jerusalem in the Middle of the Fifth Century B.C.E." Pages 19–52 in *Judah and the Judeans in the Persian Period.* Edited by Oded Lipschits and Manfred Oeming. Winona Lake, IN: Eisenbrauns, 2006.

———. "Demographic Changes in Judah between the Seventh and the Fifth Centuries B.C.E." Pages 323–76 in *Judah and the Judeans in the Neo-Babylonian Period.* Edited by Oded Lipschits. Winona Lake, IN: Eisenbrauns, 2003.

———. *The Fall and Rise of Jerusalem.* Winona Lake, IN: Eisenbrauns, 2005.

———. "Judah, Jerusalem and the Temple (586–539 B.C.)." *Transeu* 22 (2001): 129–42.

———. "Nebuchadnezzar's Policy in 'Hattu-Land' and the Fate of the Kingdom of Judah." *UF* 30 (1998): 467–87.

———. "Persian Period Finds from Jerusalem: Facts and Interpretations." *JHebS* 9 (2009): article 20. https://tinyurl.com/SBL1735d.

———. "Shedding New Light on the Dark Years of the 'Exilic Period': New Studies, Further Elucidation, and Some Questions Regarding the Archaeology of Judah as an 'Empty Land.'" Pages 57–90 in *Interpreting Exile: Interdisciplinary Studies of Displacement and Deportation in Biblical and Modern Contexts.* Edited by Brad E. Kelle, Frank R. Ames, and Jacob L. Wright. Atlanta: Society of Biblical Literature, 2011.

Lipschits, Oded, Yuval Gadot, Benjamin Arubas, and Manfred Oeming. "Palace and Village, Paradise and Oblivion: Unravelling the Riddles of Ramat Raḥel." *NEA* 74 (2011): 2–49.

Lipschits, Oded, Yuval Gadot, and Dafna Langgut. "The Riddle of Ramat Raḥel: The Archaeology of a Royal Persian Period Edifice." *Transeu* 41 (2012): 57–79.

Lipschits, Oded, Yuval Gadot, Manfred Oeming, and Benjamin Arubas. "The 2006 and 2007 Excavation Seasons at Ramat Raḥel: Preliminary Report." *IEJ* 59 (2009): 1–20.

Lipschits, Oded, and Oren Tal. "The Settlement Archaeology of the Province of Judah." Pages 33–52 in *Judah and the Judeans in the Fourth Century B.C.E.* Edited by Oded Lipschits, Gary N. Knoppers, and Rainer Albertz. Winona Lake, IN: Eisenbrauns, 2007.

Lipschits, Oded, and David S. Vanderhooft. *The Yehud Stamp Impressions: A Corpus of Inscribed Impressions from the Persian and Hellenistic Periods in Judah.* Winona Lake, IN: Eisenbrauns, 2011.

Liverani, Mario. *Assyria: The Imperial Mission.* Winona Lake, IN: Eisenbrauns, 2017.

Luukko, Mikko, and Greta Van Buylaere. *The Political Correspondence of Esarhaddon.* SAA 16. Helsinki: Helsinki University Press, 2002.

Machinist, Peter. "Achaemenid Persia as Spectacle. Reactions from Two Peripheral Voices: Aeschylus, *The Persians* and the Biblical Book of Esther." *ErIsr* 33 (2018): 109*–23*.

———. "Assyria and Its Image in the First Isaiah." *JAOS* 103 (1983): 719–37.

———. "Kingship and Divinity in Imperial Assyria." Pages 151–88 in *Text, Artifact, and Image: Revealing Ancient Israelite Religion.* Edited by Gary Beckman and Theodore Lewis. Providence: Brown University Press, 2006.

———. "The Question of Distinctiveness in Ancient Israel." Pages 420–42 in *Essential Papers on Israel and the Ancient Near East.* Edited by Frederick E. Greenspahn. New York: NYU Press, 1991.

———. "Royal Inscriptions in the Hebrew Bible and Mesopotamia: Reflections on Presence, Function, and Self-Critique." Pages 331–63 in *"When the Morning Stars Sang": Essays in Honor of Choon Leong Seow on the Occasion of His Sixty-Fifth Birthday.* Edited by Scott C. Jones and Christine Roy Yoder. BZAW 500. Berlin: de Gruyter, 2018.

———. "The Transfer of Kingship: A Divine Turning." Pages 105–20 in *Fortunate the Eyes That See: Essays in Honor of David Noel Freedman in Celebration of His Seventieth Birthday.* Edited by Astrid Beck, Andrew H. Bartelt, Paul R. Raabe, and Chris A. Franke. Grand Rapids: Eerdmans, 1995.

MacKenzie, John. "A Meditation on Environmental History." Pages 1–21 in T*he Nature of Empires and the Empires of Nature: Indigenous Peoples and the Great Lakes Environment.* Edited by Karl S. Hele. Waterloo, ON: Wilfred Laurier University Press, 2016.

MacQueen, J. G. "The Ἀσσύριοι Λόγοι of Herodotus and Their Position in the Histories." *ClQ* 28 (1978): 284–91.
Magen, Yitzhak. "Nebi Samwil." *NEAEHL* 5 (2008): 1972–76.
Magen, Yitzhak, and Israel Finkelstein, eds. *Archaeological Survey of the Hill Country of Benjamin*. Jerusalem: Israel Antiquities Authority, 1993.
Marchant, Edgar C., and Otis J. Todd. *Xenophon: Memorabilia, Oeconomicus, Symposium, Apology*. LCL. Cambridge: Harvard University Press, 2013.
Mason, Rex. "The Prophets of the Restoration." Pages 137–54 in *Israel's Prophetic Tradition: Essays in Honour of Peter R. Ackroyd*. Edited by Richard Coggins, Anthony Phillips, and Michael Knibb. Cambridge: Cambridge University Press, 1992.
Mayfield, Tyler D. *Literary Structure and Setting in Ezekiel*. FAT 2/43. Tübingen: Mohr Siebeck, 2010.
Mays, James L. *Micah*. OTL. Philadelphia: Westminster, 1976.
McKay, John. *Religion in Judah under the Assyrians*. London: SCM, 1973.
Meyer, Eduard. *Geschichte des Altertums*. 2nd ed. 5 vols. Stuttgart: Cotta, 1907–1913.
Meyers, Carol L., and Eric M. Meyers. "The Future Fortunes of the House of David: The Evidence of Second Zechariah." Pages 207–22 in *Fortunate the Eyes That See: Essays in Honor of David Noel Freedman*. Edited by Astrid B. Beck, Andrew H. Bartelt, Paul R. Raabe, and Chris A. Franke. Grand Rapids: Eerdmans, 1995.
———. *Zechariah 9–14: A New Translation with Introduction and Commentary*. AB 25C. New York: Doubleday, 1993.
Middlemas, Jill. "Prophecy and Diaspora." Pages 37–54 in *The Oxford Handbook of the Prophets*. Edited by Carolyn J. Sharp. New York: Oxford University Press, 2016.
Miller, Daniel R. "Objectives and Consequences of the Neo-Assyrian Imperial Exercise." *R&T* 16 (2009): 124–49.
Miller, J. Maxwell, and John H. Hayes. *A History of Ancient Israel and Judah*. 2nd ed. Louisville: Westminster John Knox, 2006.
Miroschedji, Pierre de. "La fin du royaume d'Anšan et de Suse et la naissance de l'Empire perse." *ZA* 75 (1985): 265–306.
Moore, Megan Bishop. "Writing Israel's History Using the Prophetic Books." Pages 23–36 in *Israel's Prophets and Israel's Past: Essays on the Relationship of Prophetic Texts and Israelite History in Honor of John H.*

Hayes. Edited by Megan Bishop Moore and Brad E. Kelle. LHBOTS 446. New York: T&T Clark, 2006.

Moore, Megan Bishop, and Brad E. Kelle. *Biblical History and Israel's Past*. Grand Rapids: Eerdmans, 2011.

Morris, Ellen. "Ancient Egyptian Exceptionalism: Fragility, Flexibility, and the Art of Not Collapsing." Pages 61–87 in *The Evolution of Fragility: Setting the Terms*. Edited by Norman Yoffee. Cambridge: McDonald Institute for Archaeological Research, 2019.

Mroczek, Eva. *The Literary Imagination in Jewish Antiquity*. New York: Oxford University Press, 2016.

Müller, Reinhard. "A Prophetic View of the Exile in the Holiness Code: Literary Growth and Tradition History in Leviticus 26." Pages 207–28 in *The Concept of Exile in Ancient Israel and Its Historical Contexts*. Edited by Ehud Ben Zvi and Christoph Levin. BZAW 404. Berlin: de Gruyter, 2010.

Müller, Yannick. "Religion, Empire, and Mutilation: A Cross-religious Perspective on Achaemenid Mutilation Practices." Pages 197–227 in *Religion in the Achaemenid Persian Empire: Emerging Judaisms and Trends*. Edited by Diana Edelman, Anne Fitzpatrick McKinley, and Philippe Guillaume. ORA 17. Tübingen: Mohr Siebeck, 2016.

Naveh, Joseph, and Jonas Greenfield. "Hebrew and Aramaic in the Persian Period." Pages 115–29 in *The Cambridge History of Judaism*. Vol. 1, *Introduction: The Persian Period*. Edited by William D. Davies and Louis Finkelstein. Cambridge: Cambridge University Press, 1984.

Naveh, Joseph, and Shaul Shaked. *Aramaic Documents from Ancient Bactria (Fourth Century BCE)*. London: Khalili Family Trust, 2012.

Niditch, Susan. *Oral World and Written Word*. Louisville: Westminster John Knox, 1996.

Nimchuk, Cindy L. "Darius I and the Formation of the Achaemenid Empire: Communicating the Creation of an Empire." PhD diss., University of Toronto, 2001.

Nissinen, Martti. *Ancient Prophecy: Near Eastern, Biblical, and Greek Perspectives*. Oxford: Oxford University Press, 2017.

Nissinen, Martti, with Choon-Leong Seow and Robert K. Ritner. *Prophets and Prophecy in the Ancient Near East*. Edited by Peter Machinist. WAW 12. Atlanta: Society of Biblical Literature, 2003.

O'Connor, Kathleen M. *Jeremiah: Pain and Promise*. Minneapolis: Fortress, 2011.

———. *Lamentations and the Tears of the World*. Maryknoll, NY: Orbis, 2002.
Oded, Bustenay. "Hayye hayomyom shel hagolim bevavel (me'ot hashishit vehahamishit lifne hasefirah) bemiqra shenitgelu le'akhronah" [Daily life of the exiles in Babylon (sixth–fifth century BCE) in the Bible and in the documents that have appeared recently]. *Bet Mikra* 63 (2018): 64–91.
Oelsner, Joachim. "Weitere Bemerkungen zu den Neirab-Urkunder." *AoF* 16 (1989): 68–77.
Olmstead, Albert T. "Oriental Imperialism." *AHR* 23 (1918): 755–62.
Olyan, Saul M. "Some Neglected Aspects of Israelite Interment Ideology." *JBL* 124 (2005): 601–16.
Pagden, Anthony. *The Burdens of Empire: 1539 to the Present*. Cambridge: Cambridge University Press, 2015.
———. *Lords of All the Worlds: Ideologies of Empire in Spain, Britain and France c. 1500–c. 1800*. New Haven: Yale University Press, 1995.
Pearce, Laurie E. "'Judean': A Special Status in Neo-Babylonian and Achaemenid Babylonia?" Pages 267–77 in *Judah and the Judeans in the Achaemenid Period: Negotiating Identity in an International Context*. Edited by Gary N. Knoppers, Oded Lipschits, and Manfred Oeming. Winona Lake, IN: Eisenbrauns, 2011.
———. "New Evidence for Judeans in Babylonia." Pages 399–411 in *Judah and the Judeans in the Persian Period*. Edited by Oded Lipschits and Manfred Oeming. Winona Lake, IN: Eisenbrauns, 2006.
Pearce, Laurie E., and Cornelia Wunsch. *Documents of Judean Exiles and West Semites in Babylonia in the Collection of David Sofer*. CUSAS 28. Bethesda, MD: CDL, 2014.
Pinker, Aron. "The Advantage of a Country in Ecclesiastes 5:8." *JBQ* 37 (2009): 211–22.
Pioske, Daniel D. *Memory in a Time of Prose: Studies in Epistemology, Hebrew Scribalism, and the Biblical Past*. Oxford: Oxford University Press, 2018.
Pongratz-Leisten, Beate. "'Ich bin ein Babylonier': The Political-Religious Message of the Cyrus Cylinder." Pages 92–105 in *Cyrus the Great: Life and Lore*. Edited by M. Rahim Shayegan. Washington, DC: Ilex/Center for Hellenic Studies, 2019.
———. "'Lying King' and 'False Prophet': The Intercultural Transfer of a Rhetorical Device within Ancient Near Eastern Ideologies." Pages 215–43 in *Ideologies as Intercultural Phenomena: Proceedings of the*

Third Annual Symposium of the Assyrian and Babylonian Intellectual Heritage Project. Edited by Antonio Panaino and Giovanni Pettinato. Milan: Università di Bologna, 2002.

Porten, Bezalel, and Ada Yardeni, eds. *Textbook of Aramaic Documents from Ancient Egypt*. Vol. 3, *Literature, Accounts, Lists*. Winona Lake, IN: Eisenbrauns, 1993.

———. *Textbook of Aramaic Ostraca from Idumea*. 4 vols. Winona Lake, IN: Eisenbrauns, 2014–2020.

Radner, Karen. "After Eltekeh: Royal Hostages from Egypt at the Assyrian Court." Pages 471–79 in *Stories of Long Ago: Festschrift für Michael D. Roaf*. Edited by Heather D. Baker, Kai Kaniuth, and Adelheid Otto. AOAT 397. Münster: Ugarit Verlag, 2012.

Rawlinson, George. *The Seven Great Monarchies of the Ancient Eastern World: History, Geography, and Antiquities of Chaldaea, Assyria, Babylon, Media, Persia, Parthia, and Sassanian, or New Persian Empire*. 3 vols. New York: Alden, 1884.

Redford, Donald B. *A Study of the Biblical Story of Joseph (Genesis 37–50)*. Leiden: Brill, 1970.

Ries, Gerhard. *Die Neubabylonischen Bodenpachtformulare*. MUS 16. Berlin: Schweitzer, 1976.

Roberts, Jimmy J. M. *First Isaiah: A Commentary*. Edited by Peter Machinist. Hermeneia. Minneapolis: Fortress, 2015.

Rollinger, Robert. "Der Stammbaum des achaimenidischen Königshauses oder die Frage des Legitimität der Herrschaft de Dareios." *AMIT* 30 (1998): 155–209.

———. "Zur Lokalisation von Parsu(m)a(š) in der Fārs und zu einigen Fragen der frühen persischen Geschichte." *ZA* 89 (1999): 115–39.

Römer, Thomas. "Transformations in Deuteronomistic and Biblical Historiography: On 'Book-Finding' and Other Literary Strategies." *ZAW* 109.5 (1997): 1–11.

Root, Margaret Cool. "Defining the Divine in Achaemenid Persian Kingship: The View from Bisitun." Pages 23–65 in *Every Inch a King: Comparative Studies on Kings and Kingship in the Ancient and Medieval Worlds*. Edited by Lynette Mitchell and Charles Melville. Leiden: Brill, 2013.

———. "From the Heart: Powerful Persianisms in the Art of the Western Empire." Pages 1–29 in *Asia Minor and Egypt: Old Cultures in a New Empire; Proceedings of the Groningen 1988 Achaemenid History Work-

shop. Edited by Heleen Sancisi-Weerdenburg and Amélie Kuhrt. AH 6. Leiden: Nederlands Instituut voor het Nabije Oosten, 1991.

———. *The King and Kingship in Achaemenid Art: Essays on the Creation of an Iconography of Empire*. Acta Iranica 19. TM 9. Leiden: Brill, 1979.

Rosenzweig, Melissa S. "Assessing the Politics of Neo-Assyrian Agriculture." *Uneven Terrain: Archaeologies of Political Ecology: Special Issue Archeological Papers of the American Anthropological Association* 29 (2017): 30–50.

———. "Cultivating Subjects in the Neo-Assyrian Empire." *JSA* 16 (2016): 307–34.

———. "'Ordering the Chaotic Periphery': The Environmental Impact of the Neo-Assyrian Empire on Its Provinces." Pages 49–58 in *The Provincial Archaeology of the Assyrian Empire*. Edited by John MacGinnis, Dick Wicke, and Tina Greenfield. Oxford: Oxbow, 2016.

Russell, John Malcolm. *Sennacherib's Palace without Rival at Nineveh*. Chicago: University of Chicago Press, 1991.

———. *Writing on the Wall: Studies in the Architectural Context of Late Assyrian Palace Inscriptions*. Winona Lake, IN: Eisenbrauns, 1999.

Schaper, Joachim. "Hebrew and Its Study in the Persian Period." Pages 15–26 in *Hebrew Study from Ezra to Ben-Yehuda*. Edited by William Horbury. Edinburgh: T&T Clark, 1999.

Schaudig, Hanspeter. "'Bel Bows, Nabu Stoops!': The Prophecy of Isaiah xlvi 1-2 as a Reflection of Babylonian 'Processional Omens.'" *VT* 58 (2008): 557–72.

———. "The Magnanimous Heart of Cyrus: The Cyrus Cylinder and Its Literary Models." Pages 67–91 in *Cyrus the Great: Life and Lore*. Edited by M. Rahim Shayegan. Boston: Ilex/Center for Hellenic Studies, 2018.

———. "The Text of the Cyrus Cylinder." Pages 16–25 in *Cyrus the Great: Life and Lore*. Edited by M. Rahim Shayegan. Boston: Ilex/Center for Hellenic Studies, 2018.

Schmitt, Rüdiger. *Wörterbuch der altpersischen Königsinschriften*. Wiesbaden: Reichert, 2014.

Schniedewind, William M. *A Social History of Hebrew: Its Origins through the Rabbinic Period*. ABRL. New Haven: Yale University Press, 2013.

Schoors, Antoon. *Ecclesiastes*. HCOT. Leuven: Peeters, 2013.

———. *The Preacher Sought to Find Pleasing Words: A Study of the Language of Qoheleth*. Part 2, *Vocabulary*. OLA 143. Leuven: Peeters, 2004.

Schwartz, Barry. "Collective Forgetting and the Symbolic Power of Oneness: The Strange Apotheosis of Rosa Parks." *SPQ* 72 (2009): 123–42.

Seux, Marie-Joseph. *Épithètes royales akkadiennes et sumériennes*. Paris: Letouzey et Ane, 1967.

Silverman, Jason M. *Persian Royal-Judaean Elite Engagements in the Early Teispid and Achaemenid Empire: The King's Acolytes*. LHBOTS 690. London: T&T Clark, 2020.

Smith, Paul A. *Rhetoric and Redaction in Trito-Isaiah: The Structure, Growth and Authorship of Isaiah 56–66*. VTSup 62. Leiden: Brill, 1995.

Smith-Christopher, Daniel L. *A Biblical Theology of Exile*. OBT. Minneapolis: Fortress, 2002.

———. *Micah*. OTL. Louisville: Westminster John Knox, 2015.

Sommer, Benjamin. "The Limits of Interpretation." Pages 85–108 in *The Pentateuch: International Perspectives on Current Research*. Edited by Thomas B. Dozeman, Konrad Schmid, and Baruch J. Schwartz. FAT 78. Tübingen: Mohr Siebeck, 2011.

Sommerfeld, Walter. "Umweltzerstörung und ökologische Krisen im Alten Orient." Pages 15–49 in *State Formation and State Decline in the Near and Middle East*. Edited by Rainer Kessler, Walter Sommerfeld, and Leslie Tramontini. Wiesbaden: Harrassowitz, 2016.

Spek, Robartus J. van der. "Cyrus the Great, Exiles, and Foreign Gods: A Comparison of Assyrian and Persian Policies on Subject Nations." Pages 233–64 in *Extraction and Control: Studies in Honor of Matthew W. Stolper*. Edited by Michael Kozuh, Wouter F. M. Henkelman, Charles E. Jones, and Christopher Woods. SAOC 68. Chicago: Oriental Institute of the University of Chicago, 2014.

Stark, Oded, and David Bloom. "The New Economics of Labor Migration." *AER* 75 (1985): 173–78.

Steck, Odil Hannes. "Der Grundtext in Jesaja 60 und sein Aufbau." *ZTK* 83 (1986): 261–96.

Stern, Elsie. "Royal Letters and Torah Scrolls: The Place of Ezra-Nehemiah in Scholarly Narratives of Scripturalization." Pages 239–62 in *Contextualizing Israel's Sacred Writings: Ancient Literacy, Orality, and Literary Production*. Edited by Brian B. Schmidt. AIL. Atlanta: SBL Press, 2015.

Stern, Ephraim. *Archaeology of the Land of the Bible*. Edited by David Noel Freedman. ABRL 2. New York: Doubleday, 2001.

———. *Material Culture of the Land of the Bible in the Persian Period, 538–332 B.C.* Jerusalem: Israel Exploration Society, 1982.

Stolper, Matthew. *Entrepreneurs and Empire: The Murašû Archive, the Murašû Firm, and Persian Rule in Babylonia*. Leiden: Nederlands Instituut voor het Nabije Oosten, 1985.

———. "The Form, Language, and Contents of the Cyrus Cylinder." Pages 40–52 in *Cyrus the Great: An Ancient Iranian King*. Edited by Touraj Daryaee. Santa Monica, CA: Afshar, 2013.

Stowers, Stanley K. "The Religion of Plant and Animal Offerings versus the Religion of Meanings, Essences, and Textual Mysteries." Pages 35–56 in *Ancient Mediterranean Sacrifice*. Edited by Jennifer Wright Knust and Zsuzsanna Várhelyi. New York: Oxford University Press, 2011.

Strawn, Brent A. "'A World under Control': Isaiah 60 and the Apadana Reliefs from Persepolis." Pages 85–116 in *Approaching Yehud: New Approaches to the Study of the Persian Period*. Edited by Jon L. Berquist. SemeiaSt 50. Atlanta: Society of Biblical Literature, 2007.

Stronach, David. "Cyrus, Anshan, and Assyria." Pages 46–66 in *Cyrus the Great: Life and Lore*. Edited by M. Rahim Shayegan. Boston: Ilex/Center for Hellenic Studies, 2018.

———. "Early Achaemenid Coinage: Perspectives from the Homeland." *IrAnt* 24 (1989): 255–83.

———. "On the Genesis of the Old Persian Cuneiform Script." Pages 195–203 in *Contribution à l'histoire de l'Iran: Mélanges offerts à Jean Perrot*. Edited by François Vallat. Paris: ERC, 1990.

———. *Pasargadae: A Report on the Excavations Conducted by the British Institute of Persian Studies from 1961 to 1963*. Oxford: Oxford University Press, 1978.

Strong, John T. "The Conquest of the Land and Yahweh's Honor before the Nations in Exile." Pages 285–322 in *Ezekiel: Current Debates and Future Directions*. Edited by William A. Tooman and Penelope Barter. FAT 112. Tübingen: Mohr Siebeck, 2017.

Stronk, Jan P., ed. *Ctesias' Persian History*. Part 1, *Introduction, Text, and Translation*. RG 2. Düsseldorf: Wellem, 2010.

Suriano, Matthew J. *A History of Death in the Hebrew Bible*. Oxford: Oxford University Press, 2018.

Tadmor, Hayim. "Nabopalassar and Sin-shum-lishir in a Literary Perspective." Pages 353–57 in *Festschrift für Rykle Borger zu seinem 65. Geburtstag am 24. Mai 1994*. Edited by Stefan Maul. Groningen: Styx, 1998.

Tal, Kali. *Worlds of Hurt: Reading Literatures of Trauma*. Cambridge: Cambridge University Press, 1996.

Tal, Oren. "Pottery from the Persian and Hellenistic Periods." Pages 266–71 in vol. 1 of *Ramat Raḥel III: Final Publication of Yohanan Aharoni's Excavations (1954, 1959–1962)*. Edited by Oded Lipschits, Yuval Gadot, and Liora Freud. Winona Lake, IN: Eisenbrauns, 2016.

Tavernier, Jan. "An Achaemenid Royal Inscriptions: The Text of Paragraph 13 of the Aramaic Version of the Bisitun Inscription." *JNES* 60 (2001): 161–76.

Thomason, Allison Karmel. "Representations of the North Syrian Landscape in Neo-Assyrian Art." *BASOR* 323 (2001): 63–96.

Thomason, Sarah G. *Language Contact: An Introduction*. Washington, DC: Georgetown University Press, 2001.

Tiemeyer, Lena-Sofia. *For the Comfort of Zion: The Geographical and Theological Location of Isaiah 40–55*. VTSup 139. Leiden: Brill, 2011.

Tolini, Gauthier. "Le rôle de la famille de Nusku-gabbê au sein d'une communauté de déportés originaires de Neirab en Babylonie au VIe siècle." Pages 591–98 in *La famille dans le Proche-Orient ancient: Réalité, symbolismes et images; Actes de la 55è RAI (Paris 2009)*. Edited by Lionel Marti. Winona Lake, IN: Eisenbrauns, 2014.

Toorn, Karel van der. *Scribal Culture and the Making of the Hebrew Bible*. Cambridge: Harvard University Press, 2007.

Torrey, Charles C. *Ezra Studies*. Repr., New York: Ktav, 1970.

Tuplin, Christopher. "The Justice of Darius: Reflections on the Achaemenid Empire as a Rule-Bound Environment." Pages 73–126 in *Assessing Biblical and Classical Sources for the Reconstruction of Persian Influence, History and Culture*. Edited by Anne Fitzpatrick-McKinley. Wiesbaden: Harrassowitz, 2015.

Tyson, Craig W., and Virginia R. Herrmann, eds. *Imperial Peripheries in the Neo-Assyrian Period*. Boulder: University Press of Colorado, 2018.

Uehlinger, Christoph. "'Powerful Persianisms' in Glyptic Iconography of Persian Period Palestine." Pages 134–82 in *The Crisis of Israelite Religion: Transformation of Religious Tradition in Exilic and Postexilic Times*. Edited by Bob Becking and Marjo C. A. Korpel. OtSt 42. Leiden: Brill, 1999.

Veen, Peter van der. "Sixth Century Issues: The Fall of Jerusalem, the Exile and the Return." Pages 383–405 in *Ancient Israel's History: An Introduction to Issues and Sources*. Edited by Bill T. Arnold and Richard S. Hess. Grand Rapids: Baker Academic, 2014.

Veyne, Paul. *Did the Greeks Believe in Their Myths? An Essay on the Constitutive Imagination*. Translated by Paula Wissing. Chicago: University of Chicago Press, 1988.

Vinel, Françoise. "La texte grec de l'Ecclésiaste et ses caractéristiques: une relecture critique de l'histoire de la royauté," Pages 283–302 in *Qohe-

leth in the Context of Wisdom. Edited by Antoon Schoors. BETL 136. Leuven: Peeters, 1998.

Voigtlander, Elizabeth N. von. *The Bisitun Inscription of Darius the Great*. London: Lund Humphries, 1978.

Volkan, Vamik D. *Bloodlines: From Ethnic Pride to Ethnic Terrorism*. Boulder, CO: Westview, 1998.

Waerzeggers, Caroline. "The Babylonian Priesthood in the Long Sixth Century BC." *BICS* 54 (2011): 59–70.

———. "The Babylonian Revolts against Xerxes and the End of Archives." *AfO* 50 (2003/2004): 150–73.

———. *Marduk-rēmanni: Local Networks and Imperial Politics in Achaemenid Babylonia*. OLA 233. Leuven: Peeters, 2014.

Wagenaar, Jan A. *Judgement and Salvation: The Composition and Redaction of Micah 2–5*. VTSup 85. Leiden: Brill, 2001.

Wasmuth, Melanie. *Ägypto-persische Herrscher- und Herrschaftspräsentation in der Achämeniden Zeit*. Stuttgart: Steiner, 2017.

Waters, Matt. *Ancient Persia: A Concise History of the Achaemenid Empire, 550–330 BCE*. Cambridge: Cambridge University Press, 2014.

———. "Ashurbanipal's Legacy." In *The Persian-Achaemenid Empire as a "World-System": New Approaches and Contexts*. PSPCAIH. Edited by Touraj Daryaee and Robert Rollinger, Wiesbaden: Harrassowitz, forthcoming.

———. "By All Means, Auramazda: Help, Support, and Protect the King." In *Contextualizing Iranian Religions in the Ancient World*. Edited by M. Rahim Shayegan. Vienna: Verlag der Österreichischen Akademie der Wissenschaften, forthcoming.

———. *Ctesias' Persica and Its Near Eastern Context*. Madison: University of Wisconsin Press, 2017.

———. "Cyrus and the Achaemenids." *Iran* 42 (2004): 73–78.

———."Cyrus Rising: Reflections on Word Choice, Ancient and Modern." Pages 26–45 in *Cyrus the Great: Life and Lore*. Edited by M. Rahim Shayegan. Boston: Ilex/Center for Hellenic Studies, 2018.

———. "Darius and the Achaemenid Line." *AHB* 10 (1996): 11–18.

———."Darius I and the Greater Glory: Ambiguity in Representation and Relationship with the Divine." In *Art/ifacts and ArtWorks in the Ancient World*. Edited by Karen Sonik. Philadelphia: University of Pennsylvania Press, forthcoming.

———. "The Earliest Persians in Southwestern Iran: The Textual Evidence." *IrSt* 32 (1999): 99–107.

———. "Parsumaš, Anšan, and Cyrus." Pages 285–96 in *Elam and Persia*. Edited by Javier Álvarez-Mon and Mark Garrison. Winona Lake, IN: Eisenbrauns, 2011.

———. *A Survey of Neo-Elamite History*. SAAS 12. Helsinki: State Archives of Assyria, 2000.

Wellhausen, Julius. *Prolegomena to the History of Ancient Israel*. New York: Meridian, 1957.

Westermann, Claus. "Micha 5.1–3." Pages 54–59 in *Herr, tue meine Lippen auf*. Vol. 5, *Die Altentestamentlichen Perikope*. Edited by Georg Eichholz. Wuppertal-Barmen: Müller, 1964.

White, Hayden. *The Practical Past*. Evanston, IL: Northwestern University Press, 2014.

Wiesehöfer, Josef. "Achaemenid Rule and Its Impact on Yehud." Pages 171–85 in *Texts, Contexts and Readings in Postexilic Literature: Explorations into Historiography and Identity Negotiation in Hebrew Bible and Related Texts*. Edited by Louis Jonker. FAT 2/53. Tübingen: Mohr Siebeck, 2011.

———. "The Role of Lingua Francas and Communication Networks in the Process of Empire-Building: The Persian Empire." Pages 121–34 in *State Formation and State Decline in the Near and Middle East*. Edited by Rainer Kessler, Walter Sommerfeld, and Leslie Tramontini. Wiesbaden: Harrassowitz, 2016.

Wijnsma, Uzume Z. "The Worst Revolt of the Bisitun Crisis: A Chronological Reconstruction of the Egyptian Revolt under Petubastis IV." *JNES* 77 (2018): 157–73.

Williamson, Hugh G. M. "Micah." Pages 595–99 in *The Oxford Bible Commentary*. Edited by John Barton and John Muddiman. New York: Oxford University Press, 2001.

———. "The Setting of Deutero-Isaiah: Some Linguistic Considerations." Pages 253–67 in *Exile and Return: The Babylonian Context*. Edited by Jonathan Stökl and Caroline Waerzeggers. BZAW 478. Berlin: de Gruyter, 2015.

———. *Variations on a Theme: King, Messiah and Servant in the Book of Isaiah*. Carlisle: Paternoster, 1998.

Wilson, Ian D. "Ezekiel as Written Text: Archiving Visions, Remembering Futures." In *Oxford Handbook of the Book of Ezekiel*. Edited by Corrine Carvalho. Oxford: Oxford University Press., forthcoming.

———. *History and the Hebrew Bible: Culture, Narrative, and Memory*. BRPBI 3.2. Leiden: Brill, 2018.

———. "Joseph, Jehoiachin, and Cyrus: On Book Endings, Exoduses and Exiles, and Yehudite/Judean Social Remembering." *ZAW* 126 (2014): 521–34.

———. *Kingship and Memory in Ancient Judah*. New York: Oxford University Press, 2017.

———. "The Song of the Sea and Isaiah: Exodus 15 in Post-monarchic Prophetic Discourse." Pages 123–47 in *Thinking of Water in the Early Second Temple Period*. Edited by Ehud Ben Zvi and Christoph Levin. BZAW 461. Berlin: de Gruyter, 2014.

———. "Yahweh's Anointed: Cyrus, Deuteronomy's Law of the King, and Yehudite Identity." Pages 325–61 in *Political Memory in and after the Persian Empire*. Edited by Jason M. Silverman and Caroline Waerzeggers. ANEM 13. Atlanta: SBL Press, 2015.

Winter, Irene. *On Art in the Ancient Near East*. Vol. 1, *Of the First Millennium BCE*. CHANE 34/1. Leiden: Brill, 2010.

———. "Touched by the Gods: Visual Evidence for the Divine Status of Rulers in the Ancient Near East." Pages 75–102 in *Religion and Power: Divine Kingship in the Ancient World and Beyond*. Edited by Nicole Brisch. Chicago: University of Chicago Press, 2008.

Wunsch, Cornelia, and Laurie Pearce. *Judeans by the Waters of Babylon: New Historical Evidence in Cuneiform Sources from Rural Babylonia in the Schøyen Collection*. BabAr 6. Dresden: ISLET-Verlag, forthcoming.

Wuttmann, Michel, Hala Barakat, Bernard Bousquet, Michel Chauveau, Thierry Gonon, Sylvie Marchand, Marc Robin, and Annie Schweitzer. "Ayn Manawir (Oasis de Kharga)." *BIFAO* 98 (1998): 367–462.

Wuttmann, Michel, Thierry Gonon, and Christophe Thiers. "The Qanats of 'Ayn-Manawir (Kharga Oasis, Egypt)." *JASR* 1 (2000): 162–69.

Zadok, Ran. *The Earliest Diaspora: Israelites and Judeans in Pre-Hellenistic Mesopotamia*. PDRI 151. Tel Aviv: Diaspora Research Institute, Tel Aviv University, 2002.

Contributors

Pamela Barmash (PhD Harvard University) is Professor of Hebrew Bible and Biblical Hebrew at Washington University in St. Louis.

Ryan P. Bonfiglio (PhD Emory University) is Assistant Professor at Candler School of Theology, Emory University and Director of the Candler Foundry.

Caralie Cooke (PhD Emory University) is an independent scholar.

Lisbeth S. Fried (PhD New York University) is Visiting Scholar in Judaic Studies and Near Eastern Studies at the University of Michigan.

Martien A. Halvorson-Taylor (PhD Harvard University) is Associate Professor of Religious Studies at the University of Virginia.

Mark W. Hamilton (PhD Harvard University) is the Robert and Kay Onstead Professor of Old Testament at Abilene Christian University.

Matt Waters (PhD University of Pennsylvania) is Professor of Classics and Ancient History at the University of Wisconsin-Eau Claire.

Ian D. Wilson (PhD University of Alberta) is Associate Professor of Religious Studies at the University of Alberta.

Ancient Sources Index

Hebrew Bible/Old Testament

Genesis
11:1–9	122
15:5	23
24:3	23
24:7	23
25:8	80
25:17	80
32:2	23
35:29	80
47:28–31	81
49	100
49:29–33	81–82
49:33	80
50:24–26	80

Exodus
1:12	107
1:19	107
15:1–21	176
32:17	103

Leviticus
26	174–76
26:18	25
26:34–35	25

Numbers
19	15

Deuteronomy
17:14–20	172
28	174–75
32	100

Joshua
24:32	81

Judges
4:20	106
5	100
20:33	105

2 Samuel
7:13	171
7:16	171
8:15	121

1 Kings
11:23–25	14

2 Kings
15:19	122
18:13	122
19:16	122
19:20	122
19:36	122
19:37	122
22–23	72–73
22:20	80
24:14–16	19
25:11–12	19
25:14–15	29
25:27–30	171
25:29	19

Isaiah
2:2–4	172
2:5	130
5:20	130

Isaiah (cont.)

5:30	130
7	128
9:1	130
10:5–12:6	176
10:17	130
11:1–5	171
13–23	128
13:8	104, 107, 110
13:10	130
14:24–27	128
17:19–24	128
18:4	130
20:1	122
21:3	104, 110
21:9	129
23:13–18	129
25:6–7	129
27:12–13	128
30:26	130
36:1	122
37:17	122
37:21	122
37:37	122
37:38	122
40–55	128, 137, 173
40:15	177
41:1	177
41:5	177
41:8–10	177
42:4	177
42:6	130
42:7	130
42:12	177
42:13	103
42:15	177
42:16	130
43:1–44:5	176
43:3	130
44–45	5
44:1–13	131
44:23	177
44:24–45:8	172
44:24–45:13	128
44:28–45:1	27
45:3	130
45:7	130
45:19	130
47:5	130
49:1	177
49:6	130
49:8–12	136
49:9	130
51:4	130
51:5	177
51:9	130
51:9–11	176
53:1	136
55:3–5	172
56–59	129
56–66	128
58:8	130
58:10	130
59	129, 135–36
59:9	130
60	58–59, 129–32
60–62	129
60:1–22	129
60:20	131
61	133–35
61:4	134
62:8	132
63–66	129
63:17–14	176
66	129, 136–37

Jeremiah

3:1	108
3:9	108
4:13	107
4:31	110
6:24–25	105
6:24–26	110
6:26	102, 104, 106–7
8:19	103
13:21	107, 110
21:8–10	178
22:23	104
24	178
25:9–13	24–25

26:17–19	98	Micah	
28:3	28	1:1	100
29:4–7	78	4:1–5:14	98–113
29:10	24–25	4:8–5:1 (ET 5:2)	97, 100–113
29:16–17	178	5:4–5	100
30:6	104, 107, 110	7:12	100
40:7	105		
40:13	105	Haggai	
41:8	105	2:14	15
42:1–22	178	2:18–19	15
43:6	178		
44:1–2	19, 86	Zephaniah	
49:24	104, 107, 110	3:8	108
50–51	123		
50:9	25	Zechariah	
50:43	104	1–8	175
51:11	25	8:7–8	177
		9:13–17	57–58
Ezekiel		12:2–4	109
7:15	105	12:3	108
33:27–29	178	12:6	109
37:1–14	82	14:2	108
38:12	108		
44:1–3	123	Psalms	
		22:3 (MT 4)	57–58
Hosea		48:6–7	104
2:25	176	48:27	110
8:13	173, 176	72	133
9:3	173, 176	78	173
9:10	173, 176	114:2	57
10:11	110		
11:1	173, 176	Ruth	
11:5	173, 176	2:18	109
11:6–9	131		
11:10–11	131	Qoheleth	
11:17–18	131	5:7–8	121
14:10	170		
		Esther	
Jonah		1:1	131
1:9	23		
		Lamentations	
Amos		2:4	58
3:1–2	173		
9:7	173	Daniel	
		5:2–3	28

Ancient Sources Index

Daniel (cont.)
9:2	25

Ezra
1–6	14–15
1:1	23
1:2	23
1:2–3	24
1:2–4	27
1:3	84
1:5	26
1:7	29–30
1:8	29
1:9–11	29
2	30–31, 88, 96
2:2	31
2:70	31
3:1–7	14
3:8–13	14
3:10–13	15
4	169
4:1	31
4:1–3	15–16
4:2	122
4:4	30–31
4:4–5	15–16
4:6–24	15–16
4:8–11	124
4:8–22	30
4:10 (MT)	124
4:13	93
4:15	22
4:24	30
5	16
5:6–17	30
5:13–15	27
5:14–16	14
6–7	11
6:3–5	27–28
6:3–12	30
6:14	16
7:6	16
7:9	78
7:11–26	16
7:24	93

Nehemiah
1:4–5	23
2:3–5	83
2:20	23
3	31
4:4	31
5:4–5	94
7	88
7:7	31
7:72	31
7:73	14
8	30
8:1	14
8:1–9	73
9:5–37	124–25
11:3	31
11:20	31
13:23–25	30

1 Chronicles
5:26	122

2 Chronicles
32:1	122
32:2	122
32:9	122
32:10	122
32:37	122
36:10	19
36:17–19	19
36:20–21	24
36:23	23

New Testament

Luke
4:18–19	134

Deuterocanonical/Apocryphal Works

Sirach
38:34b–39:3	170

2 Maccabees
5:8–10	83

Ancient Sources Index

Mesopotamian and Persian Literature

ABL 918	158
Assurbanipal, Prism H2	158
Assurnasirpal, RIMA 2:301–2	150
Black Obelisk	51
Cyprus Stela Inscription	52
Cyrus Cylinder	5, 21, 23, 27, 52, 145–46, 159
Darius I, Bisitun Inscription	22, 41, 126, 142–43, 146, 153
Darius I, Naqš-s Rustan, Inscription b	147, 150
Darius I, Persepolis, Inscription d	155
Darius, Susa, Inscription f	148
Ishtar Temple Inscription	158
Murašu Archive	91–92
Persepolis imperial tablets	37–38
Sargon Legend	152
Victory Stela of Naram-Sin	40
Xerxes, Persepolis, Inscription h	144, 156
Xerxes, Persepolis, Inscription l	147, 150

Dead Sea Scrolls

4QIsa^a (4Q55)	133
4Q372	126

Rabbinic Literature

Babylonian Talmud Megillah 16b	11
Song of Songs Rabbah 5:5	11

Greco-Roman Literature

Herodotus, *Histories*	
1.107–123	152
3.89	22
Xenophon, *Cyrus the Great*	22
Xeonophon, *Oeconomicus*	
4.8	26, 94

Modern Authors Index

Abernethy, Andrew T.	129	Ben Zvi, Ehud	30, 82, 91, 112, 164–65, 167, 172, 175–77, 179
Ackroyd, Peter R.	3, 4, 6		
Aḥituv, Shmuel	82	Berlejung, Angelika	122
Akee, Randall	79	Berlin, Adele	162
Albertz, Rainer	4, 93, 115, 164	Berman, Joshua	30, 81
Alexander, Jeffrey C.	74	Berquist, Jon L.	xv, 50, 164
Álvarez-Mon, Javier	158	Bleibtreu, Erika	153
Ames, Frank R.	85	Blenkinsopp, Joseph	85, 133–36, 177
Amiran, Ruth	86	Bloch-Smith, Elizabeth	80, 82
Andersen, Francis I.	108	Bloom, David	78
Andrews, D. K.	23	Boardman, John	44
Archi, Alfonso	140	Boase, Elizabeth	61
Arneth, Martin	133	Boda, Mark J.	101, 125, 167
Assmann, Jan	63, 68–73	Bonfiglio, Ryan P.	36, 51, 58, 59
Aster, Shawn Z.	127–28, 156	Bonnie, Rick	21
Ataç, Mehmet-Ali	156	Borger, Rykle	25, 144, 158
Attinger, Pascal	117	Borkowski, Sebastian	117
Bae, Chul-Hyun	146	Boucharlat, Rémy	149
Baker, Heather D.	159	Bousquet, Bernard	95
Barakat, Hala	95	Brady, Monica	126
Barkay, Gabriel	82	Braudel, Fernand	2
Barmash, Pamela	13, 16, 18, 68, 126, 163, 172–73, 179	Braulik, Georg	70
		Briant, Pierre	4, 116–17, 144
Barnett, Richard D.	153	Brisch, Nicole	151
Barstad, Hans M.	19, 61, 84, 85, 177	Bunimovitz, Shlomo	82
Barter, Penelope	123	Burbank, Jane	119–20, 132
Barton, John	99	Burke, Peter	2
Battista, Giovanni	4	Cardasçia, Guillaume	90, 92
Beaulieu, Paul-Alain	144, 146	Carlson Hasler, Laura	169–70
Beck, Astrid B.	124, 167	Carr, David M.	64, 67, 70
Becker, Eve-Marie	61	Carradice, Ian	54
Becking, Bob	56, 124	Carroll, Robert P.	85, 162–63, 178–79
Beckman, Gary	151	Carstens, Pernille	169
Bedford, Peter Ross	23, 26	Carter, Charles E.	87–88, 164
		Carvalho, Corrine	168

Modern Authors Index

Cassarino, Jean-Pierre 79
Childs, Brevard 98
Cogan, Morton (Mordechai) 22
Colburn, Henry P. 5
Constant, Amélie 79
Cook, Terry 168
Cooley, Robert E. 82
Coogan, Michael D. 82
Cooper, Frederick 119
Coser, Lewis A. 62–63, 68, 71
Crawford, Harriet 159
Cross, Frank Moore 72
Crouch, Carly L. 168
Curtis, John xvi, 27, 38, 159
Da Riva, Rocio 141, 144, 150
Dahood, Mitchell 57
Dandamayev, Muhammad 90, 157
Daryaee, Touraj 146, 160
Davies, Philip R. 29, 89
Derrida, Jacques 169
Dhorme, Edouard 21
Dieulafoy, Marcel 53
Dochhorn, Jan 61
van Driel, Govert 90–91, 93
Dubovský, Peter 122–23
Du Toit, Jacqueline S. 168
Edelman, Diana V. 11, 21–22, 30, 161, 164–65, 167
Eichholz, Georg 100
Eichrodt, Walther 167
Eisenstadt, Samuel N. 119, 122
Eph'al, Israel 21, 29, 85–86
Exum, J. Cheryl 82
Fales, Frederick M. 22
Faust, Avraham 82, 85–87, 89–90
Feldman, Marian H. 153, 156
Fick, Sabine 141
Finkel, Irving 144
Finkelstein, Israel 29, 85–88, 164
Finkelstein, Louis 29
Fischer, Georg 123
Fitzpatrick-McKinley, Anne 22, 156
Floyd, Michael H. 129, 165, 167, 168
Frahm, Eckhart 151
Frechette, Christopher 61
Freedman, David Noel 86, 108
Freud, Liora 125
Freud, Sigmund 169
Fried, Lisbeth S. 11, 15, 19, 23–24, 26, 28, 79, 87, 91, 93–94, 125–26, 164–65
Funk, Robert W. 87
Gadot, Yuval 88, 124–25, 164
Ganzert, Joachim 149
Gardiner, Alan H. 42
Garrison, Mark B. xvi, 38, 45, 55, 117, 126, 151, 153–56, 158
Gaspa, Salvatore 156
George, Andrew R. 145, 157
Goldingay, John 124, 129, 133, 136
Gonon, Thierry 95
Gosse, Bernard 128
Grabbe, Lester L. 5, 85, 162
Grayson, A. Kirk 149–50
Greenfield, Jonas 29
Greenspahn, Frederick E. 177
Gropp, Douglas M. 126
Guillaume, Philippe 22
Gunneweg, Antonius H. J. 14
Haak, Robert D. 165
Hackett, Jo Ann 165
Hackl, Johannes 140
Halbwachs, Maurice 62, 70–72, 75
Hallock, Richard T. 38
Halvorson-Taylor, Martien vii, 7, 33, 98, 175, 179
Hamilton, Mark W. 39, 55, 59, 112, 127, 135, 140, 142
Handy, Lowell K. 176
Hardt, Michael 118
Harger, Adam K. 123
Hayes, John H. 61
Hasselbalch, Trine Bjørnung 170
Hele, Karl S. 119
Henkelman, Wouter F. 146, 151–52, 154, 156, 158
Herrmann, Virginia R. 117
Herzfeld, Michael 125
Herzog, Ze'ev 86
Hill, Jane A. 151
Hill, John 124

Hillers, Delbert R.	99	Kuhrt, Amélie	139, 144, 147–150, 152, 155
Hock, Hans Heinrich	119		
Hoftijzer, Jean	93	Lanfranchi, Giovanni	139
Hogland, Kenneth G.	89	Langgut, Dafna	88, 124, 164
Holloway, Steven W.	176	Lambert, Wilfred G.	135
Holt, Else Kragelund	61	Lecoq, Pierre	53, 149
Horbury, William	29	Leichty, Erle	143
Hulster, Izaak de	xvi, xvii, 57–59	Leith, Mary Joan Winn	126
Hunt, Alice	164	Lemaire, André	77, 87, 93
Hurowitz, Victor (Avigdor)	26	Lemche, Niels Peter	169
Huyse, Philip	114	Leuchter, Mark	29, 169, 179
Jacobs, Bruno	144	Leuenberger, Martin	127
Janzen, David	61, 125	Levin, Christoph	30, 175–76, 179
Japhet, Sara	30	Lewis, Brian	152
Joannès, Francis	77, 117	Lewis, Theodore	151
Jobling, David	163, 180	Lichtheim, Miriam	24
Jones, Charles E.	154	Lincoln, Bruce	147, 154
Jones, Christopher M.	117, 133	Linville, James R.	167, 175
Jones, Maggie R.	79	Lipschits, Oded	5, 77, 85–88, 93, 124–25, 164
Jones, Philip	151		
Jones, Scott C.	127	Liss, Hanna	12, 162
de Jong, Matthijs J.	127	Liverani, Mario	4, 116
Jongeling, Karel	93	Luukko, Mikko	158
Jonker, Louis	164	Machinist, Peter	124, 127, 131, 151, 165, 177
Joseph, Alison L.	171		
Joseph, Brian D.	119	MacGinnis, John	8
Jursa, Michael	21, 91, 117, 140–42, 150, 159	MacKenzie, John	119
		MacQueen, J. G.	122
Kaniuth, Kai	159	Magen, Yitzhak	86, 89
Kapelrud, Arvid S.	26	Maier, Aren M.	82
Keel, Othmar	xvi, 36, 56	Marchant, Edgar C.	94
Kelle, Brad E.	63–64, 85, 167	Markl, Dominik	122–23
Kent, Roland G.	148	Mason, Rex	4
Kessler, John	176, 178–79	Massey, Douglas S.	79
Kessler, Rainer	118–19	Mattila, Raija	4
King, Rhyne	117	Mayfield, Tyler D.	168
Kleber, Kristin	140	Mays, James L.	99
Klingbeil, Martin G.	56	Maul, Stefan	144
Knoppers, Gary N.	77, 91, 93, 164	Mazar, Amichai	82
Knust, Jennifer Wright	63	McKay, John	22
Koole, Jan L.	129–30, 136	Melville, Charles	151
Korpel, Marjo C. A.	56	Meyer, Eduard	117
Kozuh, Michael	21	Meyers, Carol L.	58, 167
Kratz, Reinhard G.	168	Meyers, Eric M.	58, 167
Krüger, Thomas	121	Middlemas, Jill	85, 179

Modern Authors Index 221

Miller, Daniel R.	116
Miller, J. Maxwell	61
Miller, Marvin L.	91
de Miroschedji, Pierre	158
Mitchell, Lynette	151
Moore, Megan Bishop	63, 167
Morales, Antonio J.	151
Morris, Ellen	115
Mroczek, Eva	169
Muddiman, John	99
Müller, Reinhard A.	176
Müller, Yannick	22
Naveh, Joseph	29, 91, 93
Negri, Antonio	118
Nelson, W. David	16, 18, 172–73
Niditch, Susan	65
Nimchuk, Cindy L.	37, 43
Nissinen, Martti	165–67
Novotny, Jamie	148
O'Connor, Kathleen M.	61
Oded, Bustenay	77
Oelsner, Joachim	22
Oeming, Manfred	5, 12, 77, 85, 162
Olmstead, Albert T.	22
Olyan, Saul M.	80
Otto, Adelheid	159
Pagden, Anthony	117–18
Panaino, Antonio	147
Parpola, Simo	157
Pearce, Laurie E.	21, 26, 77–78
Perdue, Leo G.	162
Pettinato, Giovanni	147
Pinker, Aron	121
Pioske, Daniel D.	33
Pongratz-Leisten, Beate	5, 147
Porten, Bezalel	29, 126
Pratico, Gary D.	82
Radner, Karen	158
Rawlinson, George	117
Redard, Celine	149, 151, 154, 156
Redford, Donald B.	81
Ries, Gerhard	90
Ritner, Robert K.	165
Roberts, Jimmy J. M.	127–28
Rollinger, Robert	4, 139, 146, 149, 158, 160
Römer, Thomas	73
Root, Margaret Cool	xv, 37–38, 151, 153
Rosenzweig, Melissa	8
Russell, John Malcolm	143, 148, 153
Sancisi-Weerdenburg, Heleen	55, 152
Schaper, Joachim	29
Schaudig, Hanspeter	5, 21, 27, 127, 141, 146
Schmidt, Brian	32
Schmitt, Rüdiger	148, 151
Schniedewind, William M.	29
Schoors, Antoon	121
Schwartz, Barry	2, 171
Seow, Choon-Leong	127, 165
Seux, Marie-Joseph	145
Shaked, Shaul	91, 93
Sharp, Carolyn J.	179
Shayegan, M. Rahim	4–5, 21, 141, 146, 151
Silverman, Jason M.	116, 125, 146, 164–65, 172
Simpson, St. John	xvi, 38
Singer, Itamar	82
Smith, Paul A.	129
Smith-Christopher, Daniel L.	75, 108
Sommer, Benjamin	2
Sommerfeld, Walter	118–19
Sonik, Karen	151
Sonnet, Jean-Pierre	122–23
van der Spek, Robartus J.	21
Stager, Lawrence E.	82
Stark, Oded	78
Steck, Odil Hannes	129–30
Stern, Elsie	31
Stern, Ephraim	86
Stökl, Jonathan	177
Stolper, Matthew W.	90–91, 95, 117, 146, 154
Stowers, Stanley K.	63
Strawn, Brent A.	xv–xvii, 50, 57–60
Stronach, David	xvii, 4, 37, 144, 153–54
Strong, John T.	123

Stronk, Jan P.	122
Suriano, Matthew J.	79, 81, 82
Tadmor, Hayim	144
Tal, Kali	73
Tal, Oren	124, 164
Tavernier, Jan	126
Thiers, Christophe	95
Thomason, Allison Karmel	117
Thomason, Sarah G.	119
Tiemeyer, Lena-Sofia	177
Todd, Otis J.	94
Toffelmire, Colin M.	167
Tolini, Gauthier	22
Tooman, William A.	123
Toorn, Karel van der	63–66, 67, 70–72
Torrey, Charles C.	84
Tramontini, Leslie	118–19
Truschnegg, Brigitte	146, 149
Tuplin, Christopher	156
Turner, Geoffrey	153
Tyson, Craig W.	117
Uehlinger, Christoph	xvi, 38, 55–56
Vallat, François	144
Van Buylaere, Greta	158
Vanderhooft, David S.	87
VanderKam, James	126
Várhelyi, Zsuzsanna	63
Veen, Peter van der	96
Veyne, Paul	8, 9
Vinel, Françoise	121
Voigtlander, Elizabeth N. von	22
Volkan, Vamik D.	62, 63, 75
Waerzeggers, Caroline	117, 140, 159, 172, 177
Wagenaar, Jan A.	102–3, 105, 107
Wasmuth, Melanie	5
Waters, Matt	23, 68, 126, 144, 146, 151–53, 156, 158
Wellhausen, Julius	3, 176
Westermann, Claus	100
White, Hayden	32
Whiting, Robert	157
Wicke, Dick	8
Wiesehöfer, Josef	119, 146, 149, 164–65
Wiessner, Gernot	90
Wijnsma, Uzume Z.	22
Williamson, Hugh G. M.	98, 172, 177
Wilson, Ian D.	12, 18, 100, 123, 163, 166–67, 171–72, 176
Winter, Irene	151, 153
Wolfschke-Bulmahn, Joachim	149
Wunsch, Cornelia	21, 26, 77–78
Wuttmann, Michel	95
Yardeni, Ada	29, 126
Yoder, Christine Roy	127
Yoffee, Norman	115
Zadok, Ran	21, 78

Subject Index

Abraham, 80–81
Apadana, xv, xvii, 37, 48, 49–52, 54, 59
Arad, 29, 86
archer, xvi, xvii, 37–38, 40, 43, 46–48, 54–58
archives, 21, 37–38, 43–46, 65, 77, 90–92, 95, 149, 159, 161, 165–71, 174, 176, 180
art
    Egyptian, 4–5, 40–43, 51, 153–55
    Elamite, 4, 149, 153–54, 156
    Neo-Assyrian, 117
Artaxerxes I, 16 21, 26, 48, 83
Artaxerxes II, 93, 95
Assur, 142, 155
Assurbanipal, 124, 143, 152–53, 158–60
Assurnasirpal II, 150
audiences, literary, 38, 54, 113, 122, 127, 136, 137
Auramazda, 23, 41, 45, 50, 55, 59, 142–44, 150–51, 154–56
Beersheba, 29, 86–88
Bethel, 88
Bisitun (Behistun), 5, 22–23, 37, 39, 41, 43, 45, 126, 142–44, 146–47, 149–51, 153, 155–56
Black Obelisk, 51, 52, 59
burial, 79–83, 87, 90, 96, 126
Cambyses, 24, 35, 140, 157
city-state, 118, 120
corvée, 91, 93, 157. *See also* ilku
court
    legal, 77
    royal, 49, 51–52, 54, 117, 140, 158–59
    style, 37, 44–46
Ctesias/Ktesias, 122, 152

Cyprus, 52
Cyrus Cylinder, 5, 21, 23, 27, 28, 38, 52, 141, 144–46, 159–60
Davidic, 17, 72, 171–73, 176
Davidide. *See* Davidic
economics, 13, 37, 48, 78–79, 91, 106–7, 115, 117–18, 126, 129, 131, 137, 165, 168, 170
Elam(ite), 46, 117, 139, 146, 148, 157–58
elite(s), 7, 61, 75, 116, 118, 125, 140, 146, 149, 159, 165, 172
empire, 118, 119, 125
Enlil, 151
Enuma Elish, 135
Esagila, 23, 25, 29, 135, 145
Esarhaddon, 25, 122, 143, 152, 158
eschatology, 98, 107, 111
exodus, 16–18, 69, 107, 162, 166, 170–74, 176, 179
falsehood, 147
gardens, 78, 148–49, 164, 175
Gaumata, 41, 43, 155
glyptic. *See* seals
golah, 177–78,
graves. *See* burial
Hebron, 87, 88
Hesiod, 122
ideology, 9, 12, 38, 54, 56, 80, 82, 85, 125, 140, 141, 157, 162, 173
ilku, 90–93, 95–96
imperialism, 22–23, 118, 128–29, 163
Isaac, 80–81
Isis, 26, 94, 95
Jacob, 80–82, 98
Joseph, 29, 80–81, 125

Khorsabad, 51
Marduk, 24, 27, 135, 145, 151
Media, 25, 122, 143
media, 7, 9, 27, 38, 43, 48, 54, 56, 128, 131
Mesopotamia, 1, 26, 36, 39, 41–43, 51, 59, 78, 117, 120, 123, 127–28, 139–41, 144–47, 149, 151–54, 156–57, 178
Midian, 131
Moses, 152, 175
Naqsh-i Rustam, 5, 37, 39, 42, 156, 157
Naram-Sin, xv, 39, 40, 145
nation-state, 118–19, 125
Nebuchadnezzar, 1, 2, 24, 27–29, 86
Osiris, 26, 94, 95
palace, 28, 51, 53–54, 65, 93, 143, 147–48, 153, 164
paradise. *See* gardens
Pasargadae, xvii, 4, 37, 55, 144, 149, 153–54
peace, 35, 45, 50, 59, 80, 107, 132
periodization, 2–4, 6, 141, 159
Persepolis, xv-xvii, 37–39, 41–50, 55–58, 117, 123, 130, 144, 149, 151, 153, 155–57, 164
Phoenicia, 88, 120
poetry, 57, 98, 99, 102, 110, 128, 129–34, 136–37, 162, 171
prophecy, 24–25, 27, 113, 127, 165–67, 179
Ramat Raḥel, 89, 124, 125, 164
Sarah, 81
Sargon of Akkad, 142, 145, 152
Sargon II, 51, 52, 122, 152
scribalism, 33, 65–67, 71–73, 157, 169
sculpture, 4, 39, 143, 149, 153, 155, 156, 159
seal, 29, 38, 39, 44–47, 54–56, 58, 87–88, 153
Sennacherib, 28, 100, 101, 122–23, 128–29, 147–48, 152–53
Shamash, 155
statue/statuary, xv, 5, 28, 35, 37, 39, 40–42, 53
sun (disk), 50, 51, 59, 151, 154
Susa, 5, 37, 42, 53, 83, 148

Tarshish, 131, 136
taxation, 50, 52, 77, 91, 93, 95–96, 116, 117
technology, 118
Tiamat, 135
Tiglath-pileser III, 2, 122, 128
trade, 3, 68, 129, 131
utopia(n), 69, 123
Wadi Daliyeh, 126
war, 29, 73, 104, 107, 136, 160
warriors, xvi, xvii, 57, 58, 104, 106, 135, 151
women, 30, 97, 101, 103, 104–11
Xerxes, 3, 7, 16, 140–41, 143–44, 147, 150, 156, 159
Zion, 58, 101–12, 130, 177

www.ingramcontent.com/pod-product-compliance
Lightning Source LLC
Chambersburg PA
CBHW021703230426
43668CB00008B/711